Calgary Parks and Pathways

Calgary Parks and Pathways

A CITY'S TREASURES

Terry Bullick

BlueCOUCH**Books**

National Library of Canada Cataloguing in Publication
Bullick, Terry, 1958–
Calgary parks and pathways : a city's treasures / Terry Bullick. — Rev. ed.

Includes index.
ISBN 1-894739-08-6

1. Parks—Alberta—Calgary—Guidebooks. 2. Trails—Alberta—
Calgary—Guidebooks. 3. Calgary (Alta.)—Guidebooks. I. Title.

FC3697.65.B84 2006   917.123'38044   C2006-902672-6

Cover and interior photos by the author unless otherwise indicated.
Authors' photo: Norm Harburn
Map contributors: Terry Bullick, Tony and Gillean Daffern, Connections Desktop Publishing, Enviro-Tech Surveys Ltd., The City of Calgary, Harold Pinel.

Every effort was made to ensure that the information contained in this book was accurate at the time of printing. The publishers and the authors shall not be held liable for the use or misuse of information contained in this book.

Brindle & Glass thanks the Alberta Foundation for the Arts
for their contribution our publishing program.

This book is printed on 100% post-consumer recycled and ancient-forest-friendly paper. For more information, please visit www.oldgrowthfree.com.

Blue Couch Books
www.bluecouchbooks.com
is an imprint of Brindle & Glass Publishing
www.brindleandglass.com

1 2 3 4 5 11 10 09 08 07

PRINTED AND BOUND IN CANADA

To the people who create, enjoy, respect, and protect Calgary's parks, natural areas, and waterways.

Table of Contents

PREFACE XI

PARKS FOUNDATION, CALGARY: SHAPING CALGARY'S
    PARKS AND NATURAL AREAS I

A GUARDIAN OF OUR COMMUNITY'S NATURAL ENVIRONMENT 2

INTRODUCTION 6
    Sharing the Pathways • A Little Respect • Connect • Bikes and
    C-Trains • Dogs and Parks and Pathways • Fishing in Calgary •
    Distance Charts

BOW RIVER PATHWAY 12
    Calgary's Grand River • Bearspaw East • Bowness Park •
    Baker Park • Bowmont Park • Shouldice Park • Edworthy Park
    (including Lowery Gardens and the Douglas Fir Trail) • Edworthy
    Park to Prince's Island • South Bank • Prince's Island • Crescent
    Heights Connector • North Shore: Prince's Island to Nose Creek
    • North/East Shore Nose Creek to Cushing Bridge • South Shore
    Prince's Island to Fort Calgary • Fort Calgary • Centenary Park
    • Calgary Zoo, Botanical Gardens and Prehistoric Park • Pearce
    Estate Park • Cushing Bridge to Inglewood Bird Sanctuary •
    Inglewood Bird Sanctuary • Inglewood Bird Sanctuary to Beaver
    Dam Flats • Old Refinery Park • Beaver Dam Flats • Carburn Park
    • Southland Natural Park

FISH CREEK PROVINCIAL PARK 101
    Mallard Point, Bankside & Burnsmead • Hull's Wood & Sikome
    Lake • Sikome Lake • Shannon Terrace, Bebo Groves, Votier's Flats
    and Shaw's Meadows • Glennfield and Bow Valley Ranch • Fish
    Creek East and Rotary Chinook Nature Park

ELBOW RIVER PATHWAY 131
Elbow River Downstream of Glenmore Dam • Clearwater
Natural Environment Park • Griffith Woods • Glenmore Parks and
Reservoir • Weaselhead Flats Natural Area • South Glenmore Park
• East Glenmore Park • Heritage Park • Glenmore Athletic Park •
North Glenmore Park • River Park • Sandy Beach • Stanley Park •
Woods Park • Elbow Island Park • Lindsay Park • Stampede Park

NOSE CREEK PATHWAY 172
West Nose Creek Confluence Park • Laycock Park • Bottomlands
Park

DOWNTOWN PARKS 183
Downtown's +15 Walkways • Devonian Gardens • Olympic Plaza
• Shaw Millennium Park

NORTHEAST PARKS . . . . : 189
Jim Fish Ridge • Tom Campbell's Hill • Prairie Winds Park •
Airport Pathway • Rotary Challenger Park

NORTHWEST PARKS 199
Riley Park • North Capitol Hill Park • Confederation Park •
University of Calgary • Nose Hill Park • Canada Olympic Park •
Twelve Mile Coulee

SOUTHEAST PARKS 218
Western Irrigation District (WID) Canal Pathway • Reader Rock
Gardens • Elliston Regional Park • Valley View Regional Park

SOUTHWEST PARKS 227
Central Memorial Park • James Short Square • Rouleauville Square

APPENDIX 232

INDEX 233

ACKNOWLEDGEMENTS 242

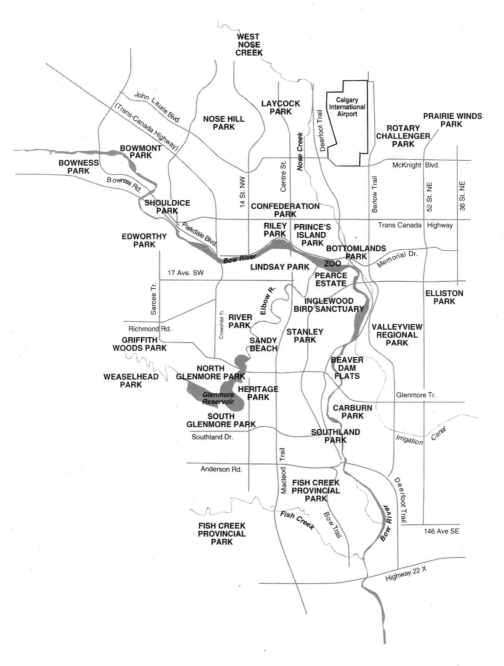

Calgary's major parks at a glance.

PREFACE

Everybody needs beauty as well as bread, places to play in and pray in, where nature may heal and give strength to body and soul.

—John Muir, environmentalist

My deep and lasting affinity for Calgary's parks and pathways began in earnest about 25 years ago while working for a construction company that was building several pathways for the City of Calgary. At the time, pathways were edged with wood and covered in "red shale." The company regarded pathway construction as painful. I, however, found the pathways delightful and began exploring them and the parks they ran through with a growing number of friends.

A decade or so later, after I had covered every official kilometre of Calgary's pathway network two or three times, the first edition of this book was published by Rocky Mountain Books. At the time, in 1991, Calgary's pathway network was going through an unprecedented and well-deserved popularity boom. Since then, that popularity has never waned—and the network has continued to grow.

Today, this network is one of Calgary's defining characteristics—a true treasure. The network runs virtually the entire length of the Bow River, the Elbow River, Fish Creek, Nose Creek, West Nose Creek, and the Western Irrigation District (WID) Canal within the city limits. Plus, the network

Shannon Terrace at Fish Creek Provincial Park.

radiates into more than 100 Calgary neighbourhoods. In all, it covers about 700 kilometres, connects more than 30 parks and natural areas, and is used and enjoyed by people of all ages with all kinds of interests and abilities. These people share a love of the outdoors and enjoy travelling from one place to another under their own power: by walking, jogging, running, cycling, in-line skating and more. It is hard to imagine Calgary without its parks and pathways.

In updating and revising this book, it's been a pleasure to once again travel Calgary's parks and pathways gathering information. I have been graciously accompanied, assisted, and supported by many people along the way, particularly Harold Pinel of the City of Calgary's Parks department and my friend Sharma Christie.

This new edition, which has been commissioned and enthusiastically supported by the Parks Foundation, Calgary, attempts to capture the same two elements the first edition focused on: the system's depth and breadth, and the many ways Calgarians and visitors can experience and enjoy it.

I would like to recognize Norm Harburn, president of the Parks Foundation, Calgary, for his unfailing patience and optimism, not only in putting this publication together, but in helping shape Calgary's parks and pathways. While Norm would adamantly shun such credit, preferring instead to see kudos go to the foundation's many volunteers and donors and the City of Calgary, his ability to negotiate for new parks, pathways, and associated projects has been formidable, good-natured, and effective.

My admiration and respect also go to the thousands of other people who have helped create one of the best urban park networks in the world. Among them is Pat Mahaffey of the City of Calgary Parks, who was my first guide and mentor to Calgary's pathways and offered invaluable advice and direction yet again on this edition. My knowledge and passion for Calgary's parks and pathways pale in comparison to Pat's. For more than two decades, he has worked as a parks planner and visionary—and he has been a pioneering bicycle commuter.

I hope those I have failed to mention by name will forgive my oversight.

Terry Bullick, Calgary, Alberta
April 2007

PARKS FOUNDATION, CALGARY: SHAPING CALGARY'S PARKS AND NATURAL AREAS

By admission, the Parks Foundation, Calgary, is a group of beautiful dreamers. For more than 20 years, we have dreamt about making Calgary a greener city filled with natural, restored, innovative, and enjoyable outdoor places and spaces.

Of course, it's taken more than idyllic imaginings to make this happen. It's taken action. Our founders, members, supporters, donors, volunteers, and community and government partners have brought vision, inspiration, and tireless commitment to the 38 key projects and numerous other projects—worth more than $100 million—that we have been a major part of since our foundation was founded in 1985.

Nowhere is the diverse geography of Alberta more apparent than in Calgary. The city's backyard is filled with mountain views, rolling foothills, sweeping grasslands, winding river valleys, old-growth forests, and thriving wetlands. We have had projects in areas such as these as well as in school and neighbourhood playgrounds.

Our projects can be found in every corner of the city, such as Jim Fish Ridge and Rotary Challenger Park in the northeast, and the Memorial Drive Tree Planting project and Bow Trail Pedestrian Bridge in the northwest. In the southwest, we proudly supported the award-winning Chevron Learning Pathway at Prince's Island and the creation of Griffith Woods Natural Area. Our projects in the southeast quadrant of the city include Valleyview Regional Park and Elliston Park.

The Parks Foundation, Calgary, is a not-for-profit organization that acts as a guardian of Calgary's outdoor and natural environment and as an advocate for amateur sport. To volunteer with, make a donation to, or learn more about the Parks Foundation, Calgary, visit: www.parksfdn.com, or contact:

The Parks Foundation, Calgary
225 – 13 Ave. SW
Calgary, Alberta T2R 1N8
P: (403) 974-0751, F: (403) 974-0758

For our 20th anniversary, we searched for a way to celebrate our accomplishments and all that Calgary's parks and natural areas have to offer. After all, this is one of the best urban park networks in the world. This book is the result of our search, and we are pleased to share it with Calgarians.

As the Parks Foundation, Calgary, begins its third decade of identifying, supporting, and collaborating on park and natural area projects, I would like to acknowledge and thank the many people—those beautiful dreamers—who have helped shape our organization and our projects.

Norm Harburn, President, Parks Foundation, Calgary
January 2007

A GUARDIAN OF OUR COMMUNITY'S NATURAL ENVIRONMENT

The Parks Foundation, Calgary, is one of the guardians of our community's natural environment. The foundation helps identify, preserve, conserve, and restore outdoor places and spaces in Calgary that have special beauty, purpose, and significance. Those places and spaces include the following completed and ongoing projects:

- Lowery (Lawery) Gardens—five kilometres of pathway built in 1985 on the south shore of the Bow River between Crowchild and Edworthy Road SW in partnership with a private donor.
- Bowness Park—the park's original 1927 fountain was removed in the 1960s; this project, supported by an anonymous donor, saw a new fountain installed in 1988.
- Prairie Winds Park—the foundation and the Northeast Regional Park Committee created this $4.5-million, 18-hectare multi-purpose park, the first major park in northeast Calgary, in 1988.
- James Short Park and Cupola—the foundation's first-ever project in 1985 funded the completion of this downtown park on the original site of James Short School. Location: Along Centre St. SW between 4 Ave. and 5 Ave.
- Heritage Escarpment—by building a pathway and adding several varieties of native plants in 1992, the foundation and the Elbow River Conservancy brought new life and appreciation to the east banks of Elbow River below the community of Parkhill.
- Outwest Park—working with the Inglewood Community Association, the foundation created a unique and distinctive gateway at the west end of Calgary's oldest neighbourhood, Inglewood.
- Peace Park—a joint project by the foundation, the Calgary Parking Authority, and the City of Calgary near 2 Ave. and 8 St. SW as part of Canada's 125th anniversary.
- Grave's Bridge Landing—new canoe docks, a boat launch, and naturalized vegetation added new life to the once run-down riverbank under Grave's bridge at Glenmore Tr. and the Bow River SW. The project was completed jointly in 1993 by the foundation and the River Valleys Committee.
- Sapper's Bridge—in 1993, the foundation, the River Valleys Committee, and the 33rd Engineer Squadron of the Canadian Armed Forces Reserves erected a wooden bridge in Beaver Dam Flats Park.

- Gerry Shaw Gardens—foundation volunteer Mike Stanford headed the efforts to create a lasting memorial for his lifetime friend Gerry Shaw. Located along the Elbow River at 30 Ave. SW; completed in 1994.
- Nose Hill Park—in 1994, the foundation and the Nose Hill Park Board spent $4,000 to preserve this sprawling park's natural habitat, flora, and fauna.
- Fish Creek to Elbow River Pathway—construction of this pathway along 37 St. SW created an important link in Calgary's comprehensive network of pathways and provided a direct route between Glenmore Park and Fish Creek Provincial Park. Completed in 1995 with the support of the Southwest Community Association.
- Memorial Drive Tree Planting—the foundation and the Royal Canadian Legion planted a new generation of trees to replace those originally planted as war memorials.
- Tom Campbell's Hill—a long-neglected escarpment overlooking Nose Creek, the Bow River, and the Calgary Zoo was restored to natural area parkland in 1995 in partnership with the Bridgeland/Riverside Community Association.
- Colonel's Island—Mrs. J. Tidswell donated an island in the Elbow River near 34 Ave. and Rideau Rd. SW to the Parks Foundation, Calgary, in memory of her late husband, Lieutenant Colonel J. E. H. Tidswell.
- Erlton/Roxboro Escarpment—in 1996, the foundation and the Erlton/Roxboro Community Association funded riverbank re-naturalization and pathway development along the Elbow River near 25 Ave. SW.
- Fish Creek Boat Launch—a boat/canoe launch and parking lot was constructed in 1996 near the Marquis of Lorne Tr. (Highway 22X) and Bow River crossing for emergency and recreational use. A joint project with the River Valleys Committee, and Friends of Fish Creek Park.
- James H. Gray Park—trees and shrubs were planted in this small park in Patterson Heights in memory of author James H. Gray who once owned the ridge and lived on the site.
- Rouleauville Square—a $1.5 million project by the foundation, the City of Calgary, and the Catholic Cathedral salutes the history of the village of Rouleauville, located in the heart of what was Calgary's French Catholic Mission district.
- Sue Higgins Pedestrian Bridge—completed in 1996 in Douglasdale, the bridge was named for former Alderman Sue Higgins, the project's primary fundraiser.
- Wildlands Park—once the site of an oil refinery, this site near the Inglewood Bird Sanctuary was completely restored and transformed

into a park in 1996 with help from the foundation, the Rotary Club of Calgary, Petro-Canada, and Ducks Unlimited Canada.

- Crowchild Pedestrian Bridge—an invaluable link that connects the pathways north and south of the Bow River under Crowchild Tr., this $1-million bridge was completed in 1997.
- Stoney Tr. Bridge Re-vegetation—four sites between the Trans-Canada Highway and Crowchild Tr. NW were reclaimed following completion of this bridge across Calgary's largest river valley.
- Airport Pathway—proof positive that if you build it they will come, a pathway constructed between the airport and McKnight Blvd. attracts thousands of users every year. Jointly funded by the foundation, Don Skinner, and the Calgary Airport Authority.
- Patterson Homestead Park—Bob Patterson donated former family farmland to the City of Calgary for a park in MacKenzie Lake near the Bow River Pathway (BRP).
- Beaulieu Gardens—once the lush backyard of the Lougheed family house, these gardens have been restored to their former beauty and complement the recently restored Lougheed mansion. Completed in 1999.
- Elbow Valley Constructed Wetlands—located along the Elbow River at 60 St. SW (off Highway 8), this project addresses environmental issues and educational opportunities and is an outdoor science classroom that has been booked to capacity since opening in 1999. A joint project with the River Valleys Committee.

Rouleauville Square salutes the history of Calgary's French Catholic Mission district.

- Griffith Woods Natural Area—at four times the size of Prince's Island, Griffith Woods Natural Area is the largest donation ever made to the people of Calgary. Truly a jewel in Calgary's treasured parks network.
- Shaw Millennium Park—hip and modern, this downtown park has been embraced by Calgary youth. A joint project between the foundation, the City of Calgary, and the 2000 Millennium Committee.
- John Simonot Commemorative Trail—a commemorative trail in Griffith Woods built in honour of the late John Simonot, a former chair of the River Valleys Committee.
- Evamy Ridge Park—a hillside park in Mission dedicated to the late Michael Evamy. Built with a donation from the Evamy family in 2002.
- Jim Fish Ridge and Rotary Park—a beautiful vantage point on the escarpment to the east of the Centre St. Bridge named for Jim Fish, a long-time parks visionary and supporter. Completed in 2002 with the support of the Crescent Heights Community Association.
- Chevron Learning Pathway—after languishing for years, the east end of Prince's Island Park was turned into a living, breathing example of a wetland. Since opening in 2003, this pathway has helped thousands of school children gain a better appreciation of this valuable ecosystem. Made possible through the support of Chevron Canada and the City of Calgary.
- Elliston Park—located along 17 Ave. SE, this southeast park is home to the city's largest stormwater lake as well as a full range of park facilities.
- Rotary Challenger Park—the world's first barrier-free park accommodates users of any age and ability.
- Harvie Passage—the taming of the weir at the headworks of the Western Irrigation District in southeast Calgary. (Future project).
- Haultain School Park—a park setting is being created around the home of the Parks Foundation, Calgary, an historical building that was once a school. (Completion 2007).

INTRODUCTION

SHARING THE PATHWAYS

Calgary's pathways are for everyone: walkers, runners, joggers, cyclists, and in-line skaters. They attract dog walkers, moms with baby strollers, and homeless people with shopping carts.

To safely enjoy the pathways, it helps to remember that any of the above could be around the next corner or right behind you. A few courtesies will keep you on the right track:

- Keep to the right—most pathway traffic is two-way.
- Slow down on hills and corners as well as under bridges and in heavily vegetated natural areas.
- Cyclists, joggers, walkers, dawdlers, and other users all have equal rights on pathways.

A few courtesies on Calgary's pathways will keep you on the right track.

- Signal when passing. When passing from behind, the tradition on Calgary's pathways is to gently ring a bike bell or call "on your left." Those being passed should move to the right as far as possible. Those passing should only do so when it's safe.
- Know the limits. The speed limit on Calgary's pathways is 20 km/h, unless otherwise posted. Speedy cyclists who find this too slow should use city streets.
- Step aside. When stopping to take in the sights or have a chat, move to the side of the pathway.
- Dog owners—know and follow the rules (see Dogs and Parks and Pathways section).

By law in Alberta, anyone under the age of 18 riding a bicycle (or riding in a bike trailer) must wear a helmet. Helmets are also recommended for cyclists over the age of 18 and in-line skaters of any age.

A LITTLE RESPECT

Showing a little respect goes a long way to making sure Calgary's outdoor areas (parks, pathways, and natural areas) can be enjoyed by everyone who uses them—both now and in the future. A little respect also ensures the plants and animals that live in Calgary's outdoors can thrive.

You can show respect by:
- Observing hours of operation and posted signs.
- Sticking to established pathways and trails. The more people stray from designated routes, the more flora, fauna, and terrain is disturbed and eventually destroyed.
- Picking up after yourself. Your litter is not someone else's treasure.
- Leaving wildlife and plants alone. No feeding, chasing, or hunting animals. No picking berries or digging up plants for your home garden.
- Keeping your dog under control, and always picking up after it.

CONNECT
The City of Calgary   www.calgary.ca/parks
Visit the City of Calgary's website to find dozens of links on Calgary's parks and pathways. The site includes the addresses of all regional parks, maps, outdoor programs, booking information, and much more. For additional information, Calgary Parks and Calgary Recreation can be reached through the City information line at 3-1-1.

Calgary Area Outdoor Council   www.caoc.ab.ca
1111 Memorial Dr. NW
Calgary, Alberta, T2N 3E4
T: (403) 270-2262, F: (403) 270-3654, E: caoc@caoc.ab.ca
Office hours: 1200 to 1700 hours, Tuesday to Friday
This umbrella group actively and passionately represents the pursuits, concerns, and interests of nearly 100 outdoor groups in the Calgary area. CAOC's mission is "to champion the needs and interests of the outdoor recreation community through representation, education, communication, and leadership." This umbrella group actively and passionately represents the pursuits, concerns, and interests of nearly 100 outdoor groups in the Calgary area. CAOC's mission is "to champion the needs and interests of the outdoor recreation community through representation, education, communication, and leadership."

BIKES AND C-TRAINS
Calgary transit users can bring their bikes on the City's C-Train for free during off-peak hours: weekdays before 0630 hours and after 1800 hours, and all day on weekends and statutory holidays.

The following rules are also in effect:
- Cyclists must walk their bikes in C-Trains and C-Train stations as well as

on C-Train platforms, pedestrian bridges, and access ramps.
- Cyclists must use the doors at the end of C-Train cars.
- Only four bikes are allowed on each C-Train car (two at each end).
- Cyclists under 16 years of age must be accompanied by an adult.
- Cyclists must give the right-of-way to other C-Train riders and remain with their bikes at all times.

Fully enclosed bike parking/storage is available at the Anderson, Brentwood, Chinook, and Whitehorn C-Train stations. Cyclists must bring their own locks.

DOGS AND PARKS AND PATHWAYS
Love it or hate it, Calgary bylaws state all dogs are to be leashed when not on their owner's property. The City exercises some flexibility in its animal control bylaws; nonetheless, dogs must be leashed on all pathways (pathways with asphalt, concrete, or brick surfaces), even on pathways in off leash areas. Currently, the one exception to this rule is at Southland Natural Area, where dogs can be off leash anywhere in the park.

A dog's leash is not to be more than two metres long and the dog must be under the owner's control at all times.

Dogs are not allowed on playgrounds, athletic/sports fields, cemeteries, school grounds, in the Glenmore Reservoir, or in areas signed by the Parks department. As well, dogs are not allowed to chase or interfere with pathway users.

Dogs in Calgary's parks and natural areas must be under their owner's control at all times.

Calgary has dozens of off leash areas for dogs and their owners to enjoy. When using off leash areas, the City of Calgary requires dog owners to:

- Maintain control of their pets and ensure pets return when called.
- Be courteous to other dogs and to owners.
- Pick up the poop. Failing to pick up after a dog can lead to a $250 fine.
- Drop the poop in garbage cans (where provided) or take home.
- Respect wildlife. Do not encourage dogs to chase, catch, or stalk wildlife. Also, frightened or provoked wildlife can attack dogs or humans. In particular, encounters with skunks and porcupines can be disruptive, painful, and costly to people and pets alike.

A full listing of Calgary's off leash areas is posted on the City of Calgary's website (www.calgary.ca).

FISHING IN CALGARY

One of the world's finest sport fishing rivers, the Bow River is famous for its brown trout and rainbow trout and is ranked among North America's top ten trout streams.

While much of the fishing along the river is of the catch-and-release variety, a licence is still required for anyone 16 to 64 years old who plans to cast a line into the Bow or any other body of water in Alberta. Anglers must also have a Wildlife Identification Number before purchasing a fishing licence.

Fishing regulations and areas can vary from year to year and it's your responsibility to know the current ones.

For information on fishing regulations and licences, visit http://www.srd.gov.ab.ca/fw/licencesys/index.html.

The Bow River is famous the world over for its brown trout and rainbow trout fishing.

DISTANCE CHARTS

Source: www.calgary.ca/parks

Bow River E	Fort Calgary	St. George's Isl Br	17 Ave. Br	Ogden Rd. Br	Southland Pedestr. Br	Douglasdale Pedestr. Br	McKenzie Pedestr. Br	Burns Ranch	Sikome Lake
Fort Calgary	0.0	0.9	3.2	6.6	12.8	17.4	22.6	24.2	25.2
St. George's Isl Br.	0.9	0.0	2.3	5.7	12.0	16.5	21.7	23.3	24.3
17 Ave. Br	3.2	2.3	0.0	3.5	9.7	14.2	19.5	21.0	22.0
Ogden Rd. Br.	6.6	5.7	3.5	0.0	5.3	9.8	15.1	16.7	17.6
Southland Pedestr. Br.	12.8	12.0	9.7	5.3	0.0	4.5	9.8	11.4	12.3
Douglasdale Pedestr. Br.	17.4	16.5	14.2	9.8	4.5	0.0	5.3	6.8	7.8
McKenzie Pedestr. Br.	22.6	21.7	19.5	15.1	9.8	5.3	0.0	1.6	2.6
Burns Ranch	24.2	23.3	21.0	16.7	11.4	6.8	1.6	0.0	1.0
Sikome Lake	25.2	24.3	22.0	17.6	12.3	7.8	2.6	1.0	0.0

Laterals: Bow River—Chestermere Lake

Bow River W	Fort Calgary	St. Patrick's Isl Br	Prince's Isl.	C-Train Br.	Crowchild Tr. Br.	Edworthy Pk. Br.	Bowness Rd. Br.	Bowness Railway Br.	Stoney Tr. Br.	Valley Ridge
Fort Calgary	0.0	0.5	2.4	3.5	6.1	9.6	12.5	17.9	20.5	22.3
St. Patrick's Isl Br.	0.5	0.0	1.9	2.9	5.5	9.1	11.9	17.4	19.9	21.8
Prince's Isl.	2.4	1.9	0.0	1.0	3.6	7.2	10.0	15.5	18.0	19.9
C-Train Br.	3.5	2.9	1.0	0.0	2.6	6.2	9.0	14.5	17.0	18.8
Crowchild Tr. Br.	6.1	5.5	3.6	2.6	0.0	3.6	6.4	11.9	14.4	16.2
Edworthy Pk. Br.	9.6	9.1	7.2	6.2	3.6	0.0	2.8	8.3	10.8	12.7
Bowness Rd. Br.	12.5	11.9	10.0	9.0	6.4	2.8	0.0	5.5	8.0	9.8
Bowness Railway Br.	17.9	17.4	15.5	14.5	11.9	8.3	5.5	0.0	2.6	4.4
Stoney Tr. Br.	20.5	19.9	18.0	17.0	14.4	10.8	8.0	2.6	0.0	1.8
Valley Ridge	22.3	21.8	19.9	18.8	16.2	12.7	9.8	4.4	1.8	0.0

Elbow River/Glenmore Res.

	Fort Calgary	Lindsay Pk.	Stanley Pk.	Sandy Beach	Glen/14 St. Br.	Heritage Pk.	Glen Ldg.	Glen S/24 St.	Glen S/37 St.	Weaselhead Br.	Glen N/37 St.	Glen/14 St. Br.
Fort Calgary	0.0	3.5	6.6	8.7	11.4	13.3	14.2	15.8	17.3	20.6	21.0	27.1
Lindsay Pk.	3.5	0.0	3.1	5.2	7.9	9.8	10.7	12.3	13.8	17.1	17.9	23.6
Stanley Pk.	6.6	3.1	0.0	2.1	4.7	6.7	7.6	9.2	10.6	14.0	14.8	20.4
Sandy Beach	8.7	5.2	2.1	0.0	2.6	4.6	5.5	7.1	8.5	11.9	12.7	18.3
Glenmore/14 St. Br.	11.4	7.9	4.7	2.6	0.0	1.9	2.9	4.4	5.9	9.3	10.0	15.7
Heritage Pk.	13.3	9.8	6.7	4.6	1.9	0.0	0.9	2.5	4.0	7.3	8.1	13.8
Glenmore Ldg.	14.2	10.7	7.6	5.5	2.9	0.9	0.0	1.6	3.0	6.4	7.2	12.8
Glenmore S/24 St.	15.8	12.3	9.2	7.1	4.4	2.5	1.6	0.0	1.5	4.8	5.6	11.3
Glenmore S/37 St.	17.3	13.8	10.6	8.5	5.9	4.0	3.0	1.5	0.0	3.4	4.2	9.8
Weaselhead Br.	20.6	17.1	14.0	11.9	9.3	7.3	6.4	4.8	3.4	0.0	0.8	6.4
Glenmore N/37 St.	21.4	17.9	14.8	12.7	10.0	8.1	7.2	5.6	4.2	0.8	0.0	5.7
Glenmore/14 St. Br.	27.1	23.6	20.4	18.3	15.7	13.8	12.8	11.3	9.8	6.4	5.7	0.0

Fish Ck./37 St. SW

	Burns Ranch	Fish Ck./MacLeod Tr.	Fish Ck./Elbow Dr.	Fish Ck./24 St.	Fish Ck./37 St.	37 St./130 Ave.	37 St./Anderson Rd.	37 St./98 Ave. Jct.	37 St./S Glenmore Pk.
Burns Ranch	0.0	5.2	6.9	10.3	12.1	13.2	15.0	16.9	18.8
Fish Ck./MacLeod Tr.	5.2	0.0	1.7	5.1	6.9	8.0	9.8	11.7	13.6
Fish Ck./Elbow Dr.	6.9	1.7	0.0	3.4	5.2	6.3	8.1	10.0	11.9
Fish Ck./24 St.	10.3	5.1	3.4	0.0	1.8	2.9	4.8	6.6	8.5
Fish Ck./37 St.	12.1	6.9	5.2	1.8	0.0	1.1	2.9	4.8	6.7
37 St./130 Ave.	13.2	8.0	6.3	2.9	1.1	0.0	1.9	3.7	5.6
37 St./Anderson Rd.	15.0	9.8	8.1	4.8	2.9	1.9	0.0	1.9	3.7
37 St./98 Ave. Jct.	16.9	11.7	10.0	6.6	4.8	3.7	1.9	0.0	1.9
37 St./S Glenmore Pk.	18.8	13.6	11.9	8.5	6.7	5.6	3.7	1.9	0.0

Nose Ck./West Nose Ck.

	Nose Ck./Bow R. Jct.	Nose Ck./16 Ave. Jct.	Nose Ck./Beddington Blvd. Pthwy. Jct.	Nose Ck. Pk.	W Nose Ck./Country Hills Blvd. Jct.
Nose Ck./Bow R Jct.	0.0	2.6	10.3	12.9	15.2
Nose Ck./16 Ave. Jct.	2.6	0.0	7.6	10.3	12.5
Nose Ck./Beddington Blvd. Pthwy. Jct.	10.3	7.6	0.0	2.7	4.9
Nose Ck. Pk.	12.9	10.3	2.7	0.0	2.2
W Nose Ck./Country Hills Blvd. Jct.	15.2	12.5	4.9	2.2	0.0

BOW RIVER PATHWAY (BRP)
CALGARY'S GRAND RIVER

In Calgary, the glacier-fed Bow River is the thread that stitches together many of the city's parks and natural areas.

Cool, clear, and quick, the Bow River flows into northwest Calgary upstream of Stoney Tr. NW. It turns, curves, and braids through the city for more than 25 kilometres, silently exiting the city about three kilometres south of the Marquis of Lorne Tr. in the far southeast corner of Calgary.

Without the Bow River, Calgary would likely not exist. Had the North West Mounted Police arrived here in 1875 and found only the Elbow River, they probably would have kept marching.

For centuries, the Bow River has sustained life on the prairies. For the plains' first inhabitants, the Bow River was a source of food, water, and transportation. Today, more than a third of Albertans depend on it for water. In Calgary, this glacier-fed river is also the thread that stitches together many of the city's parks and natural areas.

Within the city limits, pathways in one form or another run the river's entire length. Hardy cyclists can easily cover this distance in a day, although to be truly savoured and appreciated, the river and its shores are best explored in smaller, more leisurely segments.

BEARSPAW EAST

BEARSPAW EAST AT A GLANCE

LOCATION	Beneath Stoney Tr. NW at Bow River
HOURS	0500 to 2300 daily
TERRAIN	Steep, heavily forested escarpment on south banks; flat to rolling grasslands and wetlands on north shore
ACCESS	Stoney Tr. and Scenic Bow Rd. NW
	West of 85 St. and Scenic Bow Rd. NW
ACTIVITIES	Walking, hiking, cycling, birdwatching
FACILITIES	Park benches
DOGS	On leash on pathways
TRANSIT	#1, #70 (Valley Ridge Dr.), #130, #148 (Stoney Tr. NW)

To the first-time visitor, Bearspaw East is a little wild and a little remote. To regular users—most often residents of Tuscany, Scenic Acres, Valley Ridge, Bowness and other northwest communities—the area is a treasure to the more and more people who discover it every year.

Depending on your point of view, Bearspaw East is either the beginning or the end of the line, upstream of Bowness and Baker parks. As a park, the area is new in the sense that fewer than a dozen years ago, only a handful of foot trails ran through the area. But Bearspaw East has long been recognized as a vital link in Calgary's parks and pathways network and will eventually link to the Bearspaw Legacy Park (see sidebar).

In recent years, a link has been forged to Calgary's existing network with the construction of several pathways on both sides of the river and a pedestrian bridge below Stoney Tr.

The floods of 2005 weakened that link temporarily, eroding the bridge abutments, submerging the wetlands on the north shore, and cutting off the most convenient connection between the area's two solitudes: its steep, moist escarpment on the south shore and its drier, flatter grasslands on the north shore.

Bearspaw East near Stoney Tr. NW.

Pathway Description—Bearspaw East/Valley Ridge

At Valley Ridge Blvd., a paved pathway runs along Valley Ridge Park NW and the Valley Ridge Golf and Country Club, climbing from the river valley to the top of the escarpment. Travelling generally eastward, the pathway winds along the top of the escarpment, flanked by Valley Ridge homes on the right and stands of aspen trees on the left.

Occasionally, a cutline or open ridge reveals an expansive view of the river valley. Several feeder pathways link to the community and a nearby bike route on Valley Springs Dr. NW and Valley Ridge Dr. NW. Watchful travellers can also spot links to the foot trails that criss-cross the escarpment below, but many simply peter out or become difficult to follow.

Just west of Stoney Tr. NW, the paved pathway drops into the cool, shady forest and begins a long series of tight switchbacks down to the riverbank. Cyclists will want to have their brakes in good working order to navigate the twists and turns. Hikers may want to opt for the connecting foot trails that are a little less steep and a little easier on the knee joints.

The total elevation drop is about 45 metres; the actual distance travelled is several hundred metres, a distance which seems much farther when going back up the hill.

As the pathway levels and leaves the forest it approaches the Stoney Tr. Pedestrian bridge. To continue downstream, follow the gravel trail through Bowness Park.

You can also take in the sights of the river valley at the viewpoint immediately upstream of the bridge. The viewpoint is also a good access/egress point to the escarpment's foot trails.

Pathway Description—North Shore

From the north end of the pedestrian bridge at Stoney Tr. NW, the Bow River Pathway (BRP) travels east along the riverbank, passing a large red barn that is the stable for the Shriners' Al Azhar Mounted Patrol. The Al Azhar Shrine Centre also features a large meeting and banquet facility, a large, idyllic pond surrounded by lawns, trees, and pathways, and an outdoor gazebo/stage with ample spectator seating.

The pathway runs by a storm sewer runoff and, just past Stoney Tr., connects to the Nose Hill Dr. pathway. The Bow River Pathway continues east along a rolling open area, past the Bearspaw Water Intake Pump Station and into Baker Park.

Bearspaw Legacy Park

In 2003, Calgary's mayor, Dave Bronconnier, announced a $50-million Enmax Legacy Parks Plan and the addition of more than 2,300 acres of park space to Calgary in the next five years.

The plan will see three new multi-use parks created on Calgary's current outer limits (and sometimes outside its current limits): Bearspaw in the northwest, Shepard Wetlands in the southeast, and Clearwater Park, upstream of Griffith Woods, in southwest Calgary along the Elbow River.

The Bearspaw Legacy Park will be located upstream of the Bearspaw East area and will sit on more than 340 hectares (800 acres) of land. The site is described as "dramatic riverbank and escarpment lands with a mix of high quality native prairie, aspen and mountain environments. The adjacent Bearspaw reservoir provides a unique opportunity for aquatic-based activities."

The proposed park will have three distinct "zones":

- A conservation zone will feature interpretive and hiking trails
- An active zone will be created for sports activities
- An infrastructure zone will have an access road, parking, and washrooms

BOWNESS PARK

BOWNESS PARK AT A GLANCE

LOCATION	8900 – 48 Ave. NW
HOURS	0500 to 2300 daily
TERRAIN	Mostly flat and landscaped with natural areas at east and west ends; pathway winds through trees and along river and lagoon
ACCESS	About three blocks west of 85 St. on Bow Cres. NW Downstream of Stoney Tr. NW on south shore of Bow River
ACTIVITIES	Walking, hiking, cycling, paddleboats (summer), skating (winter), canoeing (on river and lagoon), fishing, picnicking, playgrounds, amusement rides, minigolf, amphitheatre
FACILITIES	Washrooms throughout; some open year-round Picnic shelters (bookings required) Outdoor theatre
CONCESSION	Lagoon Café and Cappuccino Bar open year-round
DOGS	On leash in most areas. Not allowed within 20 metres of playgrounds
BOOKINGS	To book picnic shelters and tables, call the City of Calgary at 268-3830
TRANSIT	#1, #105 (48 Ave. NW), #40 (85 St. NW)

Long before it was ever in Calgary, Bowness Park was one of Calgarians' favourite parks. When it was first built, the park just happened to be in the town of Bowness.

For close to 90 years, this park has offered year-round activities: skating and bonfires in the winter, and picnics and amusement rides in the summer.

Bowness Park was built just before the First World War by John Hextall, a land developer and speculator, who had hoped to turn the park into a weekend country retreat (see sidebar). Taking a page from New York's Coney Island, he added a number of amusement rides and attractions, among them a scale-model railway line and a

On hot summer days, nothing beats the heat like a trip to Bowness Park.

Bowness Park's west end features the Wood's Douglas Fir Tree Sanctuary.

fountain in the middle of the lagoon. Updated versions of both remain, as do the park's original and expansive picnic grounds and lagoon.

Located along the Bow River's south shore downstream of Stoney Tr. NW and across the river from Baker Park, this relatively narrow park actually extends past 85 St. NW, although its distant east end attracts far fewer visitors. A shallow lagoon runs along most of the park's southern edge, offering a tranquil setting for paddleboating in the summer, and a meandering skating surface in the winter.

Much of the park is landscaped and groomed, although its south, east, and west edges are naturally and densely forested. Bowness Park's west end features the Wood's Douglas Fir Tree Sanctuary; the east end is virtually undeveloped except for a smattering of foot trails.

A paved road loops through the park's west end and is dotted with a number of gravel parking lots.

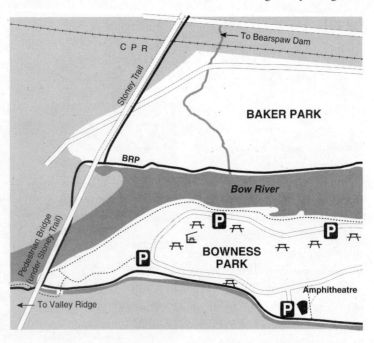

These make it easy for picnickers to reach the park's popular and well-used kitchen shelters, picnic tables, firepits, and playgrounds.

The park is generally flat and less than a kilometre wide, making the Bow River almost always within sight and easy to reach. Several groynes (constructed rock outcrops or jetties that protect the riverbank from erosion) make good viewpoints, fishing piers, and small boat launches.

Pathway Description

Immediately downstream from Stoney Tr. NW, a well established gravel trail travels east–west through Bowness Park. Starting from the west end, the pathway divides into several trails which eventually reconnect. A secondary route skirts the north shore of the lagoon's narrow west channel; another less-trodden route travels through the Wood's Douglas Fir Trail Sanctuary on the south side of the lagoon and emerges onto the grounds of Wood's Homes at the west end of Bow Cres. NW, a good three blocks west of the park's entrance on the same street.

From the main entrance to Bowness Park, a pathway travels to the Lagoon Café and Cappuccino Bar along the lagoon, which opens substantially. In the summer, a fountain in the middle sprays a column of water into the air. Weather

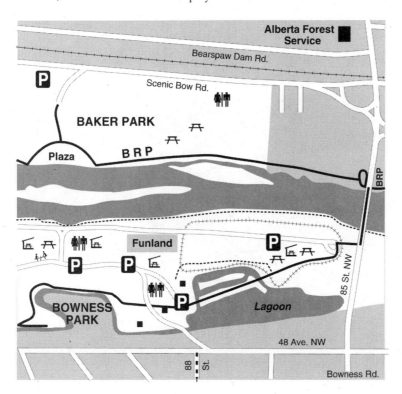

permitting in the winter, the lagoon is a well-loved outdoor skating rink with firepits and benches close to shore offering warmth and respite for frost-nipped skaters.

As the pathway continues eastward, it crosses two pedestrian bridges spanning an arm of the lagoon and a set of narrow-gauge railway tracks, then angles back toward the river and up a slight hill to the 85 St. NW bridge crossing, where it connects to the Bow River Pathway and Bowmont Park on the Bow River's north shores.

Calgary's Coney Island

Before the First World War, Bowness Park was the Coney Island of Calgary. People would flock by streetcar to the countryside retreat.

The man behind the park was landowner and developer John Hextall, who wanted to build a model suburban community where people could enjoy country life along the Bow River. Confident and brash, Hextall began selling lots for a then unheard of $1,500 but he was missing an important, and expensive, link: transportation.

Hextall struck a shrewd bargain with City Council: in exchange for a trolley car line to Bowness, he would donate parkland. Hextall had already built a golf course, bridge, and power plant. Council needed little convincing of the deal.

The first trolley car arrived in Bowness Park June 30, 1912, but with the coming of the Great War, money was scarce. Hextall died soon after and the Calgary Transit System took over park operations after the land fell into bankruptcy. The park's popularity returned after the war even though it took the better part of a morning to travel the 15 kilometres from downtown Calgary to Bowness.

Most parks in Calgary offered peace and tranquility, but the attraction of Bowness Park was the opposite: there was a merry-go-round with calliope music, a fountain that was lit at night, a large dance hall, and a state-of-the art orthophonic gramophone.

When the town of Bowness was annexed by Calgary in 1964, Bowness Park was no longer a country park but was still a great favourite with Calgarians, and remains so to this day. The park today has a number of family rides and attractions, including a scaled-down railway line.

Once the Coney Island of Calgary, Bowness Park features
a number of family rides and attractions.

BAKER PARK

BAKER PARK AT A GLANCE

LOCATION	9333 Scenic Bow Rd. NW
HOURS	0500 to 2300 daily
TERRAIN	Gently rolling with formal landscaping; pathway along river and lagoon
ACCESS	West of 85 St. on Scenic Bow Rd. NW
	East of Stoney Tr. NW on Scenic Bow Rd. NW
ACTIVITIES	Walking, cycling, picnics, weddings
FACILITIES	Washrooms (seasonal)
	Water fountains (seasonal)
	Picnic areas (bookings recommended)
	Grass amphitheatre
	River observation point and promenade
	Gazebo and arbour
DOGS	On leash
BOOKINGS	To book picnic area and other facilities, call the City of Calgary at 268-3830
TRANSIT	#40, #130, #148

The restorative powers of Baker Park's landscaped grounds are almost palpable—as are echoes of the past. The old-fashioned formality of this park is

The observation point at Baker Park offers soothing sun-baked
views of the Bow River and Bowness Park.

Trans Canada Trail

A project once headed by the late Bill Pratt, former president of the Calgary Olympic Winter Games and one of the city's greatest builders (he was cowboy-hat wearing project manager for Heritage Park, Chinook Centre, and the Stampede Grandstand), the Trans Canada Trail is "the most ambitious endeavour ever undertaken by Canada's volunteer sector."

When completed, the trail will ramble for 18,000 kilometres through every province and territory and some 800 communities. Not just a single thread, in many sections the trail is a mini-network, travelling through and to points of interest with environmental, historical, and recreational significance.

The Trans Canada Trail runs along 60 kilometres of pathways in Calgary.

A native of Ontario who came West in the 1950s and became thoroughly and completely Westernized right down to his ever-present cowboy boots, Pratt was head of Canada 125 (the organization overseeing Canada's 125th anniversary celebrations) when the trail was proposed in 1992, and is credited with establishing the Trans Canada Trail Foundation. For several years he led the fundraising effort to build the trail, an effort which included offering Canadians a metre of the trail. Supporters can still purchase a metre of trail for $50.

The trail's purpose is to "establish and maintain a recreational trail for all Canadians to allow hikers, canoeists, bicyclists, horseback riders, cross-country skiers, snowmobilers (where appropriate), and others, including the physically challenged, to explore and learn about Canada."

In Calgary the Trans Canada Trail runs:
- Along the Nose Creek Pathway from the confluence with West Nose Creek south of the confluence with the Bow River.
- Along the Bow River Pathway, on the north bank of the river from Prince's Island to the confluence with Nose Creek. On the south bank, the trail runs from Prince's Island to the south end of Fish Creek Provincial Park.
- Along the Elbow River Pathway from Weaselhead Natural Area north to the Elbow River Pathway via North Glenmore Park and the Glenmore Athletic Park.
- Along the Elbow River Pathway from Glenmore Athletic Park to the confluence with the Bow River.

A Trans Canada Trail Pavilion outlining the trail's scope, purpose, and supporters is located downstream of Prince's Island in Sien Lok Park (near Riverfront Ave. and 1 St. SW).

For further information, visit: www.tctrail.ca.

somewhat unusual for Calgary, but given that the site was once a sanatorium for First World War soldiers (see sidebar "A Venerable History"), it seems perfectly suited.

Baker Park exudes a calm orderliness, even at its sunny Sunday afternoon busiest. It's not hard to imagine frail soldiers strolling along the park's geometrical walkways or along arrow-straight allées (an avenue or walkway lined with trees).

Today, you'll also see church picnics and outdoor weddings at Baker Park. The park's mature stands of planted trees (some 1,800 of them), amphitheatre, observation point, promenade, gazebo, and arbour give groups of all sizes both a place and a reason to gather.

At 23.5 hectares (58 acres), Baker Park is not overly large, but it does feel expansive and its series of gracious open spaces is well defined and modestly private thanks to landscape architecture that has evolved over the past nine

Once a place of convalescence for soldiers, today Baker Park welcomes visitors of every description.

decades. This is a soothing, relaxing place to watch the river, people, and time go by. The promenade and sun bowl overlooking the Bow River and the Bow River Pathway are perhaps the park's most public spaces. Both quietly attract and captivate park visitors.

A Venerable History

The Baker Centre site has a venerable history. The first buildings were constructed in 1918 by the Soldiers' Civil Re-establishment Department, Government of Canada, for use as a Tuberculosis Sanatorium. The site was at that time outside Calgary's city limits. The centre was renamed the Baker Memorial Sanatorium in 1950 in honour of Dr. A.H. Baker, who retired that year after serving as director for 30 years. After 1962, use of the site gradually changed to services for the mentally and physically handicapped...Alberta Public Works, Supply and Services undertook demolition of the buildings in 1989. The remarkable stands of mature trees remaining on the site are the legacy left to us by the early gardeners at Baker Centre.

Condensed from City of Calgary Urban Park Master Plan, Baker Park, January 1995.

Pathway Description—Baker Park

The Bow River Pathway enters Baker Park east of the Bearspaw Water Intake Pump Station and across the river from Bowness Park. Hugging the river's north shore, the pathway travels past tree allées and the former sanatorium site. The rows of trees give way to a large promenade, observation point, and sun bowl in the middle of the park. The pathway continues more or less due east along the riverbank for another few hundred metres. Beyond the park's eastern edge, the pathway continues past a group home to 85 St. NW and Bowmont Park. The distance between Stoney Tr. and 85 St. NW is about 1.5 kilometres.

Family trees

Every Calgary park has its trees, but those at Baker Park stand out because so many of them—an estimated 1,800—were planted and tended by gardeners at the former sanatorium. As well as native trees and shrubs along the river's edge, Baker Park's "family" of planted tree species includes:

White Spruce	Green Ash	Colorado Spruce
Manitoba Maple	Lodgepole Pine	Bur Oak
Scots Pine	Aspen	Douglas Fir
Larch	Poplar	May Day Tree
Paper Birch	Mountain Ash	Weeping Birch
Hawthorn	Manchurian Elm	Flowering Crabapple

BOWMONT PARK

BOWMONT PARK AT A GLANCE

LOCATION	North bank of Bow River from 85 St. to Home Rd. NW
HOURS	0500 to 2300 daily
TERRAIN	Flood plain rising to steep wind-swept escarpments with well-protected ravines and valley; pathway climbs at west end of park to top of escarpment and drops back to valley floor at park's eastern end
ACCESS	85 St. and Bearspaw Dam Rd. NW (west end)
	32 Ave. and Home Rd. NW (east end)
	Silver Valley Blvd., Silver Crest Dr., Silverview Dr., Silverview Way, and 40 Ave. NW
ACTIVITIES	Walking, hiking, cycling, bird and nature watching, cross-country skiing
FACILITIES	Benches
	Observation points
DOGS	Mix of on and off leash areas with a pilot off leash area
INFORMATION	City of Calgary at 3-1-1
TRANSIT	#37, #47, #137, #147 (all via Silver Springs)

Although Bowmont and Bowness parks are within easy walking distance of one another, they are surprisingly different.

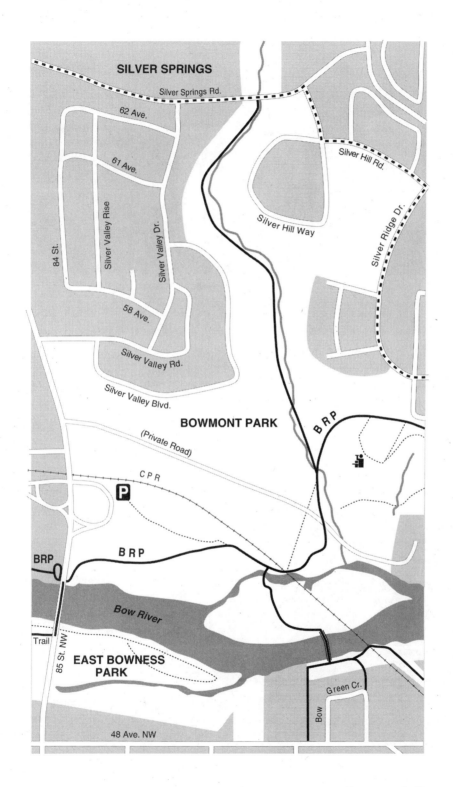

Views such as this make the climbs worthwhile at Bowmont Park.

Bowness Park's cool moist forests, manicured lawns, countless picnic tables, and amusement park rides bear little resemblance to Bowmont Park's glacier-carved coulees, prairie uplands, and native flowers.

With its southern exposure, Bowmont soaks up almost every ray of the 2,400 hours of sunlight that shine on Calgary every year. This rambling, rolling area has relatively few added amenities (several kilometres of paved pathways, an intricate web of "desire" paths—foot trails carved by users choosing to go their own way—a smattering of benches, wastebaskets and some well-placed signs), yet it lacks for nothing. Well, a washroom would be nice, given that the park spans about four kilometres from west to east. A minor point.

Long-time park users remember when the area was called Montgomery Flats. The park was renamed Bowmont—an amalgamation of the names of Bowness

On the run: the varied terrain of Bowmont Park's pathways is perfect training ground.

and Montgomery communities— in the mid-1970s. A long-ago plan envisioned Bowmont as a much more intensely developed outdoor space. Local residents vehemently rejected the notion and have spent the best part of 30 years encouraging the conservation and preservation of the park's natural environment.

This is a difficult balancing act given that in the late 1800s the area was part of the sprawling

Cochrane Ranch. As well, the railway line built on the park's west end in 1883 by the Canadian Pacific Railway (CPR) is still one of the most used rail routes in the country. The northeast section of the park was a gravel pit for 40 years and will slowly be renaturalized. And, of course, as Calgary's suburbs have grown, park use has increased. Little wonder that some precious habitat and species have been eroded or diminished. More wondrous is that a dazzling variety remains.

Among the vegetation listed in the Bowmont Natural Environment Park Management Plan of 2003 are: needle, wheat, rough fescue and June grasses, Parry's oatgrass, juniper, Prairie crocus, early cinquefoil, moss phlox, lupine, fleabane, northern bedstraw, sagewort, and goldenrod. Bowmont's riverine forests feature stands of balsam poplars with an understorey of red osier dogwood, water birch, saskatoon, wolf willow, and Canada buffalo berry.

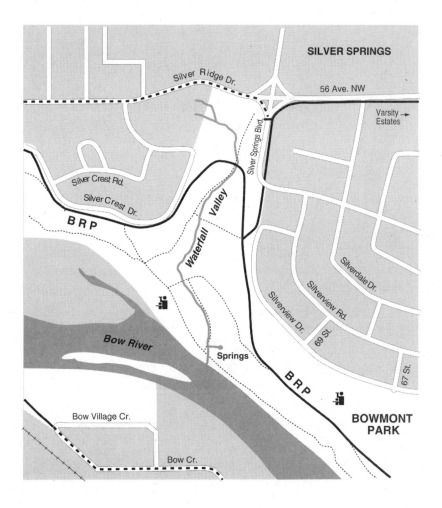

Wooded areas in the ravines also contain balsam poplar as well as trembling aspen.

Like many parks and natural areas along Calgary's waterways, Bowmont Park is long (4 kilometres) and narrow (seldom more than a kilometre). It stretches between 85 St. and Home Rd. NW on the north bank of the Bow River. The 158 hectares (390 acres) that make up Bowmont Park cover a wide variety of terrain—river flats, islands, and southwest-facing slopes and ravines. The ravines have an almost magnetic attraction, and people are inevitably drawn to them.

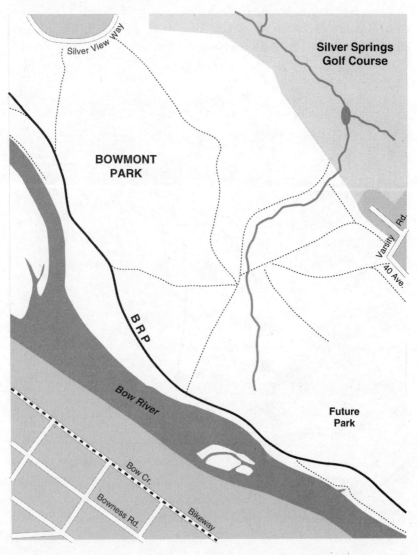

The central ravine is commonly called Waterfall Valley. In moist years, three natural springs bubble up and cascade down sandstone and shale. As water percolates through the carbonate calcium in the rocks it forms a buildup of tufa that deer use as a lick. When the springs flow in the winter, they can form a beautiful mantle of ice on the hillside. In warmer seasons, red elderberry, fragile fern, and alkali buttercup can be found here.

In April, the pale purple prairie crocus dots Bowmont's hills, signalling the pending arrival of spring. In June, plants blossom throughout the park. With only the barest of effort, more than a dozen varieties and a rainbow of colour can be spotted, especially in the flats just upstream of the existing gravel pit/concrete plant.

In spring the pale purple prairie crocus can be found nestled in the hills of Bowmont Park.

Pathway Description—Bowmont Park

The Bowmont Park section of the Bow River Pathway (BRP) is downstream of Baker Park on the Bow River's north bank. The pathway eases north slightly to avoid a marshy riverbank and zigzags east for about a kilometre through riverine forest.

As the pathway reaches the CPR railway, it branches: the south branch crosses the Bow River via a pedestrian bridge and runs a short distance before linking to an on-street cycling route on Bow Cres. NW. The Bow River Pathway continues east: past the railway bridge, the terrain opens and the route heads north, crossing a gravel access road and a second parking lot before beginning a demanding uphill climb. A fork to the north links to the community of Silver Springs. After cutting through the natural landscape of the ravine, the pathway climbs steadily for about a kilometre.

A leg-burner going up (and effortless going down), the pathway offers a few well-placed benches for rest stops and viewpoints. At the top of the ravine, the pathway intersects with a cycling route on Silver Springs Rd.

The Bow River Pathway continues east, making a steep short climb for about 300 metres, levelling out to offer a great view of Canada Olympic Park to

The shores of Bowmont Park attract visitors throughout the year.

An extensive pilot program at Bowmont Park is aimed at seeing if dogs, park users, and natural areas can co-exist.

the south, the Rockies to the west, and the river valley below.

The paved pathway winds north on top of the rolling grassy hills, and hugs Silver Crest Dr. for several hundred metres before dipping into Waterfall Valley and climbing back out of the valley's opposite side (a footpathway at the top of the valley links to 56 Ave. and Silver Springs Blvd. NW.). The pathway climbs once again, wrapping around Silverview Dr. NW.

Passing through fragrant stands of poplar and willow, the pathway begins a long, weaving descent to the river valley, below the Silver Springs Golf and Country Club. It drops quickly across a series of terraces; at the valley floor, it levels and turns right to ramble through a riverine forest. As is the case throughout the park, dozens of footpaths offer alternative routes, although many have been recently closed to protect the area.

The main pathway continues east across the flood plain, site of two excellent riverside viewing areas. Continuing east, the pathway runs past the former Klippert Construction concrete plant and gravel pit (which will eventually become part of Bowmont Park) and dense stands of shrubs. At the east end of the park, the pathway makes a long and— depending on your level of fitness—arduous climb to emerge behind the Maranatha Church at the north end of Home Rd. NW.

From here, the Bow River Pathway connects to on-street cycling routes on 52 St. NW and Home Rd. NW. The 52 St. route (the shorter of the two) rejoins the pathway near Hextall Bridge; the Home Rd. route rejoins the pathway at the east end of Shouldice Park.

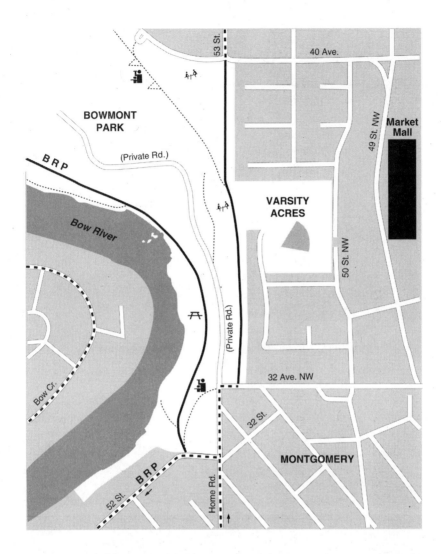

Permanent Trail Closures

Following heavy rains and flooding in 2005, the City of Calgary Parks permanently closed a number of trails along Bowmont Park's steep escarpments and riverbank. The closures are for both safety and environmental reasons. Several areas are unstable and allowing native grasses and shrubs to re-establish will prevent further erosion.

Signs clearly mark closed areas. Park users are asked to respect the permanent trail closures.

SHOULDICE PARK

LOCATION	Bowness Rd. and 56 St. NW
HOURS	0500 to 2300 daily
TERRAIN	Mainly flat plains and playing fields divided by Trans-Canada Hwy
ACCESS	Home Rd. and 13 Ave. NW
	Bowness Rd. and Monserrat Rd. NW
	Monserrat Rd. and 13 Ave. NW
	BRP downstream of Hextall Bridge, upstream of Edworthy Park
ACTIVITIES	Walking, cycling, picnics, playground, indoor swimming, soccer, baseball, tennis, football, basketball
FACILITIES	Soccer fields
	Baseball diamonds
	Tennis courts
	Basketball courts
	Washrooms (seasonal)
	Water fountains (seasonal)
	Concession (open for major sports tournaments)
	Batting cages (operated privately)
	Shouldice Swimming Pool (indoor)
	Shouldice Arena (indoor)
DOGS	On leash on pathway and within 20 metres of playgrounds and playing fields
BOOKINGS	To book soccer fields, baseball fields, tennis courts, or picnic sites, call 268-3830
TRANSIT	#40, #407, #408

Plenty of playing fields make Shouldice Park one of Calgary's best used athletic training areas.

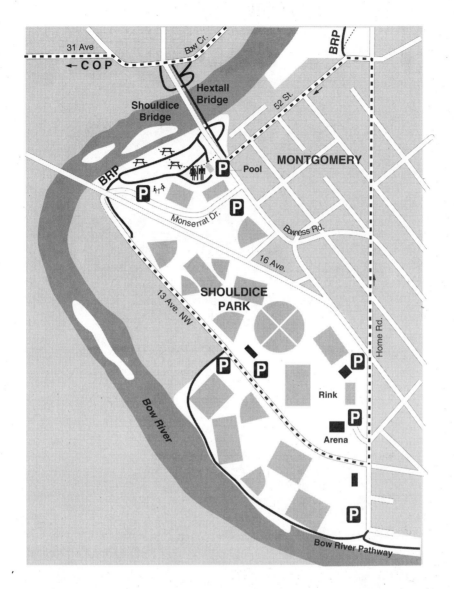

Located on either side of the Trans-Canada Highway between the Bow River and Home Rd. NW, Shouldice Park is best known as one of Calgary's largest athletic parks. The park occupies seven hectares and its amenities include riverside picnic tables, a large children's playground, an indoor swimming pool, a batting-practice cage, an indoor arena, and tennis courts.

Shouldice Park's natural area is huddled along the Bow River near Shouldice Bridge and offers a quiet stand of trees with picnic tables and gentle access to the river's edge. Away from the river, much of the park is billiard-

Shouldice Park's natural area is huddled along the
Bow River and offer a quiet stands of trees.

table flat with few trees in sight, making it an ideal field of play for soccer, football, and baseball.

Pathway Description—Shouldice Park

Past Hextall Bridge, the Bow River Pathway rises slightly to a T-intersection. The north (left) pathway loops through the park and later rejoins the main route. The south (right) pathway runs closely along the river, casually winding past a number of treed picnic sites, a playground, and tennis courts; further beyond is Shouldice Pool. The adjacent riverbank is easily scaled by people and geese alike—watch for either to appear at any time.

After passing underneath the Trans-Canada Highway, the route is along 13 Ave. NW, a bumpy gravel/oiled road, for a few hundred metres. Shortly after, the paved pathway resumes, skirting the south side of Shouldice Park's playing fields. With an ever-so-slight downhill gradient, the pathway easily covers ground to Home Rd., where, during the week, a park-and-ride lot gives cycling or running commuters the option of reducing their journey to and from downtown. On weekends and evenings, the parking lot is a convenient starting or stopping point for recreational pathway users.

Past Home Rd., the route takes a short jog along Montgomery Rd.; the pathway resumes at 43 St., where it is twinned to the Boothman Bridge at Edworthy Park.

Pathway etiquette calls for pedestrians to use the pathway closest to the river and for cyclists to use the pathway furthest from the river.

The generally flat pathway through Shouldice Park makes for easy travelling.

Going to the Dogs

For four days during the first week of August every year, Shouldice Park goes to the dogs. A sizable part of the park is home to the Alberta Kennel Club's Shows and Trials. The event attracts dog fanciers from across the province. The club itself is more than a century old (it was founded in 1904) and its member own all breeds of dogs. For information about entering or attending the annual Shows and Trials, visit www.albertakennelclub.org.

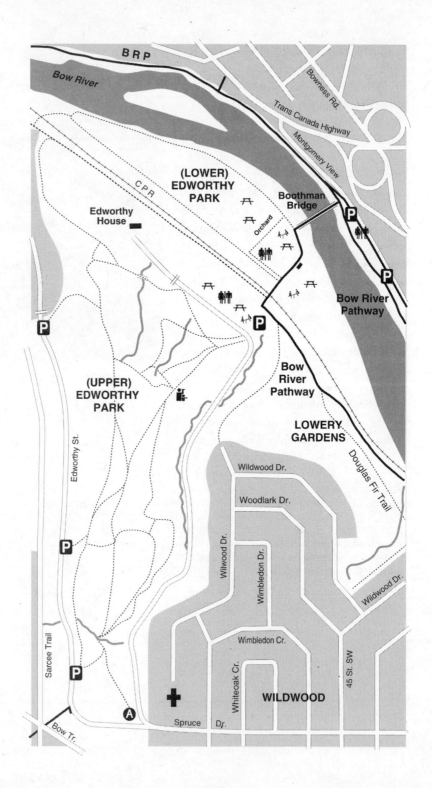

BRP

Bow River

Bowness Rd.

Trans Canada Highway

Montgomery View

(LOWER) EDWORTHY PARK

CPR

Edworthy House

Orchard

Boothman Bridge

P

P

Bow River Pathway

P

(UPPER) EDWORTHY PARK

Bow River Pathway

LOWERY GARDENS

Edworthy St.

Wildwood Dr.

Woodlark Dr.

Douglas Fir Trail

Wilwood Dr.

Wimbledon Dr.

Wildwood Dr.

P

Sarcee Trail

Wimbledon Cr.

Whiteoak Cr.

45 St. SW

P

WILDWOOD

A

Bow Tr.

Spruce Dr.

EDWORTHY PARK (INCLUDING LOWERY GARDENS AND THE DOUGLAS FIR TRAIL)

EDWORTHY PARK AT A GLANCE

LOCATION	Spruce Dr. and 45 St. SW
HOURS	0500 to 2300 daily
	Pathway along north bank closed in winter
TERRAIN	South shore of Bow River is steep escarpments, and includes the Douglas Fir Trail and large riparian forests with typically easy access to river's edge; north shore of Bow River is a rolling lawn
ACCESS	Shaganappi Tr. and Parkdale Blvd. NW
	Follow Spruce Dr. west of 45 St. SW
	Bow River Pathway
	Pathway from Strathcona
	Pathway from Cedar Cres. SW
	Pathway from Sovereign Cres. SW
	Numerous footpath connections from communities of Wildwood, Spruce Cliff, and Point McKay
ACTIVITIES	Walking, cycling, picnics, hiking, canoeing, nature watching, fishing
FACILITIES	Washrooms (seasonal)
	Water fountains (seasonal)
	Picnic areas (bookings recommended)
	Playgrounds
	Interpretive trails (Douglas Fir Trail)
DOGS	On leash on pathways, in most of the park, and within 20 metres of playgrounds and playing fields areas
	Off leash in Upper Edworthy area (off Spruce Dr. SW)
BOOKINGS	To book picnic areas, call the City of Calgary at 268-3830
TRANSIT	#1, #40, #105, #113 (from the north)
	#17, #53 (from the south)

Calgary has a number of larger parks, but it has few as diverse as Edworthy Park. This 127-hectare park has a little bit of everything: natural areas and well-used picnic areas; flat pathways and steep hiking trails; wetlands and windswept escarpments; towering trees and grasslands.

The park, which includes Lowery/Lawrey[1] Gardens and the Douglas Fir Trail, is rich with natural and human history. For centuries this area was a favourite gathering ground for Natives, who used the steep cliffs for buffalo

---

[1] Lowery Gardens and Lawrey Gardens are used equally, even by the City of Calgary, although the area is named for pioneer John Lowery.

jumps (see sidebar "Pieces of History"). In the early 1880s, the CPR constructed its main line along the south shore of the Bow River at the base of those cliffs. In the late 1800s, part of the park was homesteaded by pioneer Thomas Edworthy, who grew vegetables, raised dairy cattle, and quarried sandstone. The Douglas Fir Trail takes its name from a stately and easterly stand of Douglas fir trees—many more than 350 years old—and Lowery Gardens was a market garden in the city's earliest days.

Today, the area is within easy reach of several major roads—such as Bow Tr., Sarcee Tr., Shaganappi Tr., Parkdale Blvd., Bowness Rd., Crowchild Tr., and 16 Ave. NW. Edworthy Park is a year-round destination. People flock to the area to run, hike, explore, birdwatch, walk, fish, wade, dog walk, play, and picnic.

Pieces of History

When a heavy rainfall in the 1940s washed away part of the escarpment in Edworthy Park, a buffalo jump was exposed. Long before the arrival of European guns and horses, Plains Indians used geography to hunt buffalo. They would herd the giant animals toward the edge of a steep hill or cliff, whip them into a panic, and leave the frightened animals only one escape route: over the edge of the cliff.

In the 1880s, homesteader Thomas Edworthy cleared some of the land around the present-day park to start a market garden and dairy farm. Edworthy built an irrigation system to nurture his vegetables and, after harvesting them, hauled them eight kilometres into Calgary. Edworthy also quarried sandstone from the area, which was used to build several city landmarks: Central, Balmoral and Victoria schools, Knox United Church, and Fire Hall No. 2., Edworthy died of typhoid fever in 1904.

Another early Calgarian also recognized the area's agricultural potential. John Lowery also had a market garden about two kilometres downstream of Edworthy's homestead. Today the former vegetable plot bears his name: Lowery Gardens. In 1960 the Lowery family sold the land to the City of Calgary.

The timeworn "Brickburn" sign along the railway tracks near the park's south parking lot is one of the last reminders of a brick plant established by E. H. Crandall. The Brickburn factory manufactured the bricks used in many of Calgary's mansions. A plaque at the Boothman Bridge states: "In the 1920s factory output was up to 40,000 bricks daily. The Great Depression of the 1930s led to its closing."

The Boothman Bridge at Edworthy Park was built in the late 1970s and named after long-time Calgary Parks supervisor, Harry Boothman.

Pathway Description—Lower Edworthy (south shore)

From upstream of the Boothman Bridge to 17 Ave. SE, the Bow River Pathway is twinned on the north bank to give cyclists and pedestrians designated pathways. Typically, the pedestrian pathways are narrower and located closer to the river; the bicycle pathways are often slightly wider and more curvaceous (to discourage speeding). Accepted pathway etiquette is to follow the posted signs and use the pathways accordingly.

To explore the Edworthy Park, Douglas Fir Trail, and Lowery Gardens start at the Boothman Bridge. Three options exist on the south side of the bridge: travel east on the established pathway, west on a foot trail, or relax at the playground directly south of the bridge.

Wandering west, the foot trail cuts through a stand of trees, mainly poplars along the riverbank and rows of spruce and firs in Edworthy's one-time market garden. After about 150 metres, the trail opens up and runs adjacent to picnic tables, firepits, and playground equipment. Further along, overlooking the river, is a plaque commemorating George Edworthy which explains that the surrounding trees and orchards were planted by him in 1939 as he prepared to build a home on the site. Directly across from the plaque, almost hidden by trees, is the old Edworthy family home (now owned by the City of Calgary).

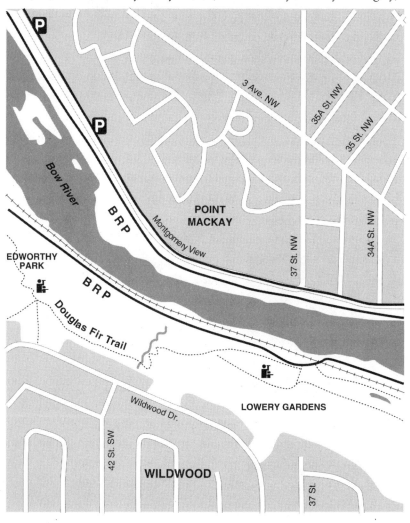

The windswept view from upper Edworthy Park.

The trail winds west through grasslands and eventually peters out along the CPR railway tracks or at the river's edge, depending on the route taken. To make a loop of the walk, cross the tracks and follow another trail back, this time closer to the Edworthy home and the north-facing escarpment (which is riddled with dozens of foot trails). On the way back are more picnic tables, firepits, and playground equipment as well as washroom facilities (closed during winter months).

Rock on: sandstone was once quarried in the Edworthy Park area.

The trail follows closely along the railway tracks and at the south parking lot intersects with several pathways. The north (gravel) trail leads quickly back to the Boothman Bridge and the east (paved) pathway skirts the foot of the Douglas Fir Trail and travels on to Lowery Gardens and points beyond in downtown Calgary.

The eastbound pathway is flanked by a steep hill and numerous foot trails lead to the top. The hill was once one of the city's most exciting toboggan runs but was officially closed several years ago after a fatal accident.

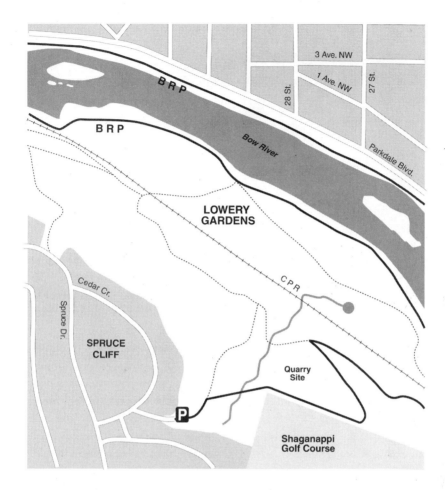

The openness of the grasslands is soon left behind as the Bow River Pathway hugs the base of the steep escarpment of the Douglas Fir Trail. The path rises slightly and is bordered by a chain-link fence that separates users from the adjacent CPR tracks.

From this point east for about a half kilometre, the trail can become dangerous and unnavigable during winter and well into the spring. Countless springs flow from the cliff and form sheets of ice that can reach thicknesses of a metre or more. This section of the pathway is officially closed in the winter; the ice can remain well into May.

Once past the stately stand of the Douglas Fir Trail, the hillside opens up. Midway along is a well established foot trail that climbs from east to west through a labyrinth of paths, bridges, steps, and stairs of the Douglas Fir Trail (see sidebar "Douglas Fir Trail").

Seasonal ice along the pathway below the
Douglas Fir Trail makes for a slippery passage.

The Bow River Pathway crosses the railway tracks and jogs north slightly along the riverbank. The route is flat and curves through stands of poplar, aspen, and willow as well as old gravel pits and a long-abandoned market garden. Given the area's flora and the pathway's meandering route, visibility can be limited.

Officially, Edworthy Park and Lowery Gardens end at the Crowchild Tr. overpass.

Pathway Description—Upper Edworthy (off Spruce Dr. SW)

Atop the escarpment overlooking the Bow River Valley just east of Sarcee Tr. is the upper section of Edworthy Park, a popular off leash dog walking and mountain-biking area.

Each of the upper area's three parking lots usually has complimentary "doggie bags," giving visiting dog-owners everything needed to pick up after their canine pals. Like other off leash areas in the city, if you're at all uncomfortable around dogs, this area is best avoided. Otherwise, the area has much to offer.

One of the constants here is the wind. It always seems to be blowing and parts of the plateau are so windswept that the trees are bent and stunted. Luckily, when taking in the views to the northeast and east, the wind is usually to your back. Several locations along the top of the escarpment overlook the new Alberta Children's Hospital, the Foothills Medical Centre, the not-so-distant downtown and, of course, lower Edworthy Park.

In May and June, it's worth visiting the plateau for its fragrant smattering of prairie flowers and shrubs, among them prairie crocus, three-flowered avens, cut-leaved anemone, western wood lily, and wolf willow.

This area lacks paved pathways, but has a well-established (almost prolific) network of foot trails across its open fields, along the shoulders of its ravines, and through its forest and valleys. Well-placed benches can be found throughout.

To reach upper Edworthy Park, take Spruce Dr. SW west of 45 St. to Edworthy St. SW; three gravel parking lots are located along the road for park users.

The Crowchild Trail Pedestrian Bridge.

Douglas Fir Trail

The Douglas Fir Trail is a demanding hiking trail in the heart of the city. Situated on a steep north-facing slope between the south access road into Edworthy Park and Lowery Gardens, its many foot trails are steep, secluded, and scented with the heady aroma of coniferous trees.

The cliff rises more than 60 metres above the Bow River and feeds it with free-flowing springs. At one time, the springs were likely a source of pure water for people in the area.

The abundance of water on the cliff can create havoc; fallen trees often lie across the narrow paths and small mudslides are not uncommon. In the winter, the springs create a thick coating of ice, making many sections of the pathway along the south shore impassable. Because the cliff faces north, this ice often lasts well into May.

The trail's steps, small bridges, and handrails have been rebuilt in recent years, but are always subject to the powerful forces of erosion—caution is advised. This is truly a wilderness area that offers many rewards for hardy explorers.

Among those rewards is wandering through a lush forest of towering Douglas Fir trees—one of the most easterly stands in southern Alberta.

Douglas Fir trees are common to the montane valleys of the Rocky Mountains and to the Pacific West Coast, where they grow much larger than in Calgary. Still, some trees in this area have a circumference of more than 1.5 metres and are estimated to be more than 350 years old.

Growing branch to branch with the Douglas Fir are White Spruce, hence the name for the community of Spruce Cliff. The two trees can be distinguished by their needles. The following description comes from *Calgary's Natural Areas: A Popular Guide* (published in 1975 by the Calgary Field Naturalists Society):

"The Douglas Fir needles are flat in cross-section; its cones have a three pointed bract with a long central spike and the mature trees have a rather irregular crown. White Spruce ... [needles are] rounded or squarish cross-section, cone with rounded scales, and tall, symmetrically pointed crown."

Living in the forest is a long list of flora and fauna including wild raspberries, chokecherries, poplars, cow parsnip, chickadees, evening grosbeaks, and red-breasted nuthatches.

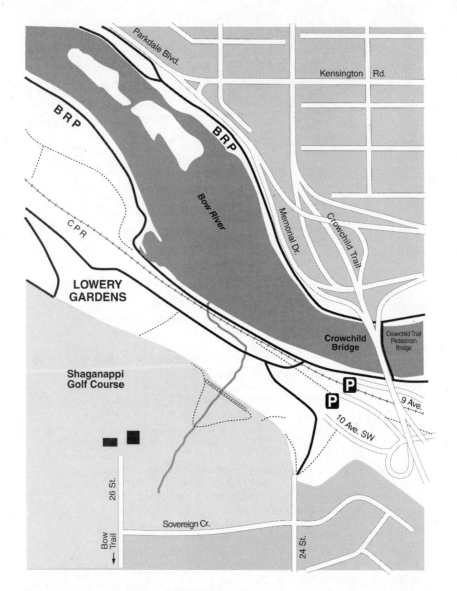

EDWORTHY PARK TO PRINCE'S ISLAND

During the summer—when people stroll, walk, cycle, roller skate, in-line skate, roller ski, picnic, chat, and even walk their ferrets—the Bow River Pathway between Edworthy Park and Prince's Island is the Deerfoot Tr. of Calgary pathways: chockablock with traffic in all directions.

Even in winter, this stretch of pathway is well travelled and the north side of the river is regularly cleared (when it actually snows) and is well lit at night.

Pathway Description—North Bank

Past the Boothman Bridge, the Bow River Pathway traverses a narrow green belt between Montgomery View, Parkdale Boulevard, and eventually Memorial Dr. NW and the Bow River for about 3.5 kilometres to Crowchild Tr. NW. Approximately 2.1 kilometres downstream (past the steep cliffs of the Douglas Fir Trail and Lowery Gardens on the opposite bank), the pathway follows along Parkdale Boulevard for about 1.4 kilometres.

This open, flat section is as easy to navigate on foot as on bike, making it ideal for families with young children.

Several nearby shops and cafés offer an excuse to stop for coffee, cinnamon buns, ice cream, and other essential fuels for pathway rambling. Among them: the Loaf and Jug (8 Parkdale Cres. NW), Leavitt's Ice Cream Store (3410 – 3 Ave. NW) and Extreme Bean (3303 – 3 Ave. NW).

For several hundred meters before Crowchild Tr., the pathway is a single route, squeezing all users onto a narrow ribbon of asphalt sandwiched tightly between Memorial Dr. and the riverbank.

A pedestrian bridge under Crowchild Tr. gives travellers the option of crossing the river and continuing downstream on the south shore or upstream to Edworthy Park through Lowery Gardens.

Kensington at Louise Crossing

Memorial Dr. and 10 St. NW is the gateway to the Kensington district, a business community densely populated with people—and places people love to visit (see www.visitkensington.com for a complete listing of current cafés, restaurants, businesses and attractions).

With more than 200 businesses, including two dozen restaurants and more than 50 specialty shops, Kensington is worth a visit any day of the year.

On sunny afternoons especially, the streets of Kensington (Kensington Rd. and 10 St. NW) are abuzz with people. They shop for everything from fresh spring tulips to fresh-baked organic bread, dine on great eats, sip fresh-roasted coffee and watch other people. This is one of the city's busiest urban villages and a wonderful departure from the malls and parking lots that are the hallmarks of most other local shopping areas.

The Kensington area is located in the communities of Hillhurst and Sunnyside, which long ago were quiet suburbs with neatly arranged rows of compact houses where many CPR workers and their families lived. For the past 25 years, Kensington, Hillhurst, and Sunnyside have been among the "trendiest" neighbourhoods in town. The revitalized business zone, with its diverse shops, rustic brick sidewalks, and wrought iron street lamps, adds greatly to area's character and lasting charm.

Downstream of Crowchild Tr., the north shore route opens up and is twinned until near 19 St. NW. A recently completed pedestrian overpass at 21 St. eliminates the need to dodge traffic to cross Memorial Dr.

Again the twinned pathway resumes and the overall route continues east, narrowing once more to a single pathway under the Mewata (14 St. NW) Bridge

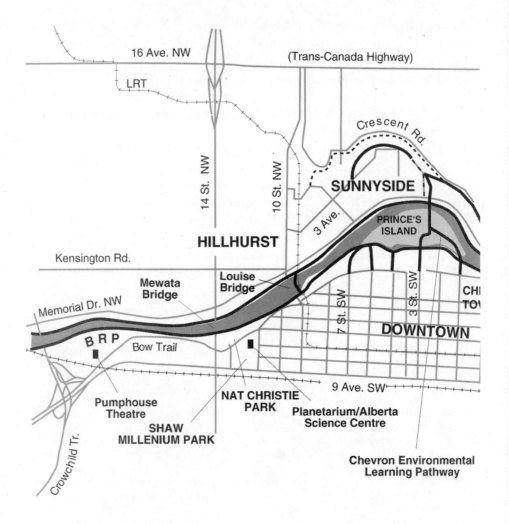

16 Ave. NW

(Trans-Canada Highway)

LRT

Crescent Rd.

SUNNYSIDE

14 St. NW

10 St. NW

3 Ave.

PRINCE'S ISLAND

HILLHURST

Kensington Rd.

Mewata Bridge

Louise Bridge

Memorial Dr. NW

7 St. SW

3 St. SW

CHI TOW

DOWNTOWN

B R P

Bow Trail

9 Ave. SW

Pumphouse Theatre

NAT CHRISTIE PARK

SHAW MILLENIUM PARK

Planetarium/Alberta Science Centre

Crowchild Tr.

Chevron Environmental Learning Pathway

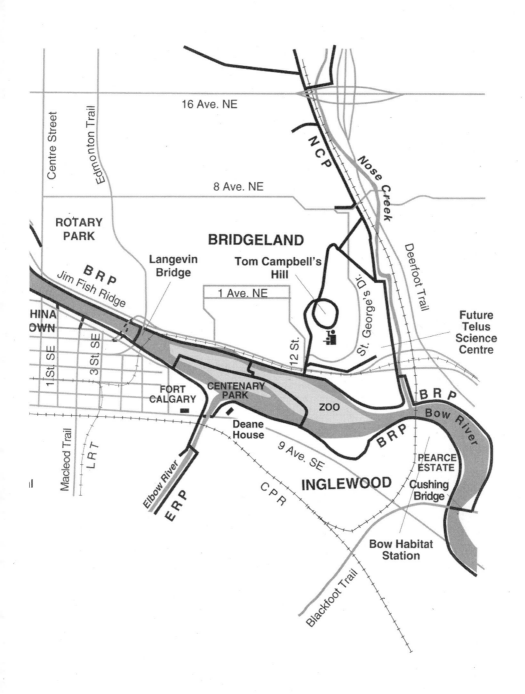

and dividing again until the Hillhurst (10 St. NW) Bridge. As a rule, twinned pathways merge into a single route as they approach bridges.

From this intersection, the Bow River can be crossed by pedestrians at the Hillhurst Bridge or by all pathway traffic via a pedestrian bridge under the Calgary's Light Rail Transit (C-Train) bridge immediately downstream. More complex than most pathway intersections, this junction is best navigated at a greatly reduced speed.

East of Memorial Dr. and 9A St. NW, the twinned pathway weaves through a stand of trees originally planted as a memorial for Calgarians who died in the First World War. A newly upgraded pedestrian bridge near 3 St. NW links the north Bow River Pathway to Prince's Island across the river and to McHugh Bluffs across Memorial Dr.

Outdoor Resource Centre
The City of Calgary's first "store-front" parks information centre is nestled in an historic firehall in the southwest corner of the Memorial Dr. and 10 St. NW intersection.

The centre is open daily from 1100 to 1830 h and features displays, guides, information, and merchandise on parks, pathways, and outdoor recreation opportunities in Calgary and throughout southern Alberta. Also check out the centre's ongoing events calendar; highlights include a variety of presentations and demonstrations on pathways, outdoor activities, healthy living, and the environment. Most events are free.

For more information, call 221-3866 or visit www.calgary.ca, click on City Living and follow the links to the Outdoor Resource Centre events listing.

SOUTH BANK

At the east end of Lowery Gardens, the Bow River Pathway follows a narrow, confined route flanked by the railway tracks and the river's edge. It's not particularly scenic, but it is serviceable. Downstream of Crowchild Tr. SW, the pathway eases away from the river, skirts a modest poplar forest and rambles past the backside of the Pumphouse Theatre, Calgary's only riverside theatre house.

A nearby viewpoint/rest stop includes interpretive signs about the city's water system—touted as one of the best in North America—Sarcee (Tsuu T'ina) elder David Crowchild (for whom Crowchild Tr. was named), and the different types of fish in the Bow River (Trout Unlimited lists rainbow trout and brown trout as the most sought after; other species include bull trout, rocky mountain whitefish, and northern pike). The rest stop includes a seasonal water fountain, unisex outdoor washroom, and benches.

Continuing east, the pathway follows along Bow Tr. and the green belt between the road and river narrows dramatically. After passing the Mewata (14 St. NW) Bridge, the pathway emerges in Nat Christie Park. The park's most notable—and arguably its only—feature is a gaggle of nine sculptures carved by artists with the Stone Sculptures Guild of North America from 60,000-year-old Paskapoo sandstone.

Across from Nat Christie Park at Bow Tr. and 11 St. SW are three city landmarks: the Alberta Science Centre/Calgary Planetarium, Mewata Armoury, and Shaw Millennium Park. All are easily recognized: the science centre/planetarium by its futuristic white dome, the armoury by its red-brick and stone Tudor/Gothic Revival architecture, and Shaw Millennium Park by its concrete skateboard playground.

The pathway continues east under the Hillhurst (10 St. SW) Bridge and past a pedestrian bridge under the northwest leg of the C-Train. While not quite as congested as the pathway on the river's opposite shore, this section is heavily travelled and users should be prepared to yield to slower moving "traffic." As the pathway approaches Prince's Island, it passes through Peace Park (2 Ave. and 8 St. SW), which was built in the early 1990s and dedicated to members of Canada's military during the country's 125th anniversary celebrations in 1992.

Compact, symmetrical, and bisected by the Bow River Pathway, this small park is easily overlooked. Those who slow down or pause here will find it offers a place for quiet respite and reflection—it's like the eye of a storm. You can sit calmly on a Peace Park

One of the nine sculptures carved into 60,000-year-old sandstone at Nat Christie Park.

The memorial arch at downtown's Peace Park was once located along Memorial Dr.

bench and a flurry of activity will continue all around you.

The park's stately sandstone memorial arch is often given no more than a passing glimpse, but this architectural feature has a proud history. It was originally part of the Strathcona Building, an office building erected east of Calgary during the First World War. The arch survived the building's demolition only to spend several years in storage. In 1985, it was erected along Memorial Dr. near the Bridgeland C-Train station in honour of those who served in WWI, WWII, and the Korean War. Only a few years later it was dismantled and assembled stone by stone at Peace Park.

Not as obvious, but every bit as impressive, are twelve elm trees planted in a circle to represent an ancient Bosco Sacro (peace grove or garden) design. Peace gardens have a long tradition in Greek, Viking, and Gaelic cultures and were originally places where people resolved their conflicts and differences.

The International Holistic Tourism Education Centre reports that in 1992, Louis J. D'Amore, founder of the International Institute For Peace Through Tourism, launched Peace Parks Across Canada as part of Canada's 125th anniversary celebrations. The program saw more than 250 national peace parks in cities, towns, and villages across Canada dedicated in 1992, most on Oct. 8 to coincide with the dedication of a national peacekeeping monument in Ottawa.

A few hundred metres past the Peace Park, the Bow River Pathway reaches Prince's Island, geographical centre of Calgary's parks and pathways network.

PRINCE'S ISLAND

PRINCE'S ISLAND AT A GLANCE

LOCATION	3 St. and 1 Ave. SW
HOURS	0500 to 2300 daily
TERRAIN	Largely landscaped, with rolling lawns and mature trees; gently sloped riverbank with rip-rap boulders on north of island; east end of island is restored natural area with pond.
ACCESS	3 St. and 1 Ave. SW

	Memorial Dr. and 3 St. NW
	Bow River Pathway between Centre St. and 10 St. NW
PARKING	Note: Prince's Island is a walk-in park and has no vehicle traffic
	Parking lot at Memorial Dr. and 3 St. NW
	On-street metered parking in Eau Claire district
	Eau Claire Market Parkade (off 2 St. SW)
ACTIVITIES	Walking, hiking, interpretive trail, cycling, picnicking, festivals and events, flower gardens, public art, canoeing, dining (River Café)
FACILITIES	Washrooms (seasonal)
	Water fountains (seasonal)
	Picnic tables
	Children's play equipment
	Chevron Learning Pathway
	River Café (gourmet restaurant, closed every January)

Calgary's beloved "royal" is not a person but a park: Prince's Island. Often mistakenly referred to as Princess Island, the park takes its name from one of the city's pioneering businessmen, Peter Prince.

When Calgary was a young town, Prince moved from Wisconsin to found the Eau Claire Lumber Company of Wisconsin and the Bow River Lumber Company in Calgary, which held lumber rights on 258 square kilometres (100 square miles) of land along the Bow and Spray rivers.

The Eau Claire Lumber Company built a mill on the Bow River, near the island that now bears Prince's name, in 1886. The district came to be known as Eau Claire and the nearby island was named for Prince. Prince died in 1925 and his lumber company operated until 1944. In 1947, his family donated the mill site to the City of Calgary. (See sidebar "Peter Prince—More than a Lumber King.")

Twenty years ago, little remained of the once thriving district. Today, Eau Claire is once again vibrant. It is decidedly more urban than industrial, teeming with restaurants, a market, hotels, office towers, and high-rise condominiums as well as its island park and connecting pathways.

While Eau Claire's development during the past two decades has been impressive and intense, it pales in comparison to the grandiose hopes a British architect had for Prince's Island and Eau Claire near the turn of the 20th century.

Thomas Mawson believed Calgary could become the ideal city, and city administrators believed in Mawson, paying him $6,000 to show them how.

Mawson's plans called for an elliptical pathway, formal gardens, boating reach, and museum on Prince's Island. Fourth St. was to cut across the island, joining the north section of the city to what Mawson envisioned would be the

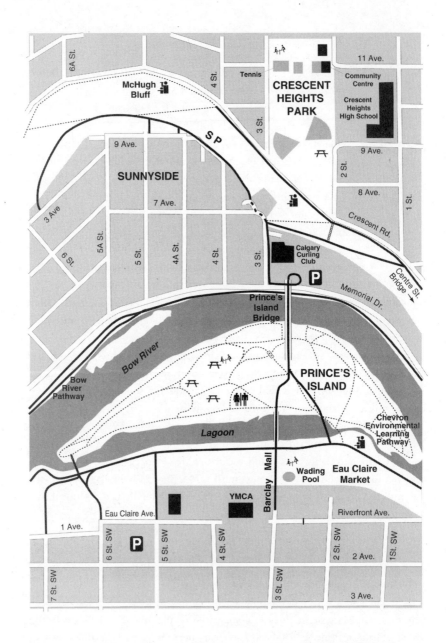

centre of town. Directly south of Prince's Island was to be a stately civic centre that embraced several architectural styles from the 19th century.

Mawson's plan was shelved. Soon forgotten, it was discovered in the 1970s behind the wall of a northeast garage and was the subject of the book *Calgary Many Years Hence—The Thomas Mawson Report in Perspective* by E. Joyce Morrow.

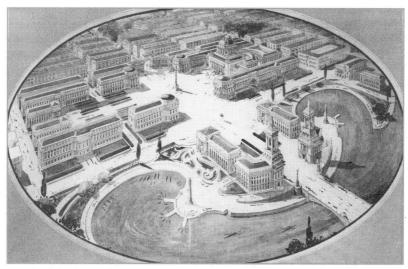

Thomas Mawson's elaborate plan for downtown Clagary was never realized.
GLENBOW MUSEUM ARCHIVES

Although never constructed to Mawson's ideals, Prince's Island is the centre of outdoor activity in the downtown core. Thousands of joggers, strollers, and cyclists cross the island daily. When weather prevails, the island hosts several festivals and gatherings—including the Calgary Folk Festival (every July), Canada Day celebrations, and Heritage Day festivities.

Far from the Madding Crowd—the Prince's Island lagoon.

Jack Leslie

Prince's Island may be named for Peter Prince but the park largely owes its existence to Jack Leslie, a former Calgary alderman and mayor in the 1960s.

As an alderman, Leslie—a realtor and then developer by profession—had stridently opposed plans to move the CPR's main line through Calgary from along 9 Ave. to along the south bank of the Bow River. The plan would have cut the island off from downtown Calgary. Leslie's resistance to the move was not a popular stance. Nor was his subsequent opposition to building a major six-lane highway along the river. Both plans would have changed not only Prince's Island, but the entire face of downtown Calgary.

Raised along the Elbow River near Sandy Beach and what later became the Glenmore Dam, Leslie wanted to protect Calgary's rivers so people could enjoy them. Yet again, this was an idea that found little political or popular support. But Leslie persisted,

Former Calgary Mayor Jack Leslie faced considerable opposition when he suggested protecting Calgary's rivers.

and while mayor from 1965 to 1969 he ushered in a plan to build the city's first red shale pathway from the Calgary Zoo to 10 St. NW.

"Some people said it was going to be a waste of money," said Leslie in the fall of 2005 at the age of 86. "It didn't matter what you did, people would always criticize you, but when we opened the first path people found the river was a place they liked."

Soon after—and with the moral and financial support of Don Harvie and Jim Fish of the Devonian Foundation—the pathway was extended to Shouldice Park and Calgary's network of parks and pathways was born. At its heart was Prince's Island.

Leslie's, Fish's, and Harvie's commitment to preserving and sharing Calgary's riverbanks and natural areas is not widely known in Calgary, but that's slowly changing. A cairn along the Bow River acknowledges the threesome as "citizens of vision."

The River Café

Perennially busy, innovative, and impressive, The River Café is as much a part of Prince's Island as summer festivals and family picnics.

Proprietor Sal Howell is one of the city's most respected and consistent restaurateurs. Under her guidance, The River Café has been a highly praised dining establishment for more than a decade.

One of the few places in Calgary you can't drive right up to, the café is worth the walk in the park required to reach it. Some would say that's its biggest charm. I say it's the menu and wine list. The River Café's wine list earned The Wine Spectator's Award of Excellence every year from 1997 to 2005. In 2005, Calgary's *Where Magazine* bestowed its best ambience award on the café.

With its fly-fishing motif and artifacts, the café is warm, rustic, and familiar both inside and out. The menu proudly strives to "use the best naturally produced ingredients in season, featuring local wholesome organic produce, meats, game, fish, and fowl." In January 2005, Fodor's Online rated the restaurant at 3.7 stars out of five. CBC Radio and Calgary Herald food reviewer John Gilchrist says the River Café is "hands down Calgary's prettiest location. I think they have become one of Calgary's very best restaurants."

Lunch for two (including wine) runs about $60 to $80; dinner is about $120. Reservations highly recommended; call 261-7670.

Chevron Learning Pathway

The Chevron Learning Pathway is an award-winning project on the east end of Prince's Island. This easily navigated interpretive trail features a series of informative signs focusing on water, water treatment, and the importance of both. Several downtown stormwater sewer lines are filtered through the area's ponds; until this constructed wetlands project was completed in March 1999, the stormwater sewer lines drained into the island's lagoon.

The constructed wetlands include three connected ponds. In the summer, the wetlands naturally "treat" 60 per cent of the water that flows through this outfall. In the winter, less water flows through the area, but it contains more contaminants; the wetlands efficiently process approximately 98 per cent of the effluent.

At the same time, the wetlands—which thrive in the shadow of Calgary's skyscrapers—are home to many waterfowl, aquatic plants, and fish. Occasionally a beaver or bald eagle can be spotted around the wetlands.

A Parks Foundation Calgary project, the Chevron Learning Pathway is part of the City of Calgary Parks public education program and is visited by thousands of school children and families every year.

The wetlands next to the Chevron Learning Pathway thrive in the shadow of Calgary's skyscrapers and are home to many waterfowl, aquatic plants, and fish.

An oasis at the north end of downtown Calgary that can only be reached by foot or bicycle, Prince's Island is an eclectic mix of lush forests, formal gardens and structures, restored natural areas, family friendly playgrounds and picnic areas, and festivities facilities. Just 20 hectares, Prince's Island can be easily discovered in a lunch-hour walk. To truly appreciate the park, however, plan to visit again and again.

Pathway Description—Prince's Island

A wide, hard-packed pathway circumnavigates Prince's Island, covering about 2.4 kilometre (including the island's east end). Travelling west from the main entrance at the south side of the island, the pathway winds along the lagoon and past the River Café (see sidebar), weaving in and out of mature trees and past "festival fields" (open grassy fields) and the east-facing Enmax outdoor stage, which opened in 2002 and is centre stage for the island's many musical and cultural events.

At the southwest end of the island, the pathway links to the Bow River Pathway across an access road, or continues around the north side of the

Public art is one of the treasures to discover at Prince's Island Park.

island. The riverside banks of the island are reinforced with rip-rap, large boulders of granite that stop erosion. The rocks are not the easiest to navigate, but they are stable.

The pathway turns east, twinning in places and passing near a children's playground and four iron sculptures. The main path advances further east, underneath the pedestrian bridge connecting the island to the north leg of the Bow River Pathway and Memorial Dr.

Beyond the bridge, the island takes on a much more natural appearance and the pathway morphs into the Chevron Learning Pathway. As it loops west back toward the main entrance, it passes another pedestrian bridge, a lookout point near a water fountain, and a small but bright formal garden. One hundred metres later, the pathway completes its route around the island.

CRESCENT HEIGHTS CONNECTOR

The climb up McHugh Bluffs, or the Crescent Heights hill as it's better known, is tough but well worth the effort. The view of downtown Calgary is picture-perfect—and regular ascents of the hill will keep heart and lungs satisfyingly fit.

As the north leg of the Bow River Pathway approaches Prince's Island, take the pedestrian bridge across Memorial Dr. NW to the Calgary Curling Club. If travelling by bike, follow the paved pathway up the hill. If travelling by foot, take the pathway or staircase. Both routes lead to Crescent Rd. NW.

If travelling by foot, the hill can be scaled up a grinding flight of stairs. The pathway joins another at the crest of the hill, which in one form or another runs the length of McHugh Bluffs, from 10 St. NW to Edmonton Tr. NE. Restoration of the bluffs has been an ongoing

Gravel gliding at Prince's Island Park.

Peter Prince—More than Calgary's Lumber King

Ambitious and determined, Peter Anthony Prince arrived in Calgary in the 1880s bent on bringing lumber to a wood-hungry town. Aside from the narrow riverine forests at some points along its waterways, Calgary's landscape was as bald as a baby's bottom.

A native of Quebec who worked in Chicago and Wisconsin before coming west, Prince was hired as general manager of the Eau Claire and the Bow River Lumber Company. His task: to log trees in the foothills and float them down the Bow River. The Calgary Public Library reports: "Prince blasted a channel in order to float logs directly to the sawmill, creating what is now Prince's Island (and is currently a park). The Eau Claire sawmill was the city's main source of lumber until the First World War, and was in operation until 1945." The mill's smokestack still stands near the Eau Claire Market.

The site of Peter Prince's sawmill later became one of the city's favourite parks: Prince's Island.

GLENBOW MUSEUM ARCHIVES

Prince became known as Calgary's lumber king, but his business kingdom included a flour mill and elevator (later the Robin Hood Mill on 9 Ave. SW), Calgary Iron Works (of which he was president), a ranch at Brooks, and a power company that evolved into Calgary Power then TransAlta.

Author, former Calgary mayor, and Alberta lieutenant-governor Grant MacEwan wrote this story of Prince in 1961 for Calgary Power's 50th anniversary:

"It all began one dark night in early Calgary when, according to the story, the sober and business-like Peter Anthony Prince of Eau Claire Lumber Company fell off a plank sidewalk and severely injured his well-groomed pride. While breathing anger at the unlighted streets, he vowed to make his adopted home the fifth community in Canada to have electric bulbs."

Prince took his oath to city council in 1889 and before long 300 flickering lights dimly lit city streets at night. (By day, Prince's electrical system powered his lumber mill.) Many Calgarians questioned if they wouldn't be better off with candles after watching the lights glow faintly with a yellowish hue. Criticism was quashed once Prince's Calgary Water Power Company delivered full power to the system, derived from a paddlewheel in the river.

Soon after, Prince built himself a manor at the corner of 4 Ave. and 2 St. SW. Today the house stands at Heritage Park. Prince died in Calgary in 1925.

City of Calgary project for several years and eventually the area will have an improved network of trails and pathways.

BOW RIVER PATHWAY—NORTH SHORE: PRINCE'S ISLAND TO NOSE CREEK

From Prince's Island, the north leg of the Bow River Pathway continues its downstream course along the river. The terrain is generally flat; the pathway itself winds subtly. As elsewhere in the downtown core, the route is often twinned as space allows. Expect bikes, runners, walkers, and strollers to share the pathway as it approaches Centre St. Bridge and Langevin Bridge (at Edmonton Tr. NE), as well as past tight squeezes between the river and Memorial Dr.

Although well used throughout the year, this section of the pathway has few formal attractions to explore. This is largely a route to be travelled, not generally a place to be visited.

At the northeast C-Train/Langevin Bridge/Edmonton Tr./Memorial Dr. interchange, the Bow River Pathway connects to a number of feeder routes and crossings. The main pathway continues east by southeast along a berm flanked by the river and Memorial Dr. Shortly after, it passes a pedestrian bridge to the Bridgeland C-Train station and—on the other side of Memorial Dr.—the Bridgeland/Riverside community. Further east, the pathway crosses the Baines Bridge at the west end of the Calgary Zoo.

From Baines Bridge and Memorial Dr., you can take Zoo Road to the south entrance of the Calgary Zoo, Centenary Park, and Fort Calgary. To reach the north zoo entrance, follow the signs to 12 St. and St. George's Dr. NE and the main entrance of the zoo. (NOTE: The Calgary Zoo cannot be directly reached from the Bow River Pathway.) The zoo's north entrance can also be reached from the Nose Creek Pathway.

The north leg of the Bow River Pathway continues past (fenced off) life-sized replicas of dinosaurs and hoodoos in the zoo's Prehistoric Park. This pathway rolls up and down along a narrow ledge overlooking the river. Watch for other

The north leg of the Bow River Pathway at Centre Street Bridge.

users around blind corners and in underpasses.

The route opens up at the east end of the zoo as it approaches the confluence of Nose Creek and the Bow River. Here, the pathway and surrounding area have a pronounced industrial feel, a theme that's common to the BRP downstream of the Calgary Zoo.

BOW RIVER PATHWAY—NORTH/EAST SHORE: NOSE CREEK TO CUSHING BRIDGE

After crossing Nose Creek, the Bow River Pathway intersects with a bridge over Memorial Dr. Cross the bridge to connect to the Western Irrigation District (WID) Pathway, which runs some 26 kilometres to Chestermere Lake, or reach Barlow Tr. NE, International Avenue (17 Ave. SE), and the Max Bell Arena.

Shortly after the bridge, the BRP reaches the WID weir, which diverts water from the Bow River into an irrigation canal system that supplies water to some 400 farmers east of Calgary. Innocuous in appearance, the weir nonetheless poses a serious risk. Swimmers or boaters caught in the weir's churning waters stand little chance of escape. (Construction of the Harvie Passage will greatly reduce this hazard).

Past the weir, the river turns south and the pathway travels next to Deerfoot Tr. for several hundred metres. This section of the pathway is perpetually riddled with weed "volcanoes"—tree roots that erupt through the asphalt.

As the BRP approaches 17 Ave. SE, it steers southwest toward the river and through a forest before crossing the Cushing Bridge over the Bow River. From here, pathway users can continue south toward the Inglewood Bird Sanctuary or north to Pearce Estate.

From this point south, the Bow River Pathway runs along a single shore of the river, crossing and re-crossing the waterway several times before reaching the city limits.

Near the confluence of the Bow River and Nose Creek.

BOW RIVER PATHWAY—SOUTH SHORE: PRINCE'S ISLAND TO FORT CALGARY

Like other sections of downtown, this twinned stretch of the Bow River Pathway is heavily used year-round; it's lit at night and cleared of snow and ice in winter.

The BRP widens to a promenade near the south entrance of Prince's Island and north end of Barclay Parade, but is still prone to crowding and confusion. Indeed, the volume and diversity of users—particularly during festivals and sunny summer weekends—combine to make this area tricky to negotiate.

The congestion usually dissipates shortly east of the Jaipur bridge. A second pedestrian bridge to the east is a less travelled link between the island and the Eau Claire district.

Moments later—whether travelling on foot or by bike—the pathway enters Sien Lok Park (see sidebar). The park's flat terrain is scattered with benches and statues, offering a reason to rest and appreciate.

This small, peaceful Chinatown park ends at the Centre St. Bridge. East of the bridge, a feeder pathway connects to the community of Chinatown and the low-slung Harry Hays Federal Building at the north end of Macleod Tr. South. The main pathway continues winding above the riverbank toward Langevin Bridge.

Five hundred metres downstream of the Langevin crossing, the pathway enters the site of Fort Calgary and connects via a pedestrian bridge to St. Patrick's Island (site of Centenary Park) and St. George's Island (site of the Calgary Zoo). Stay on the main pathway of the south side of the river to reach Fort Calgary's interpretive centre and the confluence of the Bow and Elbow rivers.

Chinatown

Chinatown is one of Calgary's great cultural diversions. Originally founded in 1910, today's Chinatown is a mix of tradition and trend, Asian and Western, and commerce and community—all crammed into six city blocks. Here you'll find ultramodern malls with the latest gadgets right next to modest herbal shops hawking centuries-old remedies and cures.

This downtown community's most visual destination is the Chinese Cultural Centre (197 – 1 St. SW, www.culturalcentre.ca, 262-5071). Modelled after the Forbidden City in Beijing, the centre is a stunning example of Chinese classical architecture. Its most striking feature is a three-storey building with gold leaf painting of 560 dragons and 40 phoenixes. The centre includes a museum, arts and crafts shop, 40,000-volume library, ongoing exhibition, and the Emperor Seafood Restaurant (265-4738).

Chinatown is also a culinary adventure where the cuisines of many regions collide, filling the street with savoury, sweet, pungent, and tempting aromas. Bakeries, restaurants, and grocery stores abound, offering Westernized Chinese dishes such as spring rolls and sweet and sour chicken along with traditional Chinese dishes such as duck's feet, bean cakes, and Peking duck. Increasingly, the cuisine of Japan, Vietnam, and Korea can also be found in Chinatown.

Popular "foodie" destinations include:

- Diamond Bakery at 101, 111 – 3 Ave. SE, 269-1888
- Dragon City Mall at Centre St. and 4 Ave. SE, 294-1338
- Gold Inn Restaurant at 107 – 2 Ave. SE, 269-2211
- Golden Happiness Bakery at 111 – 2 Ave. SE, 263-4882
- Kingfisher Seafoods Restaurant at 203, 328 Centre St. SE, 294-1800
- Ruby King Restaurant at 103 – 3 Ave. SE, 261-5656
- Silver Dragon at 106 – 3 Ave. SE, 264-5326
- Skazka Restaurant and Bar, 515 – 1 St. SE, 265-0012

Sien Lok Park

Just east of Prince's Island on the Bow River's south shore, Sien Lok Park commemorates the arrival, struggles, and contributions of Calgary's Chinese community.

The first-wave Chinese immigrants arrived in the Northwest Territories in the 1880s and worked as miners and railway workers. As their ranks grew, Chinese immigrants washed laundry and dishes, grew vegetables and laboured in kitchens in towns and cities throughout the territory. (Calgary's Chinatown district was originally founded in 1910). For decades Alberta's Chinese faced racism, discrimination and poverty, but they persevered, finding a way to bridge the gap to respect, equality, and prosperity.

Sien Lok Park salutes Calgary's Chinese community.

Sien Lok Park's cone-shaped sculpture "In Search of Gold Mountain" by Chu Honsun tells the story of these "neglected" pioneers and their search for success in a new land. The sculpture was carved from a 15-tonne piece of granite from the Hopei Province in China.

The park was constructed by the Sien Lok Society, a Calgary group dedicated to "a legacy of cooperation, advancing and preserving Chinese Canadian heritage by creating bridges between generations and cultures."

Sien Lok Park features a number of other modern and traditional sculptures and monuments.

FORT CALGARY

FORT CALGARY AT A GLANCE

LOCATION	750 – 9 Ave. SE, junction of Bow and Elbow rivers
HOURS	0900 to 1700 daily; closed New Year's Day, Good Friday, Christmas Eve, Christmas Day and Boxing Day
TERRAIN	Grassy flood plain along south shore of Bow River
ACCESS	Bow River Pathway between Langevin Bridge and Deane House Elbow River Pathway downstream of McDonald Bridge
ACTIVITIES	Walking, cycling, interpretive trails, tours, and programs; educational programs; special events, meetings, and programs
FACILITIES	Washrooms Water fountains Interpretive centre with displays, activities, and theatre General Store (featuring RCMP and Canadiana souvenirs) Replica of Fort Calgary and other buildings
DOGS	On leash on pathways and in open spaces Not permitted in Fort Calgary facilities
TRANSIT	#1
ADDITIONAL	Admission: adults $10; seniors $9; post-secondary students $9; youth $6; children six and under free; group rates and annual memberships also available

History is not simply what is recorded; it's what's experienced. At Fort Calgary, visitors can experience life in the city's earliest days of settlement. A replica fort has been left deliberately drafty to reflect the conditions the first police officers put up with in a harsh and sometimes hostile land.

Fort Calgary is the city's birthplace, one of many outposts established in 1875 by the North West Mounted Police—the forebears of the Royal Canadian Mounted Police—to run off whisky traders and expand the boundaries of a country that had yet to celebrate its 10th anniversary. History lives here— indeed, this is a national and provincial historic site—and few attractions in Calgary match Fort Calgary's passion and verve for preserving, conserving, and discovering the events and people that have forged the city.

Fort Calgary also includes grassy open spaces at the east shoulder of downtown Calgary and along the southwest shores of the confluence of the Bow and Elbow rivers and the intersection of the Bow and Elbow river pathways.

The Mounties' Arrival

The North West Mounted Police came west to fight the daring whisky traders from the United States who would stop at nothing to make a buck. The traders' currency was firewater, a deadly mixture of "rotgut" booze for which many Natives would trade almost anything. The NWMP first rounded up rum runners in Fort Whoop-Up, then moved north to Fort Macleod and Fort Edmonton.

By 1874, they had captured or chased off many illegal traders. The next year, they established forts in the Cypress Hills and sites further north, including at what would become Calgary. The Ottawa government felt having the law keepers in place before settlers arrived would eliminate many of the problems experienced in the American Wild West.

Constable George Clift King is credited with being the NWMP officer to cross the Bow River at the Fort Calgary site. Oddly enough, King—a future mayor of Calgary and one of several people called "Calgary's first citizen"—forded the river from north to south. His troop, "F" Troop, had been summoned for a surprise inspection en route to its posting along the Bow River. The battalion had crossed the Bow River further upstream and prepared for the inspection near the Red Deer River. Following the inspection, "F" Troop marched back toward the Bow from the north.

Had "F" Troop not been diverted from its original course, Fort Calgary would have been built close to the Holy Cross Hospital, at a spot marked with a coat on a stick by an advance troupe for Inspector Éphrem A. Brisebois. But when "F" Troop reached the junction of the Elbow and Bow rivers, the headstrong Brisebois decided to erect the fort there instead.

George Clift King.

Once they had wrestled the whisky traders into submission, the NWMP prepared for the 1887 arrival of the Canadian Pacific Railway and later thousands of homesteaders lured by the promise of free, fertile land. The fort was expanded in 1882 but over the years was abandoned and all but forgotten.

As Calgary prepared to celebrate its centennial in 1975, the tangled growth, creosoted tracks, and decaying buildings were excavated. Archaeologists unearthed parts of the original wooden fort and many artifacts, but were forced to re-cover them because they rapidly and uncontrollably disintegrated when exposed to oxygen.

A second Fort Calgary opened in 1978, not as a law enforcement post, but as an interpretive centre and an ambitious civic project to commemorate the people and events that had first shaped the city.

In more recent years, volunteers with the Fort Calgary Preservation Society reconstructed the 1875 fort at its original location using period tools and methods. A replica of the two-storey men's barracks was finished in 2000. The barracks includes a mess kitchen, learning centre, and Mounted Police exhibits as well as meeting and event spaces.

The Deane House

Located near the confluence of the Bow and Elbow rivers, the Deane House is the only remaining intact building from the Fort Calgary site. Designated a registered historic resource in 1978, the stately house is run by the Fort Calgary Preservation Society.

The house is named after the former superintendent of the North West Mounted Police who built it in 1906.

Richard Burton Deane budgeted $5,000 to build the house for his wife, but ended up paying $6,200. He described it as "the best . . . in Mounted Police occupancy," but his wife died before ever living there.

Deane did little entertaining in the spacious three-storey home, aside from hosting a grand social affair for Prince Fushimi of Japan in 1907. In 1914, the Grand Trunk Pacific Railway purchased the property and moved the house east from its original site at 9 Ave. and 6 St. SE to near the present site of the Fort Calgary interpretive centre. In 1929, the house was moved to again to 9 Ave.

and 8 St. SE. An engineering feat, the move across the river was documented for a magazine.

A former boarding house and artists' gallery, the house has earned a "haunted" reputation. The fabled spirits said to inhabit the house include a 15-year old boy who, suffering from epilepsy and the ridicule of his peers, committed suicide in the house in 1936. About 35 years later, a man was shot on the front porch. Shortly after, a woman was axed to death by her husband outside the house as their children watched. A fourth ghostly spirit is said to belong to someone who died after being pushed down the house's attic stairs.

Murder mystery dinner theatres have thrived at the Deane House for two decades; for times, information, and reservations, call 269-7747.

For all this mayhem, the Deane House is a soothing place to relax. The west veranda, shaded by tall poplars, overlooks the quiet Elbow River and a chef's garden blossoms with flowers, herbs, and fresh vegetables each summer on the house's east side.

The Deane House (806 – 9 Ave. SE) is open daily Monday to Friday from 1100 to 1500 h and Saturday and Sunday from 1000 to 1500 h. Reservations are recommended for lunch and afternoon tea; call 269-7747 or e-mail info@fortcalgary.com.

CENTENARY PARK

CENTENARY PARK AT A GLANCE

LOCATION	St. Patrick's Island
HOURS	0500 to 2300 daily
TERRAIN	Mixture of native and manicured open forest with balsam poplar, willow, and red osier dogwood
	Heavy brush and shrubs along shoreline
	Marshy inlet at east end of island
ACCESS	BRP (north and south shores) downstream of Langevin Bridge, via Baines Bridge on the north, 12 St. Zoo Bridge on the east, and King George (pedestrian) Bridge on the south
	Memorial Dr. and Zoo Rd. NE
ACTIVITIES	Walking, cycling, picnics, fishing, birdwatching, disc golf
FACILITIES	BBQ pits
	Picnic tables
	Playground
	Canoe/rafting egress from river
	Disc golf course (call 229-1749 for information)

DOGS	On leash throughout
BOOKINGS	To book picnic area and other facilities, call the City of Calgary at 268-3830
TRANSIT	C-Train Northeast Leg (Bridgeland Station) #1, #9

A centennial birthday present in 1975 to Calgarians from Atco Industries, Centenary Park on St. Patrick Island is often overshadowed by its adjacent neighbour, the Calgary Zoo on St. George's Island. With its superb riverside views of downtown Calgary and its quiet picnic retreats, Centenary Park is worth discovering.

Some 30 years ago, the park was built by the City of Calgary and the Calgary Zoological Society. The two organizations carved out a small network of paved and gravelled trails and installed lighting, picnic tables, and barbecue pits in the park's riverine forest.

The park can be a quiet haven from the hustle and bustle of the zoo and a peaceful diversion from the busy Bow River Pathway, although some users are alarmed by the homeless people who frequent the area.

The lazy waters around the island's south shore attract ducks and geese year-round and fishermen often wade in the river, casting fly rods for brown trout and whitefish. The flood plain at the northwest end of the island is an ideal place to watch feeding waterfowl.

Bridge over travelled waters—George King Pedestrian Bridge near Ft. Calgary.

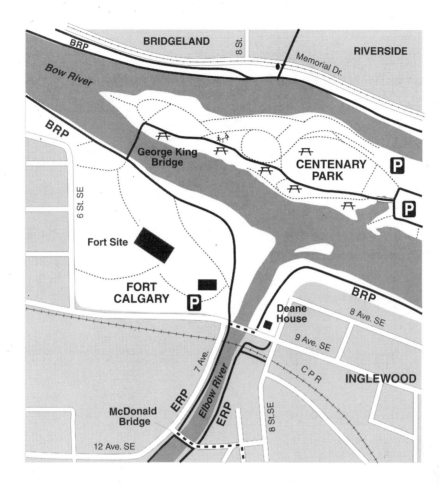

Pathway Description—Centenary Park

The Bow River Pathway arches over the King George Bridge from Fort Calgary to a grassy knoll on St. Patrick's Island and passes by an unusual sculpture by Del Anderson (a concrete tree trunk with a single branch and swing). The pathway winds east through Centenary Park, under the shade of balsam poplars close to the south branch of the river.

Several hard-packed trails and a service road criss-cross the island; one trail runs along the island's north shore overlooking the quiet and slow moving waters of the Bow's north branch.

The main pathway skirts a well equipped playground and several picnic sites before crossing an arched wooden bridge to St. George's Island. In all, the pathway runs for about 900 metres between Fort Calgary and St. George's Island.

Mallards

As in many parts of North America, the mallard (Anas platyrhynchos) is the most common duck in Calgary.

During breeding, the male is easily recognized by its shimmering green head, yellow beak, white ringed neck, tipped wings, and under plumage. Female mallards are decidedly less colourful and have mottled brown feathers.

Fish Creek Bankside—A female mallard with maturing brood.

Most mallards make their home in Calgary during the summer only, but many remain year-round, lulled by the warm and open waters around storm sewer run-offs and a comparatively abundant supply of food. As dabbling ducks, mallards feed, with their bottoms up, on water weeds and other river vegetation including seeds and small insects.

Mallards nest along shores as well as far from water. Since their legs are near the centre of their bodies, they can walk onshore with ease and have been known to nest in buildings and trees.

CALGARY ZOO, BOTANICAL GARDENS AND PREHISTORIC PARK

CALGARY ZOO AT A GLANCE

LOCATION	1300 Zoo Rd. NE
HOURS	0900 to 1800 daily
	Gates close at 1700 daily
	Closed Christmas Day
TERRAIN	Varied
ACCESS	St. George's Dr. NE
	12 St. and Zoo Rd. SE
	Bow River Pathway (north shore) downstream of Baines Bridge
	Bow River Pathway (south shore) downstream of Elbow River
ACTIVITIES	Animal and wildlife viewing, educational programs, special events, private functions, walking, picnicking, playing
FACILITIES	Botanical Gardens
	Prehistoric Park
	Conservatory
	Karsten Discovery Centre
	Destination Africa

Canadian Wilds

Kitamba Café

Gift shops

Playgrounds

Washrooms

DOGS   Not permitted (except for documented working dogs)

INFORMATION   232-9300 or www.calgaryzoo.org

TRANSIT   C-Train Northeast leg (Zoo Station)

         #1, #75, #102, #125, #126, #133, #411

ADDITIONAL   Admission: adults $16; seniors $14; youth $10; children $8; under three free.

         Memberships available

         Not allowed: balloons, bikes, tricycles, drugs and alcohol, in-line skates, scooters, balls, Frisbees, hackeysacks

         Smoking not prohibited except in three designated areas

Barely out of the shadows of downtown Calgary, the Calgary Zoo is a world of its own—and the home of animals from around the globe. Located on St. George's Island, the zoo includes the Botanical Gardens, Prehistoric Park, Destination Africa, and the Canadian Wilds as well as numerous other wildlife exhibits.

The Botanical Gardens are an impressive display of exotic and native plants that grow outdoors from spring through fall, and indoors all year-round in the glass-enclosed Conservatory. In the Prehistoric Park, life-sized and lifelike replicas of dinosaurs stand within a re-creation of their natural setting. At Destination Africa, the sights, sounds, and smells of the great continent come to life. The Canadian Wilds features our nation's largest mammals.

For more than 75 years, the Calgary Zoo has been one of the city's most popular attractions for people of any age. Whether they live in Calgary or come from 4,000 kilometres away, the visit is always worth it.

To see all the attractions, plan on spending an entire day at the zoo.

The Zoo's Canadian Wilds features the country's largest mammals, including grizzlies.

TOURISM CALGARY

The Evolution of a Zoo

In 1908, at the suggestion of William Pearce, the federal government donated three islands in the Bow River to the City of Calgary. St. George's, St. Andrew's, and St. Patrick's were given on the condition they be used for recreational purposes. The islands were literally oases on the treeless prairie: towering poplars nearly a metre in diameter stood amidst raspberry and saskatoon bushes and patches of strawberries.

Work began quickly to clear the islands. A bridge was constructed on the south side of the river and in 1909 a bandstand and dancing platform were erected on St. George's Island. Calgarians flocked to the shady island retreats to escape the prairie sun and soak up the sounds of local musicians.

At the same time, a Calgary alderman was working to establish the Calgary Zoo. Fred Currey started the zoo's collection with a menagerie of angora goats, doves, assorted finches, canaries, parakeets, and sparrows—all donated by the Vancouver Zoo. The zoo, however, wasn't ready for Currey's animals.

The predicament was solved by Fire Chief James "Cappy" Smart and the firefighters at Firehall #1 on 6 Ave. and 1 St. SE. The animals were kept in cages between the firehall and a Chinese laundry. The collection included two black bears named Major and Noodle.

The two bears, often kept on long chains, attracted the curiosity of many passersby. But when a twenty-month-old girl was mauled to death by Major, interest in all the animals waned and they were either returned to the wild or euthanized. Alderman Currey shelved his plans for the zoo.

Interest in the three island parks, however, continued: the Firth of Fourth, a small, narrow strait between St. George's and St. Andrew's islands, was made into a lagoon/swimming pool; rustic wooden bridges linked the islands together, and a large playground entertained countless children.

Calgary's 1919 yearbook gives this description: "One may go far without meeting a more lovely spot than this island . . . The driveway around it, especially during the evenings, when the long rows of electric lights throw a soft radiance across it, is really very lovely, whilst flower borders, filled with a mass of the most gorgeous blossoms, the children's playgrounds, the numerous pleasant seats, and the shady groves, with the vivid waters of the Bow on either side, comprise a series of attractions of which any city might be proud.

"Strangers, when taken through it, are unable to refrain from expressing their wonder that such luxuriant foliage should exist in the midst of a locality that is generally understood to be treeless."

Following an accidental drowning in 1920, the lagoon and swimming pool closed. The strait was filled in and the island of St. Andrew's disappeared from the map of Calgary. Changes in the river channel during the 1970s technically made the islands into one, although the names St. Patrick's Island and St. George's Island remain.

As for the zoo, Calgarians' interest returned. In 1928, at the urging of Calgary Parks superintendent William Reader, the Calgary Zoological Society was formed. The zoo's collection consisted of one black bear, one black-tailed deer, one mule deer, one whistling swan, two Guinea fowl, four long-eared owls, and two herons. Today, the zoo has more than 1,000 animals.

Since opening its gates to the public in 1929, the Calgary Zoo has expanded to include the Botanical Gardens, Canadian Wilds, Destination Africa, and Prehistoric Park. In April 2006, the zoo announced its most ambitious exhibit ever, the Arctic Shores, scheduled to open in 2010.

Pathway Description—Fort Calgary to Pearce Estate (south shore)

At the eastern edge of the Fort Calgary site, the Bow River Pathway crosses the Elbow River, winds its way past the historic Deane House (also a restaurant) and leisurely travels along the riverbank in the community of Inglewood to the Zoo Bridge, about 1.5 kilometre downstream.

Cross the bridge to reach the south entrance of the Calgary Zoo.

Continue east on the BRP past a rest stop, complete with an information plaque, bike rack, and unisex washroom.

The pathway meanders away from the river and onto New St. SE in Inglewood and passes through an open park adorned with an old-fashioned gazebo. An alternate route is to travel along New St. to 15 St. SE, past a row of architecturally inspired homes that back onto the river.

The pathway resumes—the route through Inglewood is easy to follow and well signed—and cuts through a heavily treed riverine forest and under a CPR train bridge. The railway bridge also marks an important river egress point; the WID irrigation canal's diversion weir is a few hundred metres downstream.

Just past the bridge, the BRP enters Pearce Estate Park—the 4.0 kilometre signpost marks the exact spot.

PEARCE ESTATE PARK

PEARCE ESTATE PARK AT A GLANCE

LOCATION	1440 – 17A St. SE
HOURS	**Park:** 0500 to 2300 daily
	Bow Habitat Station: to be announced
TERRAIN	Generally flat, forested terrain with wetland downstream of weir
	Manicured picnic area adjacent to main parking lot
ACCESS	North of 17 Ave. and 17A St. SE (off Blackfoot Tr. SE)
	BRP south shore downstream 12 St. Zoo Bridge or upstream of Cushing Bridge
ACTIVITIES	Walking, cycling, fishing, birdwatching, interpretive trails and programs, picnics, site tours
FACILITIES	Bow Habitat Station Visitor Centre (opening 2007)
	Snack bar
	Gift shop
	Washroom
	Elevator
	Three floors of interpretive displays and exhibits
	Sam Livingston Fish Hatchery

Pearce Estate Park Interpretive Wetland
Three self-guided interpretive trails: BP Canada Discovery
Trail, Government of Alberta Walking on Water Trail, and
Ducks Unlimited Webbed Foot Lane
Picnic areas
Wood-burning firepits (wood not provided)
WID weir (with observation deck)
Parking lot

INFORMATION For scheduled and customized tours, special events, and
programs, call Bow Habitat Station at 297-6561, visit www.
bowhabitat.gov.ab.ca or e-mail bowhabitat.info@gov.ab.ca

DOGS On leash throughout entire park

TRANSIT #1

ADDITIONAL Admission will apply to some areas of Bow Habitat Station
Visitor Centre

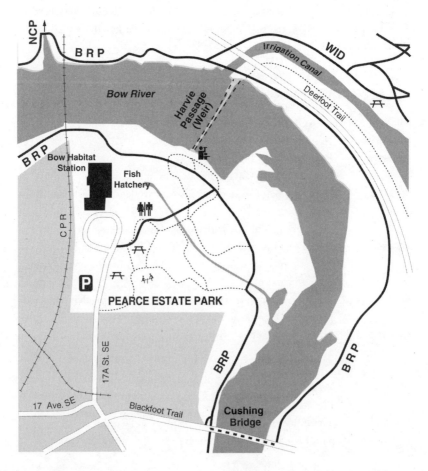

If one thing defines Pearce Estate Park, it is water. The park is home to the William Pearce Water Conservation Area and is the site of the Bow River Headworks for the Western Irrigation District (WID). First constructed in 1912, the headworks divert water to thirsty farmland east of Calgary and a fish ladder on the north side of the weir helps fish swimming upstream. The park's water theme is also the underpinning of the Bow Habitat Station and its visitor centre, Sam Livingston Fish Hatchery, and Pearce Estate Park Interpretive Wetland.

William Pearce, A Founding Father of Calgary Parks

During the 46 years William Pearce lived in Calgary, from 1884 to 1930, he was a driving force in establishing Central Park (now Memorial Park), purchasing St. Andrew's, St. Patrick's and St. George's islands, and preserving the north banks of the Bow River. He is also credited with securing federal land for Mewata Park and he once owned the land that is today a park bearing his name.

William Pearce.
GLENBOW MUSEUM ARCHIVES

Pearce left his hometown of Elgin, Ontario, to head the initial survey for the Dominion Government in Manitoba and the Northwest Territories, which included Alberta and Saskatchewan. Following his assignment, he moved to Calgary in 1884 and in 1887 was appointed superintendent of Mines.

As the chief surveyor for the Department of the Interior, he used his considerable influence to secure and preserve parkland for the city of Calgary and southern Alberta. As well, he was instrumental in establishing Canada's first national park, Banff National Park.

In the mid-1880s, Calgary was a "bald" prairie town: its only trees clumped sporadically along the riverbanks. The surrounding hills and plains were rich with native grasses and flowers but devoid of trees and shade. Pearce believed the fledgling city could be lush with trees, shrubs, and lawns, and encouraged Calgarians to plant them liberally.

Encouragement was not enough—much of the city lacked water. So Pearce formed the Calgary Irrigation Company which "offered to guarantee a water supply onto the highest points in Calgary at a cost of only $1,000, provided the owner of the lands would plant trees in abundance."

Practising what he promoted, Pearce planted thousands of trees, shrubs, and flowers on his land along the Bow River; he also built a huge sandstone and wood mansion there, modestly naming it Bow Bend Shack.

Pearce remained an active member of the community, until his death in 1930. He willed his land along the Bow River to Calgarians and it later became Pearce Estate Park.

Once endangered, American white pelicans are frequent and often numerous visitors to the weir at Pearce Estate.

JAMES MAHONEY

American White Pelicans

My son James is not readily enthralled by nature—but he, like me, was mesmerized by the antics and abilities of white pelicans at Pearce Estate Park.

The American white pelican was only recently removed from Alberta's endangered species list. For a bird still considered rare, it is surprisingly easy to spot in Calgary. As well as regularly frequenting Pearce Estate Park at the WID weir in the summer months, white pelicans are often seen near Carburn Park and Fish Creek Provincial Park.

Mainly white with black wing tips, individual white pelicans are easily distinguished on close inspection by their feather and bill markings and colourings. And after an hour of watching them, you can't help but notice these birds' personalities; pelicans can be cranky, cautious, daring, patient, and thoughtful.

The size of these birds is obvious—their wingspan can reach three metres wide and they can weigh up to eight kilograms. Other traits of these birds include:

- They fly with crooked necks, unlike whooping cranes and snow geese, which fly with outstretched necks.
- Male and female pelicans look alike.
- Pelicans are social: they fly in V-shaped formations and nest in colonies.
- White pelicans winter along the Gulf of Mexico.
- For reasons unknown, breeding white pelicans grow a fibrous knob or bump on their upper bills starting in the late winter. The growth disappears after females lay their eggs.
- White pelicans use their long bills to scoop up food in shallow water. Their bills can hold up to 20 litres of water.

As a breed, white pelicans are described by Alberta's Department of Sustainable Resource Development (previously Alberta Fish and Wildlife) as being very wary and easily startled—despite visiting the noisy city every year. "Human disturbance, even if motivated by simple curiosity and attraction, has been the most common cause of colony failure and abandonment in the past century."

How Calgary's pelicans will react to changes in habitat when the WID weir flow is changed remains to be seen.

For more information, visit Alberta Sustainable Development at www.srd.gov.ab.ca.

Discover the Bow Habitat Station

Three "sites" make up the Bow Habitat Station at Pearce Estate Park: the Pearce Estate Interpretive Wetland, the Sam Livingston Fish Hatchery, and a new visitor centre.

Squishy, oozy, and cool—those are some of the ways kids describe the Pearce Estate Park Interpretive Wetland. Created to be a living outdoor classroom, every year thousands of young students learn about the importance of wetlands and aquatic ecosystems through hands-on school field trips. As well, thousands of other people of every age learn about the wetlands through engaging and informative weekend interpretive programs.

Once a manicured area, the wetland was constructed over four years (from 2000 to 2004). Hundreds of volunteers logged 18,000 hours to help in the efforts to "renaturalize" the area and create five distinct Southern Alberta aquatic habitats. Fascinating and diverse, the wetland is part of a city-wide "revival" to restore, respect, protect, and promote these vital environments.

Major wetland partners and sponsors include BP Canada Energy Company, Ducks Unlimited Canada, the City of Calgary, Alberta Sustainable Resource Development, and the Sam Livingston Fish Hatchery Volunteer Society.

The largest indoor trout hatchery of its kind in North America, the Sam Livingston Fish Hatchery raises some three million fish a year. The hatchery raises mostly rainbow trout along with brook, brown, and cutthroat trout, and sometimes bull trout and Arctic grayling. Hatchery fish are stocked in publicly accessible lakes and ponds throughout the province. Because trout need running water and special gravel beds for breeding, they are largely unable to mate in Alberta's lakes.

The hatchery water treatment plant is big enough and sophisticated enough that it could serve a city of 50,000. The plant draws water from 11 wells on-site that take water from the largest freshwater aquifer in Western Canada. The Inglewood Aquifer starts in Sundre and was first drilled by A. E. Cross while searching for a water source for his Calgary Brewery.

Scheduled to open in 2007, the Bow Habitat Station Visitor Centre will offer spectacular educational and interpretive insight into fresh water and aquatic life in Alberta as well as the workings of the Sam Livingston Fish Hatchery. Visitors will be able to see fish as they develop from egg to fry to fingerlings. Large aquariums and life-size models will showcase the 56 species of fish found in Alberta. The centre will feature four exhibit galleries, some of the most elaborate and well-designed aquatic displays in the province, and an abundance of hands-on activities, as well as a gift shop and snack bar.

Look for the Bow Habitat Station to be one of Calgary's must-see attractions. The station will offer a number of creative, engaging, and entertaining educational and nature programs and day camps throughout the year, including the Wild Thing event, which attracts more than 5,000 people a year.

"Everything is designed to educate the general public and school students about aquatic habitats and their fish and wildlife species," says Ellen Gasser, visitor service coordinator at the Bow Habitat Station. "When you walk in the Fantastic Fish Gallery, it will feel like you're going right under the water—you'll see ducks' feet and the bottom of a boat." Visitors will also be able to crawl through a beaver lodge, step on a bog, discover an old-fashioned fishing lodge, and see sturgeon and lake trout in their natural surroundings.

The station will also lend fishing equipment (rod, reel, tackle) at no charge during the summer at the Rod Lodge. Adults must have a valid fishing licence and children under 16 years old must be accompanied by an adult. For information, call 297-6561 or visit www.srd.alberta.gov.ca/fishwildlife/bowhabitatstation.

Where beavers live, ecosystems thrive.

KEN RICHARDSON

Beavers—Engineers of the Animal World

One of nature's most industrious creatures, the American beaver (Castor canadensis) is found along all major Calgary waterways. As well as their lodges and dams, an obvious sign of Canada's national emblem is wire-wrapped balsam poplars along riverbanks, a means of quashing the beaver's insatiable appetite for the riverine trees.

The beaver is Alberta's largest rodent, weighing up to forty kilograms—more than most Golden Retrievers, points out the Provincial Museum of Alberta—and sporting a set of extra-strong, orangish incisors that never stop growing. Indeed, if a beaver doesn't wear down its teeth by gnawing on bark, wood, and leaves, its teeth will grow so long that it won't be able to eat and will starve to death.

Engineers of the animal world, beavers fell trees—including birch, poplar, willow, and aspen—for both food and shelter. They anchor logs and sticks in water, creating either lodges or stashes of food. On streams and marshes, their felled harvests result in dams and reservoirs; on fast-moving rivers, beavers keep their building activities close to shore.

Typically, where beavers live, other flora and fauna thrive. They often create ecosystems that attract and support birds, fish, amphibians, invertebrates, and plants.

Alberta's first European explorers and traders came in search of beaver pelts. At one time, beavers were hunted to near extinction for their valuable, dense, reddish-brown fur, which was used to make felt hats for affluent and fashion-conscious men in North America and Europe.

Today, beavers live throughout Alberta (except in high alpine regions) and are only selectively trapped.

Taming the Weir

By 2008, the WID Canal weir at Pearce Estate Park will be modified, removing one of the Bow River's most serious hazards. The weir will still function as intended—diverting water for irrigation. The river channel, however, will look and flow more like nature intended—similar to small rapids—allowing easier passage for fish and small boats. Canoeists, kayakers, rafters, and other river users will be able to float uninterrupted for more than 65 kilometres between the Bearspaw and Carseland dams.

Almost all of the construction for the project will be in the riverbed. In 2005, provincial engineers and hydrologists built a 1:50 scale test model of the project to test various rock structures and placements. When the project is completed, the river will have two safe midstream channels past the weir.

In September 2005, the $6.5-million project was named Harvie Passage after Calgary philanthropist Eric Harvie, whose Devonian Foundation funded many parks projects across Western Canada, including construction of several major pathways in Calgary. The project is spearheaded by the Parks Foundation,

Mesmerizing—Birds and birdwatchers are drawn to the WID canal weir at Pearce Estate.
JAMES MAHONEY

Calgary, and led by foundation volunteer Howard Heffler. The Alberta Lotteries Funds, the City of Calgary and Calgary, Foundation are providing funding. More information is available at the Park Foundation, Calgary's website, www. parksfdn.com.

Pathway Description—Pearce Estate Park

At Pearce Estate Park, the Bow River Pathway winds easily through a riverine forest, close to the river's edge. As the pathway begins to arc south, it intersects with trails for the Pearce Estate Interpretive Wetland (to the south) and the headwaters and diversion weir of the WID canal (immediately to the north).

Typically shaded and lush, the main pathway drops slightly and curves away from the riverbank and through the park's dense forest. Four hundred metres past the weir, the pathway crosses a small outflow channel from the fishery.

After flowing east–southeast from Bearspaw Dam, the Bow River begins a more south–southeast trajectory and the pathway closely follows, connecting in Pearce Estate Park to a number of feeder routes through the interpretive wetlands and to the park's main entrance and parking lot.

About 500 metres after leaving the park, the pathway reaches Cushing (17 Ave. SE) Bridge.

BOW RIVER PATHWAY—CUSHING BRIDGE TO INGLEWOOD BIRD SANCTUARY

The Cushing Bridge is an important milestone along the Bow River Pathway. Here, the routes along either shore of the river meet. South of the bridge, the pathway runs along just one side of the river, initially on the west bank. As well, the bridge connects to the WID Pathway, which runs about 26 kilometres from just below Memorial Dr. SE to Chestermere Lake.

Continuing south on the BRP, the route passes underneath the Cushing Bridge and traverses a short hill adjacent to a community park in east Inglewood. Past the park, the pathway hugs the river's shore before heading due south past a number of houses and then onto Sanctuary Rd. SE and past the entrance to the Inglewood Bird Sanctuary.

INGLEWOOD BIRD SANCTUARY

LOCATION	2425 – 9 Ave. SE
HOURS	Dawn to dusk
	Nature Centre: May to September, 1000 to 1700, daily; October to April, 1000 to 1600 except Mondays and holidays
TERRAIN	Open, flat grasslands near the Nature Centre give way to riverine forest with a lagoon and back channels; some sections of the riverbank have flat, wide gravel shores
ACCESS	East of 23 St. on 9 Ave. SE
	Bow River Pathway, south of 9 Ave. SE and north of Ogden Road
ACTIVITIES	Bird and wildlife watching, plant identification, walking, interpretive tours, tours (self-guided and guided) and educational programs
FACILITIES	Nature Centre
	Washrooms (in Nature Centre)
	Water fountains
	Interpretive displays
	Classrooms/meeting rooms
	Vending machines
	Catering available
	Wheelchair accessibility
	Petro-Canada Bird School
	Picnic tables
	Parking lot
	Colonel Walker House (provincial historical site)
DOGS	No dogs allowed
BOOKINGS	Programs, meetings, naturalists, and special events available; for details, schedules, and availability, call 221-4500
INFORMATION	221-4500, Programs: 221-4532, Playline: 268-2300 ext. 9480, Bird Alert: 221-4519. E-mail: InglewoodBirdSanctuary@calgary.ca
TRANSIT	#1
ADDITIONAL	No feeding birds or mammals
	No picking flowers, berries, or any vegetation
	No swimming in the lagoons
	No skating on the lagoons
	No cycling, horses, or motorized vehicles
	No fishing in the lagoons or along the riverbank
	No leaving designated trails
BEST VIEWING	Early morning

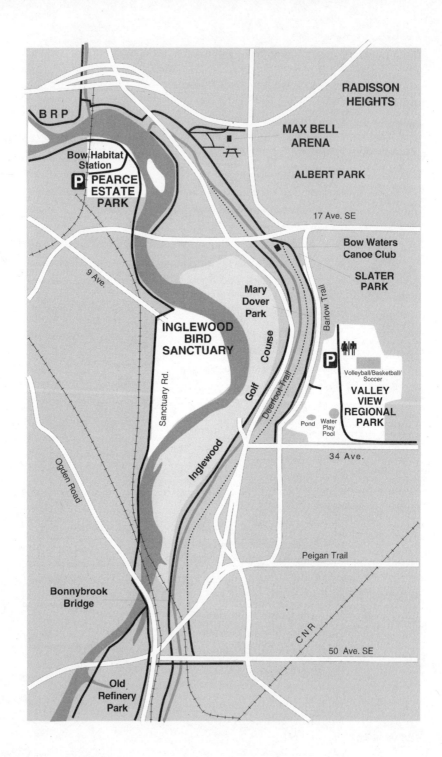

RADISSON HEIGHTS

MAX BELL ARENA

ALBERT PARK

BRP

Bow Habitat Station

P PEARCE ESTATE PARK

17 Ave. SE

Bow Waters Canoe Club

SLATER PARK

9 Ave.

Mary Dover Park

Barlow Trail

INGLEWOOD BIRD SANCTUARY

Golf Course

P

Volleyball/Basketball/ Soccer

VALLEY VIEW REGIONAL PARK

Sanctuary Rd.

Deerfoot Trail

Pond

Water Play Pool

34 Ave.

Inglewood

Ogden Road

Peigan Trail

Bonnybrook Bridge

C N R

50 Ave. SE

Old Refinery Park

For the Birds

City of Calgary Parks have recorded 216 bird species and 271 plant species at the Inglewood Bird Sanctuary. Prominent birds include bald eagles, Swainson's hawks, great horned owls, ring-necked pheasants, gray partridges, and a range of warbler species.

The provincial department also says the sanctuary's backwaters and old channels, now a chain of lagoons, are one of the best places in Alberta to see wood ducks. Other sanctuary wildlife include common goldeneyes, muskrats, beavers, white-tailed and mule deer, coyotes, foxes, and long-tailed weasels.

Everyone who enjoys birds and birding must always respect wildlife, its environment, and the rights of others, says the American Birding Association. The association's code of ethics is for the protection and conservation of birds. This version is condensed; the full version is posted at http://birdcomp. fanweb.ca (Nature Calgary).

Chirps off the old block—guided group tours let birdwatchers
share in the thrill of sighting more than 210 species of birds.

Promote the welfare of birds and their environment:

- Support the protection of important bird habitat.
- Exercise restraint and caution during observation, photography, sound recording, or filming.
- Keep well back from nests and nesting colonies, roosts, display areas, and important feeding sites.
- Before advertising the presence of a rare bird, evaluate the potential for disturbance to the bird, its surroundings, and other people in the area.
- Stay on roads, trails, and pathways where they exist; otherwise keep habitat disturbance to a minimum.
- Respect the law and the rights of others.
- Practice common courtesy in contacts with other people.
- Group birding requires special care.
- Respect the interests, rights, and skills of fellow birders, as well as those of people participating in other legitimate outdoor activities.

Bird monitoring

Since 1992, the Calgary Bird Banding Society has operated a migration monitoring station at the Inglewood Bird Sanctuary. Carried out mainly by enthusiastic volunteers, bird monitoring is a way to track bird populations and, says the Canadian Migration Monitoring Network, is crucial for bird conservation.

The annual Breeding Bird Survey across North America counts birds every summer in their breeding grounds. The network's website says: "This count is particularly valuable because most birds are fairly faithful to their breeding grounds, reducing the variation in the counts. Also, changes in bird populations can be compared directly with changes in the breeding habitat."

Monitoring by Calgary Bird Banding Society confirms the following species are regularly spotted at the sanctuary.

- American crow
- American goldfinch
- American robin
- Baltimore oriole
- Black-billed magpie
- Black-capped chickadee
- Cedar waxwing
- Chipping sparrow
- Downy woodpecker
- Eastern kingbird
- European starling
- Gray catbird
- House wren
- Yellow-rumped warbler
- Northern flicker
- Orange-crowned warbler
- Red-breasted nuthatch
- Tennessee warbler

- Western wood-pewee
- White-crowned sparrow
- White-throated sparrow
- Wilson's warbler
- Yellow warbler

In all, 216 bird species have been recorded at the sanctuary; additional species include:

- American kestrel
- Bald eagle
- Belted kingfisher
- Bufflehead
- Common goldeneye
- Common merganser
- Gray partridge
- Killdeer
- Lesser scaup
- Mallard
- Northern pintail
- Spotted sandpiper
- Wilson's snipe

For more information about bird sightings, call the Inglewood Bird Sanctuary Bird Alert information line at 221-4519.

Seasonal Sightings

What you could find—and when—at the Inglewood Bird Sanctuary:

- Warblers during August and September
- Uncommon species of gull (mew, Thayer's, Iceland, glaucous-winged, and glaucous) in spring and late fall
- American kestrel, northern flicker, western wood-peewee, least flycatcher, eastern kingbird, and Baltimore oriole in summer
- Migrating songbirds through August and September
- Black-capped chickadees and white-breasted nuthatches during the winter

The Inglewood Bird Sanctuary is made for strolling, stopping, watching, and listening. True birders will shuffle through the sanctuary for hours with their binoculars and field guides in the hopes of seeing or hearing a particular species.

The Inglewood Bird Sanctuary was once the largest urban sanctuary in the Dominion. Today, it covers 79 acres, and for some 50 years has provided shelter and food along the Bow River for 216 different bird species every year.

As well, more than 265 species of plants have been identified at the sanctuary along with six species of fish and more than a dozen mammals. And each year more than 50,000 people visit.

The sanctuary does all this while sharing a section of the Bow River Valley with Deerfoot Tr., a flight path for the Calgary International Airport, a golf course, and a nearby industrial district.

This is one of the gems of outdoor Calgary. It never fails to surprise, delight and amaze. It steadfastly remains a place of urban solitude and it consistently offers visitors the opportunity to see and learn about a wide variety of birds, plants, and mammals every day of the year.

The waters, shores, and forests at the Inglewood Bird Sanctuary attract thousands of birds—and more than 50,000 people each year.

Volunteers often patrol the sanctuary's packed trails, eager to help birdwatchers and nature lovers identify their finds. Quite often they carry binoculars, cameras with telescopic lenses, and sanctuary brochures. Some are mobile librarians with bird and flora guidebooks in their backpacks. Volunteers also sport their own colourful "plumage": fluorescent orange vests.

Free bird and plant checklists are available from the sanctuary's Nature Centre. The centre also offers a number of guided and interpretive tours and programs. Plus, the Bird Alert telephone line is regularly updated with the latest bird sightings.

Using Calgary's Natural Areas

When you respect the flora, fauna, and habitat in Calgary's natural areas, you help protect and conserve these fragile urban environments. Their future depends on people using common sense and observing rules and hours of operation.

- Off leash dogs can wreak havoc with wildlife; give way to wildlife and always clean up after your pet.
- Exploring less-travelled areas can be exciting, but can also disturb wildlife and erode habitat.
- Feeding wild animals is discouraged. So is picking berries, flowers, or any vegetation—anywhere.

Nature suffers silently. Park and pathway users are encouraged to report damage or abuse by calling the City of Calgary at 3-1-1.

Sanctuary Pathway Description—Inglewood Bird Sanctuary

About 2.5 kilometres of paved pathways and unpaved footpaths radiate from the Nature Centre, across open grasslands and into mature riparian forests. All are flat and easy to navigate. Keeping to the trails is one of the foremost rules at the sanctuary.

On Talk about Birds at www.weaselhead.org, City of Calgary naturalist Dave Elphinstone writes that the sanctuary has three terraces or levels: "The upper terrace is covered mainly by restored grassland, cultivated trees and shrubs; the interpretive centre and the Walker House are situated upon it. Balsam poplar trees dominate the middle terrace, while the lowest terrace is an area that is often flooded in spring and is dominated by willow."

Another geographical feature at the sanctuary is the lagoon, once a channel

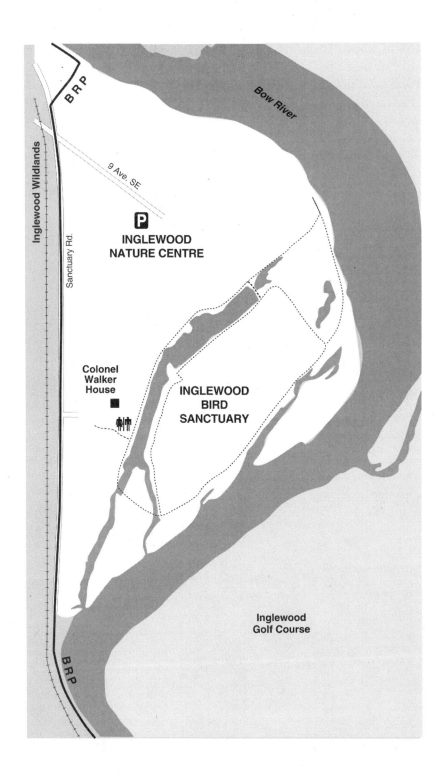

of the Bow River. With several bridges and observation decks, the lagoon offers excellent and slightly elevated viewpoints of migrating and nesting waterfowl. The lagoon is also home to many beavers, and their lodges are easily spotted. (The beavers' insatiable appetite for trees is also evident—stumps dot the banks and many trees have been wrapped with wire to fend off the gnawing rodents.)

Additional sanctuary pathways lead to the Bow River's gravelly shores; those at the north end of the sanctuary are ideal vantage points for observing waterfowl, gulls, and a number of birds of prey, particularly bald eagles.

Across the river are the serene greens of the Inglewood Golf Course and the constant rattle and hum of Deerfoot Tr.

Inglewood Bird Sanctuary History

Calgary's citizen of the 20th century, Colonel James Walker, once owned the land that today is the Inglewood Bird Sanctuary. The third house he built on the site in 1910 stands today and served for many years as the Sanctuary's office and interpretive centre.

In 1925, Banff naturalist George Pickering leased a parcel of the Walker land to create a bird sanctuary for migrating birds. The location was ideal because that particular section of the Bow River seldom froze over. In 1929, Walker's son Selby requested that 59 acres become the Federal Migratory Bird Sanctuary.

For nearly 25 years, Pickering managed the sanctuary, receiving only a meagre wage and stipend. When the provincial government retired Pickering at the age of 65, he stayed on at the sanctuary as an unpaid worker for another seven years.

Pickering estimated in 1950 some 6,000 birds stopped at the sanctuary during spring and fall migrations. By the 1960s, the birds were still migrating to the sanctuary, but it had fallen from public favour. Because it attracted thousands of birds in the flight path of McCall Field (then Calgary's airport), some people felt it posed a safety hazard to planes. It was also a common sanctuary practice to feed the

visiting birds, an increasingly expensive undertaking.

On Sept. 5, 1970, the Calgary Herald reported: "Virtually no one goes there now, most of the birds have gone and many of the water control and bird-banding facilities have fallen into disrepair."

That same year, the City of Calgary astutely purchased the sanctuary lands and has worked ever since with the community to protect and promote the virtues of the site—and to protect the thousands of birds that continue to stop along this section of the Bow River.

Colonel James Walker's third home was once the bird sanctuary's office and interpretive centre.

A Refined Environment

The Inglewood Wildlands Park, located next to the Inglewood Bird Sanctuary, was not so many years ago the site of an oil refinery. In the past three decades, it has been transformed from a decaying and abandoned industrial site to an "evolving natural area" with nearly a dozen distinct areas, including a pond, thornbush thicket, wildflower meadow, fruit orchard, and berry bushes. The area's evolution is ongoing—both surface and underground remediation of the site will take years to complete.

Contractors and volunteers have worked together to plant more than 35,000 trees, shrubs, grasses, and other flora, including a rare native plant (sandhills cinquefoil), transplanted from a development site near Symon's Valley in northwest Calgary. In 1997, the Rotary Club of Calgary Olympic received an Emerald Award from the Alberta Foundation for Environmental Excellence for its work at Wildlands Park.

The club's work at the site has been supported by Petro-Canada (the landowner and educational program partner), City of Calgary Parks (which maintains the park), landscape architect Len Novak (who designed the park), the Inglewood Wildlands Society, and the Parks Foundation, Calgary.

The City's vision for the wildlands is that it "will become a river valley site dominated by a mosaic of grasslands, shrubs, and riparian woods: a functional adjunct to the Inglewood Bird Sanctuary to be freely accessed and enjoyed by both wildlife and the public." Much work remains.

BOW RIVER PATHWAY—INGLEWOOD BIRD SANCTUARY TO BEAVER DAM FLATS

Comedian Jerry Seinfeld once said: "Sometimes a road less travelled is less travelled for a reason." For the Bow River Pathway between the Inglewood Bird Sanctuary and Beaver Dam Flats, two reasons spring to mind.

First, the setting. The pathway winds its way through Calgary's grittiest industrial district—Alyth—home to the CPR's Alyth Yard and the Bonnybrook Water Treatment Plant. Plus, the river valley is shared by Deerfoot Tr.—see next point.

Second, the noise. The whine of railway cars—akin to off-key divas—can be grating and abrupt enough to make your heart skip a beat. The thrum of Deerfoot Tr. is largely inescapable.

So this isn't the most scenic and serene stretch of pathway in the city. Nor is it the most travelled. But some redeeming qualities can still be found. The river is quiet, wide, and majestic, its rippling surface shimmering like crushed velvet. The birdlife is diverse and industrious, scouring the river's waters for food, teaching offspring to manoeuvre, and building shore-side nests. And if ever there was a place to lose yourself in the drone of urban life and rhythm of walking, running, and cycling—this is it.

At the end of Sanctuary Rd. SE, the pathway narrows and skirts the CPR's train yard. A catwalk-like bridge under a train bridge demands attention—inevitably this is where pathway traffic comes face to face.

The pathway crosses the river at Ogden Road and forks shortly thereafter; follow the west (right) fork through an opening in the chain-link fence to remain on the main route through Old Refinery Park. Telltale signs of the 2005 floods are evident just upstream of the Calf Robe Bridge: small dunes of silt and jumbled piles of wood and garbage are still scattered across the gravel shores.

Just beyond the Calf Robe Bridge, the pathway reaches Beaver Dam Flats.

A bonny ride—the Bow River Pathway at the Bonnybrook Bridge.

Pathway Hotline
For information about current pathway closures and detours, call the City of Calgary at 3-1-1 or visit www.calgary.ca/parks and follow the links to Pathway Openings, Closures, and Detours.

OLD REFINERY PARK

Blink and you could miss this park at the north end of Beaver Dam Flats. Located between the Bonnybrook Bridge and Beaver Dam Flats, the park sits on the old Esso Refinery site and has been undergoing remediation for several years. That work is expected to continue. Meanwhile, the park does offer several benches and picnic tables, although most visitors simply traverse the park rather than stop and linger. Plus, the river's shore is rich in feeding and nesting waterfowl.

BEAVER DAM FLATS

LOCATION	62 Ave. and 16 St. SE
HOURS	0500 to 2300 daily
TERRAIN	Flat riverine forest in flood plain backing onto a steep west facing escarpment
ACCESS	Bow River Pathway south of Calf Robe Bridge (Deerfoot Tr.)
	Bow River Pathway north of Graves Bridge (Glenmore Tr.)
	West of Lynnview Way and 62 Ave. SE (closest major intersection: Glenmore Tr. and 18 St. SE)
	No direct vehicle access
ACTIVITIES	Walking, hiking, cycling, bird and animal watching, guided nature walks, cross-country skiing, boating (non-motorized), fishing
FACILITIES	Paved pathways and gravel trails
	Washrooms (seasonal)
	Water fountain (seasonal)
	Playground
	Picnic tables
	Firepits
DOGS	On leash on pathway
	On leash in park, unless otherwise noted
	On leash within 20 metres of playground
BOOKINGS	For guided nature walks, call 221-4532; to book picnic areas and other park facilities, call the City of Calgary at 268-3800
TRANSIT	#24, #36, #41, #730, #770

Located on the eastern shores of the Bow River, south of the Calf Robe Bridge and north of Graves Bridge, Beaver Dam Flats is another river valley park flanked by traffic. Although adjacent to two of Calgary's busiest roads— Deerfoot Tr. and Glenmore Tr.—Beaver Dam Flats can only be reached by the Bow River Pathway.

The park's semi-isolation is part of its charm—and one of the reasons flora and fauna thrive here. True to its name, Beaver Dam Flats is a haven for beavers, which are attracted to the park's lush riverine forest.

The forest's quiet sentinels are balsam poplars. Wrinkled, wizened, and stooped with time, these giant trees have withstood timeless seasons, the vagaries of industry, and of course the unrelenting appetite of Castor canadensis, the American beaver.

The City of Calgary's animal control officers wage a constant but gentle battle against the beaver to prevent flooding of this low-lying area. Signs of both sides' engagement—chewed-off and wire-wrapped tree trunks—are easily spotted along the park's channels and wetlands.

Because of its diverse habitats, the park also attracts and supports a wide variety of birds, mammals, and plants. Among them: American white pelicans, double-breasted cormorants, bald eagles, coyotes, and white-tailed deer.

Beaver Dam Flats shares many of the serene qualities of nearby Carburn Park—both are natural sanctuaries to people and wildlife—although it suffers more from the indignities of careless users. (The washrooms have been vandalized so many times that they are seldom open.)

The park's densely vegetated riverside "flats" butt up against a steep, west-facing escarpment. Windswept and grassy, the escarpment has its own distinct prairie ecosystem. In early spring, prairie crocus, moss phlox, and early blue violet lend colour to the bleached hillside. And the crest of the escarpment offers a sweeping, somewhat gritty panorama of the river valley as well as roadways, railways, the city skyline, and distant mountains.

10 Cool Things About Balsam Poplar

- The Latin name for balsam poplar is Populus balsamifera.
- Balsam poplars grow up to 25 metres high.
- These towering trees can live for 150 years.
- Many birds depend on live and dead balsam poplars for nesting, including flickers, owls, hawks, eagles, nuthatches, woodpeckers, and a number of tree-nesting ducks.
- The seeds of these fast-growing trees need floods to germinate.
- More than 30,000 poplars have been planted along the Bow River.
- Balsam poplar is also known as balm-of-Gilead, black cottonwood, black poplar, and tacamahac.
- Tree buds contain salicylic acid, the main ingredient in aspirin.
- Poplars have a distinct, fresh aroma, especially when budding in spring and when their leaves turn in the fall.
- Both male and female poplars produce catkins.

Useful dead or alive—many birds depend on live and dead balsam poplars for nesting.

Pathway Description—Beaver Dam Flats

After passing underneath a CNR Railway line south of the Calf Robe Bridge on Deerfoot Tr. SE, the Bow River Pathway enters Beaver Dam Flats. A narrow strip of trees and shrubs separates the pathway from the riverbank. The flat, gently winding pathway veers inland slightly and soon forks. The tines rejoin at the washrooms and playground located in the middle of the park. From this hub, the Bow River Pathway begins a short, steep climb up a grassy escarpment. The pathway follows the escarpment's edge south through Lynnwood Ridge for several hundred metres before once again descending to the valley floor—via some hairpin corners—where it ducks under Graves Bridge (Glenmore Tr. SE) and enters Carburn Park.

Additional hard-packed trails in Beaver Dam Flats travel to the riverbank at the south and west ends of the park. Plus a well developed network of desirable paths weaves across the flood plain and its wetlands and back channels

Dropping a line—Sunday morning fishing near Graves Bridge SE.

at the south end of the flats. Sapper's Bridge connects the flat's south end to the terrace below the escarpment. The grand timber bridge was built by a volunteer corps of sappers—the military nickname for engineers—from the 33rd Engineer Squadron of the Canadian Armed Forces, with the support of the Parks Foundation, Calgary, and the River Valleys Committee.

CARBURN PARK

CARBURN PARK AT A GLANCE

LOCATION	8925 – 15 St. SE
HOURS	0500 to 2300 daily
TERRAIN	Generally flat, riverine forest along flood plain with escarpment at north end
ACCESS	BRP south of Graves Bridge
	BRP north of Eric Harvie Pedestrian Bridge (Southland Natural Area)
	South of Riverbend Dr. and Riverview Dr. SE (closest major intersection: Glenmore Tr. and 18 St. SE)
ACTIVITIES	Walking, hiking, cycling, guided nature walks, fishing, picnics, boating (non-motorized; lagoon and river), cross-country skiing
FACILITIES	Three man-made lagoons, two with wheelchair accessibility
	Parking lot
	Washrooms (seasonal)
	Water fountains (seasonal)
	Picnic tables and shelters
	BBQ pits/camp stoves
	Playgrounds
DOGS	On leash on pathway
	On leash in park, unless otherwise noted
	On leash within 20 metres of playground
	On leash in picnic areas
INFORMATION	For guided nature walks, call 221-4532; for picnic areas and other park facilities, call the City of Calgary at 268-3800
TRANSIT	#36, #41, #75, #136, #731, #734
ADDITIONAL	Please don't:
	Swim in the lagoons
	Skate on the lagoons
	Explore the adjacent islands (they're wildlife sanctuaries)

When Carburn Park opened in 1986, it was remote, obscure, and seldom visited. Two decades of explosive growth in Calgary have changed all that. Today, this reclaimed gravel pit (see sidebar "It was the Pits") is surrounded by a well-established neighbourhood (Riverbend), is well known, and is used passionately throughout the year.

Like the nearby Beaver Dam Flats, Carburn is a flat park on the flood plain of the Bow River's eastern shore. Carburn lacks the dramatic escarpment that

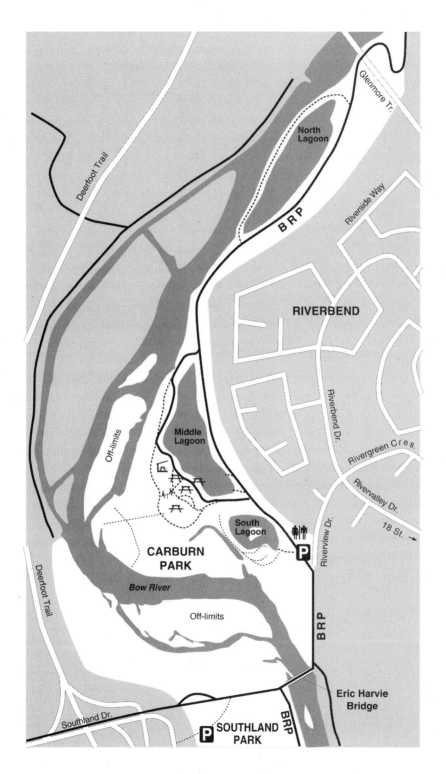

North Lagoon

Glenmore Tr.

Deerfoot Trail

BRP

Riverside Way

RIVERBEND

Off-limits

Middle Lagoon

Riverbend Dr.

Rivergreen Cres.

Rivervalley Dr.

South Lagoon

Riverview Dr.

18 St. →

CARBURN PARK

Bow River

Off-limits

BRP

Deerfoot Trail

Eric Harvie Bridge

Southland Dr.

BRP

SOUTHLAND PARK

A Rose is a Rose...

Calgary's most widespread rose is the Common Wild Rose (Rosa woodsii), a close relative to the Prickly Rose (Rosa acicularis), the floral emblem of Alberta since 1930 and the most widespread rose native to Canada. The two species are nearly identical with five pinkish, heart-shaped petals and five sepals, and both grow in moderately moist, grassy areas along roadsides and riverbanks and in open woods.

Common Wild Roses develop rose hips rich in Vitamin A and C.

Prickly and common wild roses often bloom in June, bearing numerous, lightly scented flowers with bright yellow stamens. In late summer, both develop deep pink or scarlet rosehips. Native Indians used the Vitamin A and C laden hips in a variety of ways: the leaves for tea, the outer bark for smoking, and the entire (dried) fruit for decorative beads. Today, rosehips are also used in jams, jellies, marmalades, syrups, and juices.

Other members of the rose family include chokecherry, saskatoon berry, wild gooseberry, wild red raspberry, and cinquefoil.

is part of Beaver Dam Flats, but the two parks share many similarities such as a majestic riverine forest and an abundance of wildlife and native plants.

With its wide and well-defined pathways and trails, Carburn Park is an ideal area for bicycles, baby strollers, and wheelchairs. For the more adventurous and more mobile, a gravel service road offers an alternative route along the western section, plus a series of trails is scribbled across the entire area. Park users are encouraged to stick to the pathways and well-established trails to reduce erosion and habitat damage.

Water is a predominant feature at Carburn—the park has two man-made lagoons immediately west and north of the main parking lot and a third south of Graves Bridge. The lagoons' quiet waters are well suited to novice paddlers, but are off limits to swimmers. Likewise, in winter skating is prohibited due to the lagoons' uneven and unstable ice surfaces.

Thick with balsam poplars, wolf willow, saskatoons, and red osier dogwood, the park's riverbanks are soothing and fascinating—the shores teem with waterfowl and fish, and it's not unusual to see a bald eagle circling overhead. Carburn Park combines with a natural area across the river and three nearby islands (these adjacent areas are all closed to visitors) to make up one of the most populated and diverse winter wildlife areas in Calgary. The nearby islands are also part of this rich wildlife area, and because of this, visiting them is strongly discouraged. The small wetland basins at the park's southern end are exceptionally rich habitats and worth exploring.

A word of caution: the floods of 2005 undercut many riverbanks along the Bow River, leaving them highly unstable. Indeed, significant sections of Carburn Park's riverbanks were washed away, especially at the park's north end between the river and the lagoon. In other places, new channels and flows were created.

In Carburn Park, much of the damage has been restored; some sections of trail along the north lagoon's western edge remain washed out and extreme caution is advised.

Watching the river go by—the quick flowing waters of the Bow River attract and fascinate.

Bald Eagles

The bald eagle is Canada's largest bird of prey. It is also the national bird of the United States of America.

One of only two eagles in North America (the other is the golden eagle) and the only eagle exclusive to the continent, Haliaeetus (sea eagle) leucocephalus (white head) has a wingspan of more than two metres, stands about 75 centimetres high and often weighs more than seven kilograms.

Some 70,000 bald eagles range widely across North America. Those that nest in Alberta are thought to migrate each fall to the southern United States, where the species has been listed as endangered or extirpated (no longer living in the wild) for three decades.

In Canada, the bald eagle is more common than in the United States. In Calgary, bald eagles frequently soar during the winter above the Bow River between the Inglewood Bird Sanctuary and Fish Creek Provincial Park. In February 2006, the City of Calgary and the Calgary Field Naturalists' Society (Nature

Wildlife Checklist
Animals regularly seen in Carburn Park include:

Birds
- American white pelican
- Bald eagle
- Black-capped chickadee
- Canada goose
- Cliff swallow
- Common merganser
- Double-breasted cormorant
- Franklin's gull
- Great blue heron
- Great horned owl
- Ring-billed gull
- Tree swallow
- Wood duck

Fish
- Northern pike
- Rainbow trout
- Brown trout

Mammals
- Coyote
- White-tailed deer
- Eastern grey squirrel

Calgary) Bird Alert reported: "Observers in Calgary could be on the lookout for possible nesting activity by bald eagles along the Bow River, especially in southeast Calgary. In the past two years, nesting activity there has started around mid-February."

It's thought some bald eagles overwinter in their nesting habitat if their fishing areas do not freeze over. The bald eagle hunts and scavenges for fish, aquatic birds, and small mammals. As hunger dictates, a bald eagle will eat virtually anything—using its hooked beak, powerful talons, and pincer-like spiked feet to catch, carry, and then rip apart food. *Hinterland Who's Who* says, "generally, the adults are likely to hunt and kill, whereas the younger birds rely more heavily on scavenging and piracy."

An estimated 2 to 20 bald eagles migrate annually to winter in Calgary, often to Carburn Park where the duck population provides a steady food source.

Mature bald eagles are readily identified by their white heads ("bald" refers to white not lacking in feathers) and white tails, but immature birds of the species are often confused with the golden eagle. The difference is that young bald eagles have whitish feathers on the front underside of their wings; golden eagles have whitish feathers on the rear underside of their wings.

Nurturing the Riverine Forest

Carburn Park is home to one of the city's most striking examples of a riverine forest. These concentrated habitats along the shores of rivers in Southern Alberta are seldom more than a couple of hundred metres wide.

The most prominent feature of a riverine forest is typically its gnarled balsam poplars. Like other riverine forests in Calgary, the one in Carburn Park has many old stands but almost no new natural growth of balsam poplars. Added to this is the fact that many of the mature poplars there are nearing the end of their lives.

A City of Calgary press release in 2003 said "balsams regenerate best under naturally dynamic river regimes, which damming of the Bow River has prevented." That year the City, RiverWatch, Calgary Board of Education, Trans Canada, and students from T. B. Riley Junior High School planted 1,800 balsam poplars at the northeast corner of the Inglewood Bird Sanctuary. In all, some 30,000 balsam poplars have been planted along the Bow River.

The floods of 2005 created very "dynamic river regimes," but it remains to be seen if those conditions will lead to any natural germination and growth of balsam poplars in Calgary.

Pathway Description—Carburn Park

The Bow River Pathway travels south under Graves Bridge on Glenmore Tr. SE to enter Carburn Park. On the opposite shore is the Graves Bridge Boat Launch.

The pathway divides at the north end of the park's middle lagoon. The western branch runs through the park's picnic and playground area and links to a number of foot trails leading to the river's edge. The east branch continues south to the parking lot and seasonal washrooms before leaving the park. Some 300 to 400 metres south, the pathway reaches the Eric Harvie Pedestrian Bridge and a gazebo at its east end.

Here pathway users have two choices: the BRP continues across the bridge to Southland Natural Park, and the regional pathway continues south along the river's eastern shore, linking to a number of community pathways in Riverbend.

It was the Pits

Carburn Park was once part of Senator Patrick Burns' vast prairie empire (a sprawling 450,000 acres) and at one time was the right-of-way for a railway line that was to have run between Calgary and Montana. In 1961, the land became City of Calgary property, and in the early 1980s a gravel company caught city council between a rock and a hard place, so to speak, when it applied for the area's gravel excavation rights. In return for the rights, Burnco Rock Products agreed to pay $800,000 to develop a park once the gravel pit was mined.

Reaction to the decision was mixed because the area's grasslands were stripped away. A precious expanse of native flowers and grasses was lost forever.

Pathway Description—Deerfoot Meadows

From Glenmore Tr. to close to the north end of the Southland Natural Area, the Bow River Pathway runs along both sides of the river. The pathway on the west shore is relatively new, and begins at Graves Landing, on the west side of the Graves Bridge on Glenmore Tr. SE (and reached via the very east end of Heritage Dr. SE).

Traffic is a given along the pathway at Deerfoot Meadows.

Graves Landing is a favourite fishing hole, boat launch, and an emergency Calgary Fire Department boat launch. Designed by well-known architect Bill Milne—also the founding chair of the Calgary River Valleys Committee—it is one of his many "public service" contributions to Calgarians. Milne doggedly lobbied for the pedestrian bridge that runs under Crowchild Tr. at the Bow River and for years was a patient but determined advocate of redesigning the weir at the headworks of the Western Irrigation Canal. He also helped usher in a City bylaw

Look but don't enter—a wildlife area at Deerfoot Meadows is strictly off limits.

limiting boats on Calgary's waterways to non-motorized versions only (except, of course, the Fire Department's emergency craft). Graves Landing was officially opened by Premier Ralph Klein in 1993.

South of Graves Landing, the Bow River Pathway veers south-southwest along Heritage Dr. SE and then along a dense riverine forest. At the Deerfoot Tr. SE on/off ramp, the pathway takes a sharp turn south. To the east of the pathway is a little-known natural area. Unlike its sister sanctuary to the north, the Inglewood Bird Sanctuary, this area—previously home to the old Cominco plants—is strictly off limits to the public. To the west of the pathway is traffic—and lots of it. Indeed, the pathway and entire interchange surrounding Deerfoot Meadows are part of the largest-ever private civil engineering project in Calgary.

At Heritage Meadows Way SE, the pathway connects to a regional pathway that climbs up Heritage Dr. SE to 79 Ave. SE.

Directly adjacent to Deerfoot Tr., the Bow River Pathway is flanked on either side by two metre high chain-link fences. A series of perfunctory benches and garbage cans give the illusion that people would actually want to stop and sit a spell along this route, but this is not the most inviting of routes. And, for now, it leads nowhere—ending abruptly before reaching Southland Natural Park. Secure fencing at either end of the gap ensures you must return the same way you came. The gap is, however, on the City of Calgary's pathway priority list and could be obsolete as early as 2007.

SOUTHLAND NATURAL PARK

SOUTHLAND NATURAL PARK AT A GLANCE

LOCATION	Southland Dr. east of Deerfoot Tr. SE
HOURS	0500 to 2300 daily
TERRAIN	Flat riverine forest and grassy fields
ACCESS	BRP downstream of Carburn Park
	BRP upstream of Lafarge Construction plant (Anderson Rd. SE)
ACTIVITIES	Walking, cycling, dog walking, birdwatching, fishing, and cross-country skiing
FACILITIES	Parking lot
	Fountain (seasonal for humans and dogs)
DOGS	Off leash, including on pathways
BOOKING	Not available
TRANSIT	#39

Located on the Bow River's west shores, Southland Natural Environment Park is best known as a dog walking park. A 2002 pathway survey by the City of Calgary found that nearly 41 per cent of Southland Natural Park users visit the area with their canine pets, compared to eight per cent of overall pathway users.

This is one of four natural areas along the Bow River between the Calf Robe Bridge and Anderson Rd. SE. Heavy use in Southland Natural Park, however, has had dramatic effects on park wildlife and habitat. This, combined with substantial riverbank damage from the floods of 2005, will see a new "protection strategy" developed for the park's natural areas. The City of Calgary has already installed a 1.2 metre high fence north of the Eric Harvie Pedestrian Bridge to keep people from the slumping riverbank. The City also plans to build a small missing link of pathway to connect with the pathway on the western edge of the Deerfoot Meadows Natural Area and to address conflicts between off leash dogs, their owners, and other park users.

The possibility that off leash use at the park could change greatly concerns the many dog owners who come across the city to roam with their animals. For more than a decade,

Strolling through the grasslands at Southland Natural Park.

this area has been a place where dogs can run freely. In fact, the park's pathway is the only one in the city that doesn't require dogs to be on leash: even in other off leash areas, dogs must be leashed along the pathway (as well, dogs must be leashed in all park and natural area parking lots).

Southland Natural Environment Park's grassy fields, open forests, and easily reached riverbanks are endlessly fascinating for dogs and humans alike.

Pet Etiquette

In May 2006, the City of Calgary offered Peace in the Parks—its first course for dog owners using Calgary parks. The evening-long course was held at Southland Natural Park and Bowmont Natural Park and covered dog safety, park etiquette, bylaws, and exercises as well as a practicum on park use. For information about further dog owner courses, call 3-1-1.

Giving Birth to a Forest

Southland Natural Park is one of six BP BirthPlace Forests in Calgary. The BP BirthPlace Forest program began in 2000 and is the largest "green" initiative in Calgary's history and is part of the City of Calgary's Forever Green program, to involve Calgarians in addressing the city's tree shortage. Every year, more than 6,000 trees are planted to celebrate the birth of new Calgarians. In 2003, 1,000 trees were planted at Southland Natural Park.

BP Canada Energy Company, Golden Acre Garden Sentres Ltd., and the Calgary Health Region sponsor the forest program. Other BP BirthPlace Forests include:
- Elliston Park—7,600 trees in 2001
- Silver Springs (NW)—7,500 trees in 2002
- McCall Lake Golf Course—3,500 trees in 2003
- Blackfoot Tr. and Glenmore Tr. SE—6,000 trees in 2004
- McCall Outlook (overlooking Deerfoot Tr. NE)—more than 6,000 trees in 2005

Pathway Description—Southland Natural Areas

At the west end of the Eric Harvie Pedestrian Bridge, the east entrance to Southland Natural Park, the route branches to the north (trail) and the south and west (pathways).

The Bow River Pathway travels south across the park, wandering in and out of the western edge of a riverine forest for about 1.2 kilometres. As the pathway reaches the Lafarge Construction plant, the right of way squeezes onto a narrow shelf between the river's edge and Lafarge property. This is one of the most uninviting sections of the BRP, made all the less welcoming when the pathway is regularly closed to accommodate Lafarge traffic at the south end of the plant.

The north route, a wide gravel trail, arcs north and west across the park. For about 500 metres, the pathway is set well back from the river's edge. Attempts to close and fence off this section of the park have proven futile; the area is still heavily overused. Park users opting for this route will find it a one-way route; the north end of the path—about 800 metres upstream of the bridge—is well fenced off.

The west route—a three metre wide paved regional pathway—cuts across the park to Southland Dr. SE, where it begins a long steady climb into Acadia. The pathway crosses Deerfoot Tr. SE and Blackfoot Tr. SE before reaching Archwood Rd. SE, where it joins an on-street cycling route.

Southland Natural Park is Calgary's busiest off leash area.

Pathway Description—Southland Natural Area to Fish Creek Provincial Park

South of the Southland Natural Area, the Bow River Pathway runs along a narrow shelf between the river and Lafarge Canada's main Calgary plant. Pitted with weeds and badly eroded in some sections, this is a utilitarian stretch of the pathway. In 2005, the pathway sustained major flood damage near the junction with Lafarge's private bridge. This junction is also subject to short, periodic closures to accommodate Lafarge's day-to-day operations.

South of the Lafarge Plant, the pathway dips under Deerfoot Tr. SE and then makes a long and arduous climb into the community of Diamond Cove. After running along the escarpment on the east side of the community, the trail descends back to the river valley.

The Bow River Pathway crosses Sue Higgins Pedestrian Bridge just upstream of Fish Creek Provincial Park. Built in the past 15 years, this section of the Bow River Pathway is almost as rich in birdlife as the Inglewood Bird Sanctuary. For a good part of the route, Fish Creek Provincial Park's Mallard Point—a massive island and protected wildlife area—is visible across the river. The sprawling island is off limits to humans but a haven for deer, coyotes, and beaver as well as dozens of species of birds.

All ashore—a temporarily abandoned boat near Southland Natural Areas.

This long, ambling and sometimes demanding section is without a doubt one of the true gems in Calgary's entire network of pathways. Running behind—and connecting in several places to—the communities of Douglasdale, McKenzie, and Mountain Park, the pathway travels through, near, or over flood plains, riverine forests, grasslands, wetlands, and escarpments for more than six kilometres before linking with the pathway on the east side of Fish Creek Provincial Park.

This is one of the reasons tens of thousands of people enjoy living in Calgary's "deep south."

Wildlife of every description, mountain views that force you to stop and look, brisk air that fills your lungs with satisfaction, the sound of honking geese (especially an hour or so before dusk), the like-it-or-leave-it suburban architecture, and the quiet power and isolation of the river combine to make this one of my most recommended journeys in Calgary. It's worth visiting—any time of the year, any time between sunrise and sunset.

Thousands of geese land along the shores of the Bow River south of Deerfoot Trail.

FISH CREEK PROVINCIAL PARK

FISH CREEK PROVINCIAL PARK AT A GLANCE

LOCATION	15979 Bow Bottom Tr. SE
HOURS	Vary seasonally, typically 0800 to 2000 in summer and 0800 to 1600 in winter
TERRAIN	Varies from steep spruce forests at west end to open rolling grasslands at east end; see individual area descriptions
ACCESS	See individual area descriptions
ACTIVITIES	Walking, hiking, cycling, bird and wildlife watching, dog walking, fishing, boating, swimming, cross-country skiing, picnicking, and educational and archaeological programs
FACILITIES	Shannon Terrace Environmental Learning Centre
	Washrooms and water fountains (usually locked one hour prior to park closing)
	Amphitheatre
	Picnic shelter, picnic areas and BBQ pits
	Bow Valley Ranch Visitor Centre
	Historical Bow Valley Ranche
	Annie's Kitchen
	University of Calgary Archaeology Field Station
	Lake Sikome and Lake Sikome concession
	Playground
	McKenzie Meadows Golf Course
	Boat launch
DOGS	On leash at all times; banned from Lake Sikome
INFORMATION	Call 297-5293 or visit www.fish-creek.org; picnic shelters and areas cannot be reserved; availability is on a first-come, first-served basis
TRANSIT	#3, #28, #35, #44, #56, #81, #83, #156, #736, #763, #764, #765, #766
ADDITIONAL	Park speed limit is 30 km/h
	Liquor is prohibited in all public areas
	Use only signed trails

Fish Creek Provincial Park is many things to many people: a diverse natural area, a neighbourhood park, a refuge for wildlife, and a living classroom and laboratory for students from grade school to university. It is rich in history—and a place where memories are made. People come here to run their fingers across knee-high grasses, listen to the melody of songbirds, contemplate reflections in

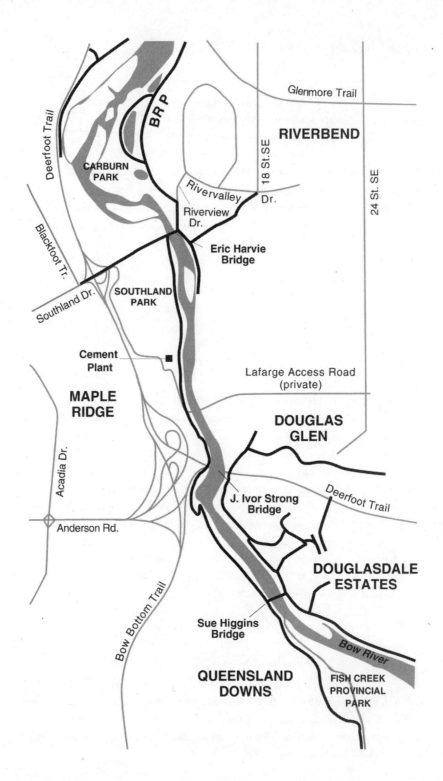

Quiet backwaters of the Bow River at Bankside in Fish Creek Provincial Park.

mirror-clear ponds, search for the first flowers of spring, bask in the aroma of warm fall afternoons, and marvel at the glow of the setting sun.

"This is some people's wilderness and it's where people get away from life's stresses and pressures," says Wayne Meikle, a parks planner who has worked at Fish Creek since 1979. "It's a very simple life here and I think that's a big attraction."

Shaped like a reclining question mark, Fish Creek Provincial Park is stretched along 19 kilometres of Fish Creek from the Tsuu T'ina (Sarcee) Reserve to the Bow River. Marvellously diverse, the park contains almost every habitat found in the Calgary area: grasslands, escarpments, oxbow lakes, spruce forests and riverine forests. More than a dozen different areas make up the park. From west to east along Fish Creek they are: Shannon Terrace, Bebo Grove, Raven Rocks, Marshall Springs, Votier's Flats, Glennfield, Heron Flats, and Bow Valley Ranch. From north to south along the Bow River they are: Mallard Point, Bankside, Burnsmead, Hull's Wood, Chinook Ridge, Sikome Lake, East Fish Creek, Rotary Chinook Natural Area, and the Lafarge Lands.

World-Class
At 1,430 hectares (some 203 hectares more than Nose Hill Park), Fish Creek Provincial Park is Calgary's largest park. It's also Alberta's only and Canada's largest urban provincial park. Fish Creek Provincial Park measures up internationally as well, and is one of the largest contiguous urban parks on the planet. It is the envy of and model for park planners and administrators around the world.

Weekend pleasures—a rod, a reel, and a river at Bankside in Fish Creek Provincial Park.

In the past ten years, the park has grown by some 400 hectares, with the purchase of the Lafarge Lands—the old gravel pits—on the west banks of the Bow River south of the Marquis of Lorne Tr. (Highway 22X). The reclaimed gravel pits will be turned into a series of engineered wetlands over the next two to three years.

Divided neatly by Macleod Tr. S, the park's west end is a narrow valley with steep north- and south-facing slopes; the valley floor is rich parkland dotted with aspen forest. East of Macleod Tr., the Fish Creek Valley widens into sunny grasslands and the escarpments soften. This moisture-rich valley supports many different species of vegetation as well as dozens of species of wildlife.

Since 1990, park use has steadily increased from one million to more than three million visitors per year. Originally created in the mid-1970s for $15 million, Fish Creek Provincial Park suffered more than $7 million of flood damage in 2005. Thirty years of intensive use and adjacent development—in conjunction with the 2005 flood—have left their mark on the park, but it continues to evolve and fascinate.

A Torrent of Change

Fish Creek Provincial Park was one of Calgary's hardest-hit natural areas during the floods of June 2005. Helicopters removed eight of the park's 18 pedestrian bridges after they were damaged beyond repair; more than 50 per cent of the park's pathways were damaged or destroyed, including sections of the Trans Canada Trail. The park's water monitoring station was also swept away. As well, "without a doubt there are stories of wildlife survival and loss that will never be known," said the park's website in 2006.

Nature's destructive fury, however, is almost always tempered by its restorative powers. So it is in Fish Creek. The flood purged the creek bottom, deposited rich silt, improved fish-spawning grounds and created new creek channels and wildlife and plant habitat. Flood damage also led park planners to momentarily pause and contemplate the park's future.

The result is that much of nature's course will be left to its own devices (as is the standard practice in the park). Damaged pathways and bridges will be repaired and/or relocated in stages through to the fall of 2007.

A two-year park restoration plan calls for:

- Construction of a paved east–west pathway from 37 St. SW to the Bow River.
- Construction of several paved north–south regional pathway connectors.
- Replacing some pedestrian bridges using federal engineering standards.
- A single-track unpaved pathway to be developed for multiple use (pedestrians and cyclists).
- Closing the park to equestrian use.

Other recent changes and long-term plans in the park include:

- Extending the paved pathway south of the Marquis of Lorne Tr. SE.
- Purchasing additional land south of present-day boundaries.
- Restricting bike use to designated pathways (part of changes to Alberta's Park Act).

In many ways, the flood "naturalized" the park, says park planner Wayne Meikle, and "people are learning to live with its changes. You can't fight nature because nature will win—we're working with nature, not against it."

Fish Creek Provincial Park Wildlife Checklist

Which wildlife have you seen in Fish Creek Provincial Park? Alberta Sustainable Development lists the following among the park's wildlife residents.

Amphibians
- Boreal chorus frog
- Tiger salamander

Birds
- American goldfinch
- Bald eagle
- Black-capped chickadee
- Blue jay
- Raven
- Canada goose
- Common merganser
- Eastern kingbird
- Great blue heron
- Great horned owl
- Hairy woodpecker
- Downy woodpecker
- Northern flicker
- Pileated woodpecker
- Red-breasted nuthatch
- Red-tailed hawk
- Ring-necked pheasant
- Ruffed grouse
- Swainson's hawk

Fish
- Brook stickleback
- Brown trout
- Longnose sucker
- Rainbow trout

Mammals
- Little brown bat
- Meadow vole
- Pocket gopher
- Porcupine
- Muskrat
- Beaver
- Snowshoe hare
- Mule deer
- White-tailed deer
- Coyote
- Red Squirrel
- Richardson's ground squirrel
- Shrew
- Weasel

Reptiles
- Red-sided garter snake
- Wandering garter snake

MALLARD POINT, BANKSIDE AND BURNSMEAD

LOCATION Mallard Point—south of Bow River Pathway and Sue Higgins Pedestrian Bridge on west shore of Bow River

Bankside and Burnsmead—south of Mallard Point and east of Bow Valley Ranch Visitor Centre

HOURS Vary seasonally, typically 0800 to 2000 in summer and 0800 to 1600 in winter

TERRAIN Flat, expansive grasslands; riverine forest along west shore of Bow River

ACCESS Mallard Point—end of Canyon Meadows Dr. SE

Bankside and Burnsmead—east of Bow Bottom Tr. SE

ACTIVITIES Walking, cycling, bird and wildlife watching, picnicking, fishing

FACILITIES Washrooms and water fountains: year-round at Mallard Point, seasonal at Bankside and Burnsmead (May through September)

Picnic areas

Parking lots

DOGS On leash at all times

INFORMATION Call 297-5293 or visit www.fish-creek.org; picnic shelters and areas cannot be reserved, availability is on a first-come, first-served basis

TRANSIT #28, #713

ADDITIONAL Park speed limit is 30 km/h

Liquor is prohibited in all public areas

Use only signed trails

Pathway Description—Mallard Point, Bankside and Burnsmead

South of the Bow River Pathway and the Sue Higgins Pedestrian Bridge on the west shore of the Bow River is the northernmost point of Fish Creek Provincial Park, the Mallard Point area.

True to its name, the area is alive with mallards as well as with other waterfowl and songbirds. Deer and coyotes also inhabit the area.

The pathway divides shortly after entering the park: an unpaved trail travels along the river's shore and another trail meanders through the riverine forest for several hundred metres before crossing the expansive grasslands.

The two trails intersect several times at the north end of Mallard Point but are well separated across the flood plain. Both trails are wide, well-maintained, and easy to navigate. The paved pathway is virtually pancake-flat and wide open to sun and wind, and is flanked by the estate homes of Deer Run. Several paved

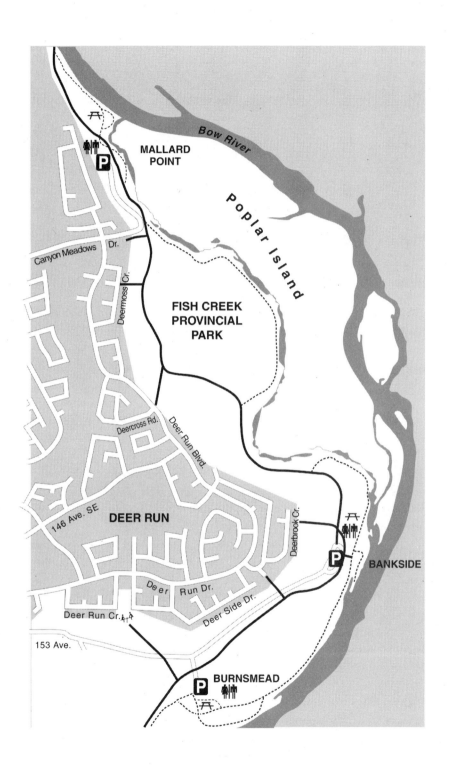

Sunday best—Pathway users redefine the weekend dress code.

connections link the route to the neighbouring community.

The unpaved trail gently rolls up and down a channel of the Bow River; much of this route was rebuilt in 2005 and is in excellent condition. Across the seasonal river channel is Poplar Island, the largest island in Calgary, a wildlife sanctuary closed to all human use. The island's abundant wildlife can be easily observed from either side of the river (the Bow River Pathway runs along the east shore of the river) and is most active at dawn and shortly before sunset.

The paved and unpaved pathways intersect in several places, but remain distinct. For the most part, the paved pathway leisurely ambles south through grasslands, which in summer and fall grow knee-high grasses. The unpaved pathway continues to wind through the shade and coolness of the riverine forest, usually within 50 to 100 metres of the river's edge.

Downstream of Burnsmead, the paved pathway and an unpaved path continue, running parallel to each other around the Fish Creek Water Treatment Plant. As they approach Bow Bottom Tr. SE, they separate slightly before reaching Fish Creek. Pathway users can continue west to Bow Valley Ranch and the creek's upper reaches, or south to Hull's Wood and Sikome Lake.

Downstream of Bankside, the paved pathway is twinned; the easterly leg links to a pedestrian bridge across the Bow River. (See: Pathway Description—Burnsmead to Chinook Nature Park.)

Pathway Description—Burnsmead to Chinook Nature Park
Across the river the pathway splits east and south. The east leg is a series of very steep hairpin curves up the escarpment into the community of McKenzie. The

south leg cuts across a wide flood plain and joins the river's edge directly across from the confluence of the Bow River and Fish Creek. From there the paved pathway hugs the western edge of McKenzie Meadows Golf Course. On either side of the bridge over the Bow River, the pathway runs along an access road. Downstream of the bridge, the east pathway enters the Rotary Chinook Natural Area; the west pathway ends at the Lafarge lands.

Coyotes and Conflicts

Coyotes (Canis latrans) are amazingly adaptable to city life. They inhabit virtually every natural area in the city and are often seen loping unabashedly through city streets and alleys. Smart and social, coyotes are simultaneously admired, feared, and loathed by Calgarians. For their part, coyotes instinctively avoid human contact, although they can seem undaunted by it.

In 2005, Calgary's coyote population was estimated to be 1,000. As human and coyote populations increase, so too does the contact—and conflict—between the two species. In 2005, a coyote was shot after two young children were reportedly attacked by coyotes in northwest Calgary. Coyote attacks in Calgary, or anywhere else in North America, are exceptionally rare—fewer than 20 have ever been substantiated. Attacks on dogs and cats, however, are more common, especially at night and when coyotes are defending their territory. Thus, coyotes have earned many a human opponent.

Coyote proponents can easily and regularly observe this species of canine in the city. Coyotes are common in parks and communities along all Calgary waterways and in and around Nose Hill, Currie Barracks, and golf courses.

Coyotes are smaller than wolves and bigger than foxes. They resemble light-coloured, fine-boned German shepherds with bottlebrush tails, and feed on small mammals (rabbits, gophers, and mice), birds, plants (fruit and grasses), carrion, and garbage.

Coyotes mate for life—although they have been known to mate fleetingly with larger dogs. Male and females share in hunting, housekeeping, and pup-rearing. Each spring, in late April and early May, litters of 5 to 12 pups are born.

The City of Calgary offers these basic tips to prevent conflict between people and coyotes:

- Always supervise small children if coyotes are in the area.
- Teach your children never to approach coyotes or other wildlife.
- Keep dogs on a leash—especially in areas coyotes are known to frequent. Coyotes are also attracted by dog feces. Please clean up after your pet, especially in natural area parks.
- Clean up all loose garbage and put garbage in approved waste receptacles with the lids on.
- Never feed coyotes or leave pet food (including bird seed) outdoors.
- Carry a shrill whistle and portable alarm with you in areas frequented by coyotes.

Coyotes are smart, social inhabitants of Calgary's natural areas.
KEN RICHARDSON

Soft shoulders—a weekend walker takes the side trail near Mallard Point at Fish Creek Provincial Park.

Pathway Description—Burnsmead to Bow Valley Ranch

To reach Bow Valley Ranch and Fish Creek West from Burnsmead, take the pathway across Bow Bottom Tr. SE and turn north. The pathway forks at the parking lot: the paved pathway reaches the Bow Valley Ranch area along the treed base of the north escarpment; the unpaved trail skirts the south side of the Bow Valley Ranch parking lot. Approximate distance between Burnsmead and Bow Valley Ranch is 1.6 kilometres.

At a crossroads—checking directions at Bankside in Fish Creek Provincial Park.

Pathway Description—Burnsmead to Sikome Lake via Hull's Wood

From Burnsmead, follow the paved or unpaved path west about 1.1 kilometres toward Bow Bottom Tr. SE. From there, turn south to cross Fish Creek: a series of unpaved trails runs along the east side of Bow Bottom Tr. through Hull's Wood to Sikome Lake; the paved pathway runs along the west side of Bow Bottom Tr. Approximate distance between Burnsmead and Sikome Lake: 2.0 kilometres.

Pathway Description—Bow Valley Ranch to Sikome Lake

Take the paved pathway east of the Bow Valley Ranch area. At Bow Bottom Tr. SE, turn south and cross Fish Creek to reach the lake. Approximate distance between Bow Valley Ranch and Sikome Lake is 1.4 kilometres.

HULL'S WOOD AND SIKOME LAKE

LOCATION	Downstream of Burnsmead; southeast of Bow Valley Ranch
HOURS	Hull's Wood—vary seasonally, usually 0800 to 2200 in summer, 0800 to 1800 in spring and fall, and 0800 to 1600 in winter
	Sikome Lake—1000 to 2000 daily, mid-June to Labour Day weekend
TERRAIN	Hull's Wood—open grasslands; riverine forest along west shore of Bow River
	Sikome Lake—engineered lake and shore flanked by marshy forest and east-facing plateau
ACCESS	South end of Bow Bottom Tr. SE
	East of Sun Valley Blvd. SE
ACTIVITIES	Walking, hiking, cycling, bird and wildlife watching, picnicking, fishing, boating, swimming
FACILITIES	Washrooms and water fountains (seasonal, usually locked one hour before park closing)
	Picnic areas
	Playground
	Engineered lake (treated water)
	Parking lots
	Concession
	Playground
	Pay phone
DOGS	On leash at all times in Hull's Wood
	Pets not allowed at Sikome Lake
INFORMATION	Call 297-5293 or visit www.fish-creek.org; picnic shelters and areas cannot be reserved; availability is on a first-come, first-served basis
TRANSIT	#78, #178, #710
ADDITIONAL	Park speed limit is 30 km/h
	Liquor is prohibited in all public areas
	Use only signed trails

SIKOME LAKE

A family destination, Sikome Lake is an engineered lake near Bow Bottom Tr. and Marquis of Lorne Tr. SE. Extensive development has made this area the most "unnatural" part of Fish Creek. But Sikome Lake is blissfully popular on hot, sunny days, when families are more interested in a safe, clean beach than untouched

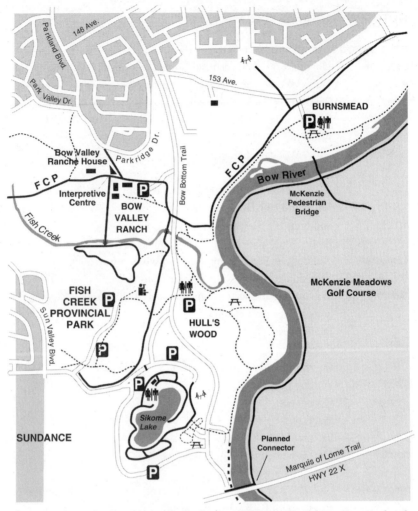

forests and grasslands. Open annually from mid-May to the Labour Day weekend, the lake's water is treated and lifeguards are on duty, making it ideal for swimming, wading, and splashing. Note: Sikome Lake will be closed in 2007.

The sandy shores of Sikome Lake are laced with trails, roads, and parking lots—and well-placed signage makes wayfaring a cinch. The lake's perimeter also includes a concession/snack bar, indoor washrooms and change rooms, a playground, and picnic areas. Children under 12 must be supervised by adults to use the lake and its facilities. For health reasons, pets are not permitted at the lake.

As weather allows, Sikome Lake is used for ice skating in winter months.

Sikome Lake can be reached by Bow Bottom Tr. SE south of the community of Deer Run or by the park entrance east of Sun Valley Blvd. SE.

Off the main track at Shannon Terrace in Fish Creek Provincial Park.

Boat Ramp

The boat ramp on the west shore of the Bow River between Sikome Lake and the Marquis of Lorne Tr. bridge is open year-round as weather and conditions allow. Hours vary by season; park gates are usually open from 0800 h to sunset (around 1800 h in spring and fall, 2200 h in summer, and 1600 h in winter).

The ramp is an access point for floating downstream (to destinations such as the Carseland Dam) and an egress point for those travelling downstream from points such as the weir at Pearce Estate Park or the Graves Landing under Glenmore Tr. SE.

By the fall of 2007, a second ramp and additional parking will be added.

SHANNON TERRACE, BEBO GROVE, VOTIER'S FLATS AND SHAW'S MEADOWS

SHANNON TERRACE, BEBO GROVE, VOTIER'S FLATS AND SHAW'S MEADOWS AT A GLANCE

LOCATION	Fish Creek Valley between 37 St. and Macleod Tr. SW
HOURS	Vary seasonally, usually 0800 h to 2200 h in summer, 0800 h to 1800 h in spring and fall, and 0800 h to 1600 h in winter
TERRAIN	Steep creek valley with spruce forests on north-facing

escarpment and grasses, shrubs, and aspens on south-facing escarpments. Creek runs through riverine forest and grasslands

ACCESS   Shannon Terrace and Fish Creek Environmental Learning Centre: Woodpath Rd. south of 130 Ave. SW

Bebo Grove: 24 St. south of Anderson Road SW

Marshall Springs: north of Evergreen Blvd. SW

Votier's Flats: south end of Elbow Dr. SW

Shaw's Meadows: Shawnee Gate north of James McKevitt Rd. SW

Plus numerous pathway connections to/from Woodbine, Woodlands, Evercreek Bluffs, Evergreen Estates, Millrise, Canyon Meadows, Shawnee Slopes, Canyon Meadows and Fish Creek, Lacombe C-Train Station

ACTIVITIES   Walking, hiking, cycling, bird and wildlife watching, educational programs

FACILITIES   Washrooms and water fountains (seasonal, usually locked one hour before park closing)

Picnic areas

Parking lots

Viewpoints

Fish Creek Environmental Learning Centre

Willan's Ranch

DOGS   On leash at all times

INFORMATION   Call 297-5293 or visit www.fish-creek.org; picnic shelters and areas cannot be reserved, availability is on a first-come, first-served basis.

TRANSIT   #3, #35, #56, #156, # 763, #764, #765, #766, #778, #779

ADDITIONAL   Park speed limit is 30 km/h

Liquor is prohibited in all public areas

Use only signed trails

Pathway "Prescription"

Until 2005, the west end of Fish Creek Provincial Park was a labyrinth of trails— paved and unpaved, as well as foot and horse trails. Heavy rains throughout June 2005 affected every pathway in the area. Many were washed away overnight in severe flooding, others along ridges and creek banks will erode and slump for years to come, and still others may be rerouted, merged or closed.

By the fall of 2007, the park's pathways are expected to be considerably different than they were in May 2005. Because of this, detailed pathway descriptions for many parts of Fish Creek are not provided in this book. For current routes, park visitors are encouraged to obtain an up-to-date park map

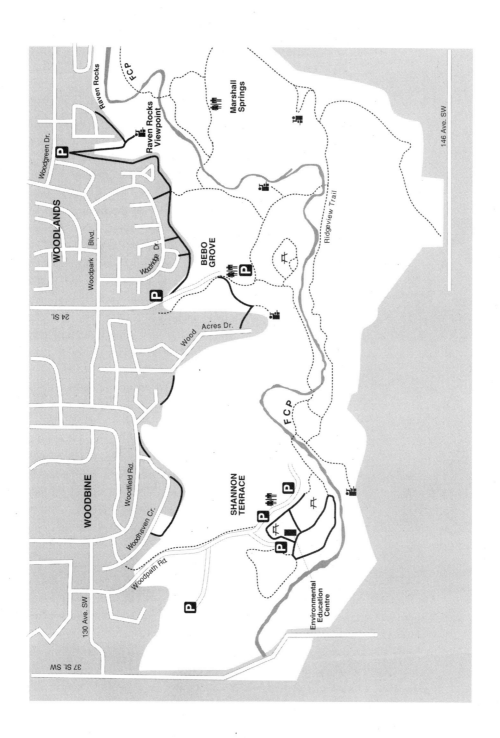

from the Fish Creek Environmental Learning Centre or the Bow Valley Ranch Visitor Centre. Park visitors are also encouraged to use only signed trails and to stay off damaged, closed, or decommissioned pathways and trails.

Shannon Terrace Description

Shannon Terrace, the westernmost point of Fish Creek Provincial Park, sits in a narrow, steep valley, and was named after ranchers Joseph and Margaret Shannon. The valley's north facing wall is thick with stands of white spruce, a moisture-loving tree that only began to grow in the valley when grass fires all but stopped scouring the landscape clean every few years. The forest, which covers less than two per cent of the park (about 34 hectares), is cool and damp, offering welcome respite from sun and heat during sun-baked summer and fall days and capturing snow and ice in the winter.

The well-travelled Ridgeview Trail that ran through and above the forest since the park opened was permanently closed in 2005.

Closer to the valley floor and the creek's shore, the spruce wane and stands of aspen and pockets of shrubs and grasslands thrive. The floods of 2005 greatly changed the creek bed; new channels have been rawly and hurriedly carved and some former channels left abandoned and dry. Large piles of deadfall and deposits of silt not only line the creek's new shores, but are strewn haphazardly along what was the high-water mark, sometimes dozens of metres from the water's edge.

Up the creek—Fish Creek shortly after it arrives in Fish Creek Provincial Park.

Once little more than a meandering trickle, Fish Creek has become a much more powerful waterway, in part because stormwater from more than a dozen surrounding communities drains into it. It will continue to evolve in the years ahead.

Fish Creek Environmental Learning Centre

The Fish Creek Environmental Learning Centre is a resource centre for educational groups interested in the park's natural history and its many ecosystems.

Teachers and group leaders primarily use the centre as a starting point for guiding their students and participants through the west end of Fish Creek Provincial Park.

The wheelchair-accessible centre includes a classroom setting and prior to visiting teachers can attend workshop courses on a broad range of natural park-related topics. In turn, they can pass on the information to their students.

Once owned by the Mannix family, the Fish Creek Environmental Learning Centre is located in Shannon Terrace at 13931 Woodpath Road SW. Other nearby facilities include picnic facilities, an amphitheatre, washrooms, and drinking water. The creek is within a three-minute walk of the centre.

The centre is open year-round Monday to Friday from 0815 to 1600 h; for further information, call 297-7827.

Willans Ranch

One of several ranchers in the Fish Creek Valley, Norman Willans was born in England and educated in Germany. He immigrated to Canada at the age of 15 and studied at the Agricultural College at Guelph, Ontario, before working and then homesteading in the Priddis area. For more than 30 years he worked for ranching baron Patrick Burns as a cattle buyer and as the manager of the Bow Valley Ranche, where he, his wife Maud, and their family lived until 1923.

Willans was forced into retirement due to failing eyesight, and his family purchased ten acres of land east of Shannon Ranch. In the 1930s, the family built "an old-fashioned" ranch house—called Cozy Cabin—and several outbuildings echoing the architecture of 50 years earlier. The Willans' barn and a storage shed still stand a few hundred metres east of the Shannon Terrace parking. For many years, park staff used the barn to stable their patrol horses.

Viewfinder—looking northeast from Willans Ranch across Fish Creek Valley.

Stargazing

The Royal Astronomical Society of Canada, Calgary Centre, holds regular Star Nights, rain or shine, several times a year at Fish Creek Provincial Park's Shannon Terrace area. Society members bring extra telescopes for the public to use. The astronomical outings include displays, star charts, computer games, talks and discussions about planets, stars, and even nocturnal wildlife, to introduce night watchers to the marvels that exist after sunset and beyond the orange glow of urban lights. These evenings are one of the few ways people can visit and experience the park after hours. For information, visit http://calgary.rasc.ca.

Bebo Grove and Marshall Springs

Downstream of Shannon Terrace, Bebo Grove (on the north side of the Fish Creek Valley) and Marshall Springs (on the south side of the valley) are melting pots for nearly all habitats in the park. Spruce forest, aspen stands, grasslands, riverine forest, and springs all collide in the narrow valley. The diversity of these areas is engaging at any time of the year, but it can be absolutely riveting in the fall, when the hills and valley are awash in blazing red shrubs, gleaming golden aspen, shimmering striated grasses, and smouldering grey spruce. Add a clear Alberta afternoon—with achingly azure skies and the purple-hued eastern slopes of the Rocky Mountains—and you have a picture-perfect autumn scene, and one worth the climb from the valley floor to the escarpment's crest.

Backcountry in the city—biking in Canada's largest urban park.

Across the valley, Marshall Springs flows year-round. It is one of 16 springs in the park and feeds a number of nearby bogs. The area is named for E. T. Marshall, a former landowner.

Downstream of Bebo Grove and Marshall Springs, Fish Creek turns sharply to the north as it flows toward Raven Rocks.

Raven Rocks

Geologically speaking, the Fish Creek Valley is part of the Porcupine Hills Formation, a bedrock formation carved during the Paleocene period (55 million

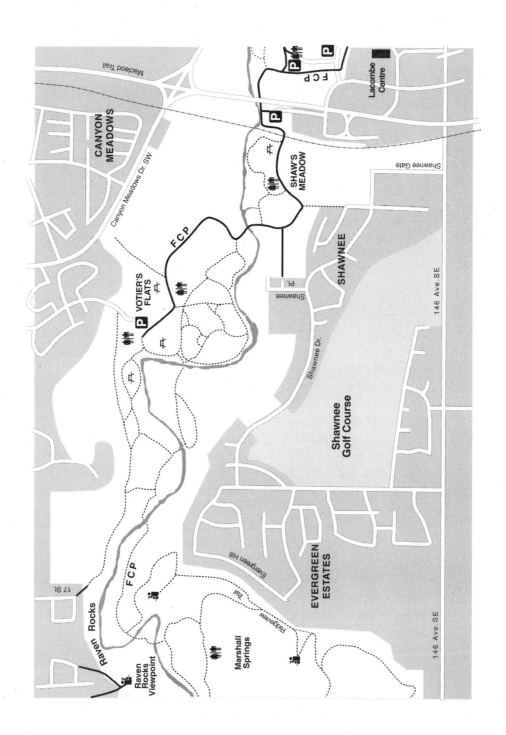

On the rocks—a family gathers on the water worn stones of Fish Creek.

to 65 million years ago), when dinosaurs were on the decline and mammals were on the rise.

"The sandstones, shales, and siltstones of the Porcupine Hills Formation were laid down when fast-moving water entered the still waters of deltas, lakes, and swamps," writes Anna Robertson in her 1991 book, *Fish Creek Provincial Park: A Guide to Canada's Largest Urban Park*.

The best example of the Porcupine Hills Formation in Fish Creek Provincial Park is at Raven Rocks, an outcrop of hard sandstone east of Bebo Grove (between 24 St. and Elbow Dr. SW) on the north side of the valley. Elsewhere in the park and throughout Calgary, such deposits of rock have been eroded into gravel, sand, and silt, but those at Bebo Grove have withstood time, wind, and weather. A similar outcropping of the Porcupine Hills Formation can also be found in Bowmont Natural Area's Waterfall Valley. The grassy tops of the rocks overlook Fish Creek Valley's eastern and western reaches. This is undoubtedly the most encompassing, dramatic view in the park and verges on breathtaking during colourful sunrises and sunsets. Note: A preservation zone below Raven Rocks is off limits to park visitors.

Buffalo Pounds and Jumps

Long before European settlers discovered the agricultural potential of Fish Creek Valley, native tribes had been using it for harvesting buffalo.

Blackfoot tribes rounded up buffalo into pounds, or *piskuns*, in the valley until the mid-1700s. The huge animals were chased into brush-and-buffalo-skin-lined pens also called "kettles of blood." Unable to see beyond the pen's temporary walls and flanked by hunters armed with arrows and spears, the bison were easily slaughtered. Few ever escaped the ambush.

Following their quick slaughter, native women would rush into the "kettles of blood" to butcher and clean the buffalo carcasses.

Native tribes also slaughtered bison upstream in the Fish Creek Valley at Raven Rocks on the south-facing hills west of Macleod Tr. There, natives chased herds over the cliffs where the animals either fell to their death or were wounded seriously enough to make them an easy kill.

Native life on the prairies revolved around bison, which provided wandering tribes with food, clothing, and shelter.

Cool Digs

Dig into the past with the University of Calgary's Archaeology Interpretive Centre at Fish Creek Provincial Park. It's one of the best ways to understand and appreciate how people have lived at the park for more than 8,500 years. Centre visitors go behind the scenes to learn about the over 70 archaeological sites in the park and to delve into the working lives of archaeologists.

Part of the U of C Archaeological Field School based at the park, the interpretive centre offers a number of educational programs for students in Grades one to six and is geared to hands-on learning. Students explore the site of John and Adelaide Glenn's original log cabin (the first European settlement in the Calgary area), an 8,000-year-old buffalo kill site, a 5,500-year-old native campsite, and William Roper Hull's historic—and grandly restored—Bow Valley Ranche House. History, culture, and school lessons have never been more interesting.

Program costs are modest—$4 per student for a half-day field trip in 2006. For further information, contact the University of Calgary's Archaeology Interpretive Centre at Fish Creek Provincial Park at 271-6333 or www. fp.ucalgary.ca/arkyeducation.

The Archaeology Interpretive Centre is located in the Bow Valley Visitor Centre off Bow Bottom Tr. SE.

Votier Flats and Shaw's Meadow

Named for early European pioneers, Votier Flats (James Votier) and Shaw's Meadow (Sam Shaw) are a mix of riverine forest and open grasslands, once used extensively for farming and ranching. Here it's easy to understand what has attracted native people, European settlers, and park visitors to the valley for thousands of years: it is an oasis. One hundred and twenty-five years ago, the surrounding plateaus—now dense with houses, condos, and apartments—were dry and windswept, and vegetation seldom grew higher than a buffalo's knee.

Reflecting on nature—a seasonal wetland at Votier Flats.

By comparison, the valley was and remains moist and cool; balsam poplars form colonnades over the creek. Nearby marshes and bogs cleanse ground and stormwater as well as the air. Walking through the forest you can smell and feel pockets of earthy freshness and musky compost. Step out of the trees and shade onto the grasslands and the aroma changes again. Some days the air is fragrant with sage or clover, other days with budding willow and the barest hint of rose.

As elsewhere in the park, the valley floor is easily navigated and the escarpments take a bit more effort to climb and descend.

The Shaws of Midnapore

When settlers came west, they usually brought only the essentials. Sam and Helen Shaw brought a little more, including a prairie schooner wagon, five

Helen Shaw.
GLENBOW MUSEUM ARCHIVES

teams of oxen, cows, chickens, sheep, farm machinery, grain, clothes, medicine, and one ready-to-assemble 30-ton woollen mill. The Shaws had left a comfortable life, their servants, and an ornamental garden in Kent, England, to homestead in the Northwest Territories. But they would not leave the conveniences and technology of the Industrial Revolution.

They had originally planned to settle in the Peace River area, but dire tales of bitter winter weather forced them to rethink their destination. After trekking from the end of the railway line in Swift Current, the Shaws opted to settle in the Midnapore area, south of Calgary. In the late 1880s, they built a log cabin with a sod roof, just south of Fish Creek and west of what would become Macleod Tr. SE.

Originally a chemist, Sam Shaw became a

homesteader, postmaster, storekeeper, rancher, and manufacturer of woollen goods. The woollen mill, set up in the Fish Creek Valley, was Alberta's first. Shaw soon found a steady market for his goods and for several years ran the Midnapore Woollen Store in downtown Calgary.

A series of interpretive signs and a sculpture in Shaw's Meadow highlight the family's industrious efforts.

Memorial Forest

Each year the McInnis & Holloway Funeral Home plants several thousand "living tributes" in memory of people who have died. McInnes & Holloway began planting memorial forests at Shaw's Meadow in Fish Creek Provincial Park in 1996 and has since planted more than 20,000 trees (aspen, poplar, spruce, saskatoon, dogwood, wolf willow, schubert, and chokecherry). The company also maintains each memorial forest, and posts the names of those remembered on its website (www.mhfh.com). The memorial forest in Shaw's Meadow is off Macleod Tr. and Bannister Rd. SE.

GLENNFIELD AND BOW VALLEY RANCH

GLENNFIELD AND BOW VALLEY RANCH AT A GLANCE

LOCATION	Fish Creek Valley between Macleod Tr. S and Bow Bottom Tr. SE
HOURS	Vary seasonally, usually 0800 to 2200 in summer, 0800 to 1800 in spring and fall, and 0800 to 1600 in winter
TERRAIN	Open grasslands with riverine forests
ACCESS	Glennfield—Bannister Rd. SE off Macleod Tr. S
	Bow Valley Ranch Visitor Centre—Bow Bottom Tr. south of 153 Ave. SE
	Plus numerous pathway connections to/from Lake Bonaventure, Lake Bonavista, Midnapore, Sundance, Parkland, the Canyon Meadows, and Fish Creek-Lacombe C-Train Station
ACTIVITIES	Walking, hiking, cycling, bird and wildlife watching, educational displays and programs, dining
FACILITIES	Washrooms and water fountains (both seasonal and year-round, usually locked one hour before park closing)
	Picnic areas with fire stoves (water and power available from May to September in west shelters and year-round in east shelter)
	Parking lots
	Bow Valley Ranch Visitor Centre
	Bow Valley Historic Ranche
	The Ranche Restaurant

Annie's Café and Bakery (seasonal)

University of Calgary Archaeology Field School at Fish Creek

DOGS On leash at all times

INFORMATION Call 297-5293 or visit www.fish-creek.org; picnic shelters and areas cannot be reserved, availability is on a first-come, first-served basis

TRANSIT #28, #44, #83, #712, #713, #760, #761

ADDITIONAL Park speed limit is 30 km/h

Liquor is prohibited in all public areas

Use only signed trails

The Glenns of Fish Creek

Often acknowledged as the first Europeans to settle in the Calgary area, and as Calgary's first citizens, John and Adelaide Glenn built a log cabin at the confluence of Fish Creek and the Bow River in 1873. John had already sought his fortune in California's gold rush and explored the Peace country and Fort Edmonton before marrying Adelaide Belcourt and travelling up the Whoop-Up Trail north from Fort Benton, Montana, to settle in the Calgary area.

The couple's cabin at Fish Creek served as both hearth and counter. As well as living in the sod-roofed cabin, the Glenns ran a trading post from it, serving the Hudson's Bay Company, local Sarcee (Tsuu T'ina) Indians and, later, the North West Mounted Police. The couple eventually settled in two more areas in the Fish Creek Valley. They built a second home and several outbuildings near what is today the Bow Valley Ranch Visitor Centre. In 1879, the Glenns sold their homestead to the Dominion Government; the government used one solidly constructed building as a supply house in their efforts to teach Blackfoot people about European farming. Some years later, William Roper Hull bought

the land from the government and built his prairie mansion, the Bow Valley Ranche House, a short distance from the Glenns' home.

The Glenns' third home in Fish Creek Valley was located near Macleod Crossing. The couple thrived in the valley for many years, raising six children and successfully growing a variety of agricultural crops. The couple's role in Fish Creek

Around the bend—Fish Creek takes a turn at Glennfield.

history is encapsulated in an interpretive display in the Bow Valley Ranch Visitor Centre.

One of the buildings the Glenns constructed at their second homestead stood across from the Visitor Centre until 1998. By then, vandals and time had taken their toll on the house and what hadn't rotted was taken apart by the University of Calgary's Department of Archaeology Field School. The department is working with the park and The Ranche at Fish Creek Restoration Society to rebuild the cabin, and in the winter of 2006, Dale Walde, director of the University of Calgary's Archaeology Field School at Fish Creek, reported work had started on a cut-away version of the Glenn Building inside the Visitor Centre.

The exact site of the Glenns' original sod-roofed hut near the Bow River has yet to be discovered.

Glennfield to Bow Valley Ranch

East of Macleod Tr. S, the floor of Fish Creek Valley widens and the sweeping grasslands that define Shaw's Meadow continue in Glennfield. The spruce trees on the north-facing slopes begin to thin, but the riverine forest clearly marks the creek's meandering route east to the Bow River. The valley floor of Glennfield—the third home of the Glenn family in the Fish Creek Valley—is easily navigated on foot, but these wide open fields are particularly well suited to cycling.

So inclined—the uphill grind out of the Fish Creek valley at Glennfield.

Glennfield's most visible—and well used—feature is a sheltered picnic area, which includes ample parking and seasonal washrooms, and is surrounded by a spidery network of pathways and trails that travel in all directions.

Glennfield's grasslands are a mix of native and introduced species, the most common of the latter being awnless brome brought from Australia to Canada by William Roper Hull. Native grasses include blue grama, June grass, and wheat grass.

About three kilometres downstream of Glennfield is a great blue heron colony (see sidebar), a protected area closed to all visitors. The area can, however, be observed from a viewpoint on its southwestern edge.

A kilometre past the colony, the creek and main park pathway wind past the historic Bow Valley Ranch site and the Bow Valley Ranch Visitor Centre.

Annie's Bakery and Café

Adjacent to the Bow Valley Ranche House, Annie's Bakery and Café is a perennial favourite among park visitors and foodie critics. Open seasonally in what used to be the ranch foreman's house, this bustling, wholesome eatery serves some of the biggest muffins, sandwiches, and cinnamon buns you'll ever find. The ideal reward and nourishment after a day in the park. For hours and information, call 225-3920.

Bow Valley Ranche House

When built in 1896, the Bow Valley Ranche house was acclaimed as one of the finest country homes in the Northwest Territories. Today, more than a century later, it is home to one of the city's finest restaurants.

Designed by Calgary architect James Lewellyn Wilson for businessman William Roper Hull, the sandstone house originally cost $4,000. It was a princely sum, but Hull wanted to reflect his wealth and lavish hospitality on his guests. He didn't disappoint. His spirited parties attracted countless visitors from across southern Alberta; Calgary partygoers readily travelled for two hours by horse and buggy to reach the sprawling, well-appointed house.

In 1902, Hull sold the Bow Valley Ranche to Patrick Burns, who reportedly purchased the house for his new bride, Eileen Ellis. The ranch became a part of Burns' 450,000-acre agricultural empire, but a golden era of entertainment faded from the valley. Burns was a man of business, not pleasure. The home's social standing languished until Patrick Burns' death and the arrival of his hospitable nephew, Michael John Burns, who revived many of the traditions of Alberta's ranching culture. The Burns family owned the house and surrounding ranch until the provincial government purchased them for Fish Creek Provincial Park in 1973.

For the next 18 years, the house was used for little more than historical tours. In 1995, Larry and Mitzie Wasyliw formed The Ranche at Fish Creek Park Restoration Society to return the Gothic Revival house and its grounds to their former grandeur. Four years later—and after raising several hundred thousand dollars—the house was reopened as The Ranche Restaurant.

Forced march—climbing the escarpment at Glennfield.

The stately restaurant is operated by the Canadian Rocky Mountain Resorts family of companies. For reservations, call 225-3939, e-mail info@theranche.com or visit www.crmr.com/theranche.

Bow Valley Ranch Visitor Centre

Also the park's administrative hub, the wheelchair-accessible Bow Valley Visitor Centre features a theatre, fireplace, year-round indoor washroom, and water fountain. The centre's exhibit hall currently has a display on 15,000 years of life in the valley as well as a full-size tipi. Numerous educational programs for students in kindergarten to Grade six are offered at the centre. Maps, brochures, and park updates are readily available for all park users.

Plain and simple—an afternoon pedal across the wide
grasslands of Fish Creek's Glennfield area.

The centre is open Monday to Friday from 0815 to 1200 h and from 1300 to 1630 h. For current program descriptions and bookings and general park information, call 297-5293.

FISH CREEK EAST AND CHINOOK ROTARY NATURE PARK

FISH CREEK EAST AND CHINOOK ROTARY NATURE PARK AT A GLANCE

LOCATION	Bow River valley east shore, south of Marquis of Lorne Tr. SE
HOURS	Vary seasonally, usually 0800 to 2200 in summer, 0800 to 1800 in spring and fall, and 0800 to 1600 in winter
TERRAIN	Steep, west-facing escarpment overlooking flood plain with engineered ponds and wetlands
ACCESS	Off McKenzie Blvd. and Marquis of Lorne Tr. SE (follow signs to McKenzie Meadows Golf Course)
	Fish Creek pathway east shore, downstream of Burnsmead
	Numerous pathway, connections to and from McKenzie and Cranston
ACTIVITIES	Walking, hiking, cycling, bird and wildlife watching
FACILITIES	McKenzie Meadows Golf Course (open to public)
	Gazebos and benches
DOGS	On leash at all times
INFORMATION	Call 297-5293 or visit www.fish-creek.org

Rotary Chinook Nature Park

One of Fish Creek Provincial Park's newest additions, this 55-hectare area south of Marquis of Lorne Tr. SE along the east shore of the Bow River was jointly restored by the Province of Alberta and the Rotary Club—Chinook. Although not well known, once discovered Rotary Chinook Nature Park is not soon forgotten. Its most notable features are two depleted gravel pits that have been turned into engineered wetlands, creating a birdwatching area. The wetlands also capture stormwater runoff from nearby Deerfoot Tr. SE.

The nature park's west-facing escarpment is tangled with densely vegetated ravines, slumping gravel outcrops and determined prairie grasses. The top of the escarpment—which is best reached by a twisting, leg-burning paved pathway south of the ponds—offers exceptional views of the river valley and the not-so-distant foothills and Rocky Mountains. The pathway continues past the park boundary to join a regional route along the escarpment and the western edge of Cranston.

Lafarge Meadows

The area south of Marquis of Lorne Tr. SE (Highway 22X) on the west shore of the Bow River in Fish Creek Provincial Park is known as Lafarge Meadows. The meadows—59.5 hectares in all—are expected to remain closed to public use until at least the fall of 2007. During the closure, Lafarge Meadows—once a series of highly productive gravel pits owned by Lafarge Canada Inc. and mined for more than 30 years—will undergo extensive reclamation and be turned into a chain of wetlands. Other plans for the area include pathways, archaeological studies, educational facilities and programs, and wildlife viewing areas.

Fish Creek Provincial Park now extends past Highway 22X and will continue to grow southward.

Norm Harburn of the Parks Foundation, Calgary, at
Rotary Chinook Nature Park along the Bow River.

It will take more than 40 years for the wetlands to fully mature following the completion of the project. By 2054, the wetlands will treat an estimated two million cubic metres of stormwater a year from surrounding roads and communities. Long before that, however, the area will become a vital extension of the park's wildlife corridor, pathway network, and "living classroom" space.

As well as being the project's former landowner, Lafarge Canada Inc. is the project's largest corporate sponsor and is working with the Province of Alberta and numerous other community groups and businesses to transform the area into a prized natural habitat.

McKenzie Meadows Golf Course

Although oddly out of character with much of Fish Creek Provincial Park, the McKenzie Meadows Golf Course was added to the park in 1999. It's been a popular destination ever since. The 18-hole championship course below the community of McKenzie (off McKenzie Blvd. and Marquis of Lorne Tr. SE) was designed by Gary Browning and bills itself as Calgary's finest public golf facility. The course is open May through October; the pro shop is open daily from March to October, and Monday to Friday (0900 to 1700 h) from November to February. For tee times, call 257-2255.

ELBOW RIVER PATHWAY

ELBOW RIVER DOWNSTREAM OF GLENMORE DAM

Calgary's second major pathway system—the Elbow River Pathway—runs
along the Elbow River through Griffith Woods and from the Weaselhead Natural
Environment Park to the Bow River. By nature a quiet waterway, but prone to
powerful surges in spring runoff, the Elbow River is Calgary's "residential" river,
with hundreds of homes backing onto its shores. And, of course, this stretch
includes a number of major city parks, including Sandy Beach, River Park,
Stanley Park, Woods Park, and Lindsay Park.

The Elbow River Pathway's narrow and sometimes steep banks are lined
with dense riverine forests. Unlike the Bow River, there is virtually no industry
along the Elbow, unless you count Stampede Park, home of the annual Calgary
Stampede ("The Greatest Outdoor Show on Earth"), and the Pengrowth
Saddledome. Instead, a good stretch of the Elbow River Valley is the setting
for some of Calgary's grandest homes, in communities such as Rideau Park,
Riverdale Park, Britannia, Elbow Park, and Mission. House-watching can
definitely be considered an activity along the pathway.

Parks along the Elbow River are a little more compact and a little less "wild"
than those along the Bow River. These are parks that can be easily explored and
easily reached by car, bicycle, or foot.

Typically reduced to little more than a trickle during the summer months,
the Elbow River's lazy currents and winding channels are perfect for floating
in rubber rafts and inner tubes. And its many flat banks attract hundreds of hot
weather waders and sun worshippers.

Besides drawing people to its shores, the Elbow River attracts many
animals. Beavers, especially, thrive to the point of peskiness; sometimes the
large rodents are trapped and moved by the provincial government. Waterfowl
find an abundance of food along the river's lush shores.

Humans can also find an abundance of food near the shores of the Elbow
River, particularly in the Mission area (on 4 St. SW between 17 Ave. and 25
Ave. SW). The strip's diverse business district features a wide range of popular
eateries and coffee shops within easy walking/cycling distance of the pathway.
Among them: The Wildwood, Earl's Tin Palace, Second Cup, Starbucks, Planet
Coffee, Aida's, Original Joe's, The Mercado, and the James Joyce Pub.

Elbow River—Innocent to Torrent
The source of the Elbow River is Elbow Lake in the Elbow–Sheep Wildland

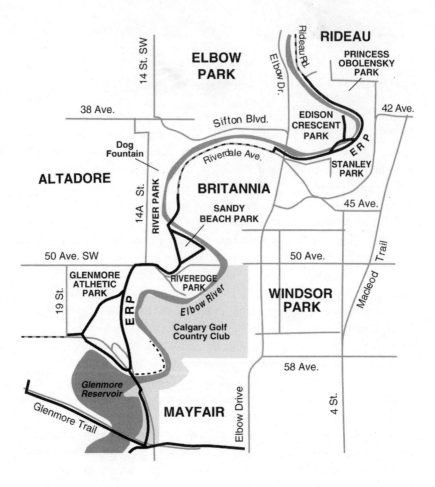

Area of Kananaskis Country. Considerably smaller than the Bow River, the frigid Elbow River tumbles through limestone canyons in the front ranges and foothills of the eastern slopes of the Rocky Mountains, then makes a dramatic plunge at Elbow Falls, upstream of Bragg Creek, and cuts a swath through the farming and ranching country west of Calgary. Travelling east, the river flows across the Tsuu T'ina Nation Indian Reserve and then into the Glenmore Reservoir in Calgary.

Natural Resources Canada says "because of a lack of glaciers in the Elbow River valley, recharge of the river relies on annual winter snowfall. Soils in the watershed of the Elbow River near its headwaters lack the absorbing power of many old-growth soils, so the Elbow River is particularly susceptible to flash flooding during intense thunderstorms."

The river's most recent flood was in 2005, when it spilled over its banks both upstream and downstream of the Glenmore Reservoir, creating whole new channels, wiping out trees and shoreline, and indiscriminately filling nearby basements with water, sludge, and muck.

Over the course of centuries, the seemingly innocuous Elbow River has exhibited considerable determination and might by carving steep cliffs along its shores. Etched out of sediment left from glaciers, these cliffs have powdery fine soil, perfect for nesting, and subject to constant erosion.

CLEARWATER NATURAL ENVIRONMENT PARK

Although outside city limits, Clearwater Park is a City of Calgary owned natural area on the Elbow River, located 7.2 kilometres west of Sarcee Tr./Glenmore Tr. SW on Highway 8. Located in exceptional natural surroundings, the park features a rare white spruce ecosystem, four large tipis (complete with wooden floors and wood-burning heating stoves), washrooms, a cook room, firepits, and a festival tent with picnic tables.

Not currently open for general public use, Clearwater is expected to become a major Calgary park and a link to Griffith Woods, creating a memorable and unique western park along the banks of the Elbow River. For now, the park can be booked for the day or overnight by schools, church groups, Cubs, Scouts, Girl Guides, and other non-profit or charitable organizations.

Clearwater is open from Easter through mid-September annually, and the city promotes it as an ideal destination for overnight "backyard" camping close to home, as well as for team building activities, nature appreciation, orienteering, and outdoor games.

GRIFFITH WOODS

GRIFFITH WOODS AT A GLANCE

LOCATION	Discovery Ridge Blvd. and Discovery Ridge Link SW
HOURS	0500 to 2300 daily
TERRAIN	Heavily forested natural area with extensive wetlands, oxbow channels, and lakes on Elbow River flood plain
ACCESS	Discovery Ridge Blvd. and Discovery Ridge Link SW
	West end of Discovery Ridge SW
ACTIVITIES	Walking, hiking, cycling, bird and wildlife watching, guided nature walks, dog walking, cross-country skiing, picnicking
FACILITIES	Washrooms and water fountains

Picnic tables and benches
DOGS   On leash at all times
INFORMATION City of Calgary 3-1-1
TRANSIT   #438, #439

With its mirror-like oxbow wetlands and cool inviting forests, Griffith Woods is a strikingly beautiful environmental area in southwest Calgary. Located in Discovery Ridge along the Elbow River across from the Tsuu T'ina Nation Indian Reserve, the park sits on some 90 acres of lands donated to Calgarians by Wilbur Griffith's Power Farms.

Griffith, a wealthy rancher and oilman originally from Texas, also owned the nearby Pinebrook Golf Course for several years. He was in his late nineties when he officially made the three million dollar donation to the Parks Foundation, Calgary, in 2000. His decision didn't sit well with surviving family members, but as nearby communities grew—and new ones such as Richmond Hill, Discovery Ridge, and East Springbank emerged—Griffith's conviction to protect and preserve the land was unflappable. His decision resulted in the largest single donation of private land in Calgary's history. Griffith died at the age of 101, just months after touring the park's new pathways in a golf cart.

An environmental plan in 1997 revealed that the area contained 31 plant species rare to Calgary, including the northern green bog orchid and the lady slipper orchid, a species rare in the greater Calgary area, but common at Griffith

Getting a bearing—checking the pathway map at Griffith Woods.

Griffith Woods is known for its mirror-like oxbow wetlands and cool inviting forests.

Woods. The area is also home to young balsam poplars. Mature balsam poplars are abundant in Calgary's river valleys, but natural new growth is rare.

Equally rich in wildlife, the park is home to dozens of mammal species and about 70 species of birds (see sidebar "Wildlife in Griffith Woods").

Although used at various times for agriculture, gravel mining, and utilities (a large power line right-of-way cuts a wide swath through a good section of the area), Griffith Woods is largely undisturbed. It is, however, constantly changing as the unruly Elbow River is subject to flooding and regularly shifts channels and courses. This was especially the case in 2005, when the river overflowed its banks during a major and powerful flood.

As resilient as it is delicate, Griffith Woods has a number of environmental reserves, closed to general use to nurture flora and fauna. Park users must stay on designated pathways and trails and keep out of protected areas—and they have, for the most part, since the park opened in 2002.

What lies beneath—below the water's surface, aquatic life thrives in Griffith Woods.

Pathway Description—Griffith Woods

A series of winding, looping pathways and trails travels through Griffith Woods' distinct vegetation communities (including aspen forest, white spruce forest, upland low shrub, native grassland, and wetland). These pathways and trails are generally flat and oriented east–west between the river and the houses that rim the southern edge of Discovery Ridge. Among the network is a kilometre-long gravel trail named for the late John Simonot, a former chair of the Calgary River Valleys Committee. The trail runs through a number of natural features, explained with interpretive signs.

Quiet and pristine, Griffith Woods is a treat to discover and a joy to revisit.

Wildlife in Griffith Woods

The Griffith Woods Natural Area Management Plan notes the following wildlife can be expected or seen in the park:

- Coyote
- Red fox
- Moose
- Muskrat
- Swainson's hawk
- American kestrel
- Rufous hummingbird
- Black-backed woodpecker
- Red-eyed vireo
- Boreal chorus frog
- Tiger salamander
- Wandering garter snake

For a full listing, see the Griffith Woods Natural Area Management Plan (page 22) on the City of Calgary website (www.calgary.ca).

GLENMORE PARKS AND RESERVOIR

Glenmore, Gaelic for "big valley," is one of Calgary's favourite recreational areas. This sweeping expanse of land in the city's southwest has six parks (North Glenmore Park, Weaselhead Flats Natural Area, South Glenmore Park, East Glenmore Park, Heritage Park, and Glenmore Athletic Park) woven together with a slender thread, 16 kilometres of the Elbow River Pathway.

The parks and the Elbow River Pathway wrap around Calgary's largest body of water, the 429-hectare Glenmore Reservoir. Fed by the Elbow River and constructed in the 1930s, the reservoir supplies half the city's drinking water. The reservoir's shores—600 hectares of City of Calgary parks—provide a startling variety of terrain, views, and activities.

The fiercely stewarded Weaselhead Flats Natural Area's wetlands are a tangle of foot trails, natural areas, and wildlife. At Heritage Park, life as it was a century ago is displayed at Canada's largest historical village. South Glenmore Park is home to the Variety Park Spray Deck, a wet and wild playground for children of all ages and abilities. South Glenmore Park also harbours the Glenmore Sailing School. And the Glenmore Athletic Park is the field of play for dozens of organized sports teams and events.

Although Glenmore has no sandy beaches and swimming is strictly forbidden in the reservoir, water is this area's single biggest attraction. Water-based activities are abundant, especially sailing, rowing, and canoeing. And many people find solace and comfort in simply watching Glenmore's waters and the teeming life attracted to them. Bald eagles, beavers, tundra swans, American white pelicans, common goldeneyes, and black-capped chickadees are just a few of the species sighted in the valley.

WEASELHEAD FLATS NATURAL AREA

WEASELHEAD FLATS NATURAL AREA AT A GLANCE

LOCATION	Southwest of 66 Ave. and 37 St. SW
HOURS	0500 to 2300 daily
TERRAIN	Heavily forested natural area in river valley with wetlands, oxbow lakes and flood plains
ACCESS	66 Ave. and 37 St. SW
	90 Ave. and 37 St. SW
	Elbow River Pathway
ACTIVITIES	Walking, hiking, cycling, bird and wildlife watching, guided nature walks, dog walking, cross-country skiing, picnicking
FACILITIES	Seasonal washrooms and water fountains
	Picnic tables
DOGS	On leash
	Not allowed in reservoir and many areas adjacent to the reservoir
INFORMATION	For guided nature walks call 221-4532; for park or picnic site bookings, call 268-3830
TRANSIT	#18, #47, #63, #733
ADDITIONAL	No wading or swimming in reservoir
	No skating or walking on ice
	Do not pick or transplant any plants
	Stay on designated trails

Weaselhead Flats was named after a Sarcee chief who made his camp in the heavily wooded area along the Elbow River near the present day Glenmore Park

Fully composed—nature is always perfectly arranged at Weaselhead Flats.

and Tsuu T'ina (Sarcee) Indian Reserve. Weaselhead lived in the area for about 50 years beginning in the late 1800s.

In the 1900s, the area was used by the military as a training ground, and soldiers dug many a foxhole and trench southwest of the bridge in Weaselhead to prepare for action overseas. Some of the area's paths were first carved out by huge military tanks.

Remarkably, much of Weaselhead is rugged, little-touched wetlands, and forests bounding the Elbow River. A virtual rainbow of flora and fauna thrive in this cool, moist valley. The Calgary Field Naturalists Society has identified more than 450 species of plants in Weaselhead Flats; the Weaselhead Society lists more than 150 species of birds on its comprehensive website (www.weaselhead.org). Both groups ardently promote the protection and preservation of Weaselhead Flats.

Pathway Description

On the north bank of the reservoir, west of 37 St. SW, the Elbow River Pathway drops into the Elbow River Valley and Weaselhead Flats, the headwaters of the Glenmore Reservoir. As the pathway reaches the valley floor, it makes a sharp turn south, travelling across the flats for about 300 metres before reaching the reservoir's delta.

Less than 20 years ago, the pedestrian bridge across the river was a giant overhead sign; today it's a well engineered structure. Foot trails radiate from either side of the bridge. Those who choose these less-travelled routes are reminded to tread lightly as the area and its inhabitants are easily disturbed.

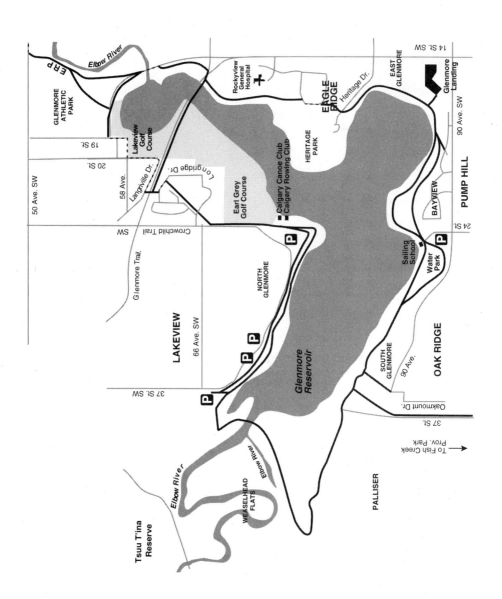

Crossing Weaselhead—the pedestrian bridge at the west end of the Glenmore Reservoir.

Past the pedestrian bridge, the Elbow River Pathway runs southwest in a relatively long, straight line. The wide-cut pathway is surrounded by spruce, aspen, and several types of shrubs. On closer inspection, plants such as elephant head, silverweed, creeping juniper, and cut-leaved anemones can be spotted. Also look for porcupines, red squirrels, and, closer to the wetlands, muskrats.

Across the valley floor, the pathway turns east around a number of scenic bogs and ponds, crosses Beaver Pond Bridge, and climbs steeply out of the flats. At the top of the plateau are a handful of secluded viewpoints, perfect for picnics or pausing while your calf muscles recover after the climb.

Heading east, the pathway winds in and out of aspen woods above the reservoir's steep-walled shores. One of the major foot/ski trails carved through the forest is the Jackrabbit Trail, named after pioneering cross-country skier Jackrabbit Johannsen, who lived to be 111. This intimate and sheltered route offers many opportunities to spot wildlife. This wide trail runs from Beaver Pond Bridge east to the Sailing School for about 4.8 kilometres.

At the top of the escarpment, the Elbow River Pathway runs flatly across open fields to South Glenmore Park.

SOUTH GLENMORE PARK

SOUTH GLENMORE PARK AT A GLANCE

LOCATION	South shore of Glenmore Reservoir, along 90 Ave. between 24 and 37 St. SW
HOURS	0500 to 2300 daily
TERRAIN	Open, grassy plateau above steep forested banks of the reservoir
ACCESS	90 Ave. and 18 St. SW (Bayview escarpment)
	90 Ave. and 24 St. SW
	West end of 90 Ave. SW
	Elbow River Pathway
ACTIVITIES	Walking, hiking, cycling, bird and wildlife watching, guided nature walks, dog walking, cross-country skiing, picnicking, sailing, tennis, spray playground
FACILITIES	Seasonal washrooms and water fountains

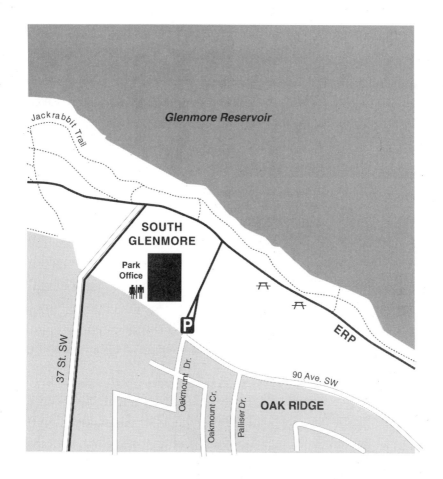

	Picnic tables and shelters
	Tennis courts
	Calgary Sailing School
	Variety Park Spray Deck
DOGS	On leash
	Not allowed in reservoir and several areas adjacent to the reservoir
INFORMATION	For guided nature walks call 221-4532; for park or picnic site bookings, call 268-3830
TRANSIT	#79, #80, #775, #780
ADDITIONAL	No wading or swimming in reservoir
	No skating or walking on reservoir ice
	Do not pick or transplant any plants
	Stay on designated trails

South Glenmore Park Pathway Description

Southeast of Weaselhead Flats, the Elbow River Pathway continues along a plateau above the reservoir into South Glenmore Park. An open grassy field gradually widens on the south side of the pathway.

The pathway passes a park maintenance building (which has public indoor washrooms) near 90 Ave. and 37 St. SW. East of this point, the pathway is cleared in the winter to the Glenmore Dam and right through to the Bow River.

From 37 St. to the Sailing School, the pathway is twinned and typically open and flat, winding slightly at times to add variety. The parking lot at 24 St. SW is one of the Glenmore area's major hubs and includes the Sailing School, the Variety Park Spray Deck (open to all, but built especially to accommodate disabled users), seasonal washrooms, and a viewpoint complete with interpretive signage about the reservoir. Past the Sailing School, the pathway hugs a terrace along the water's edge. After making a sharp turn to the east (right) the pathway enters East Glenmore Park.

Glenmore Sailing School

Every summer, the Glenmore Sailing School (8415 – 24 St. SW) offers nautical adventure and instruction for every level and every age of sailor. Surprisingly,

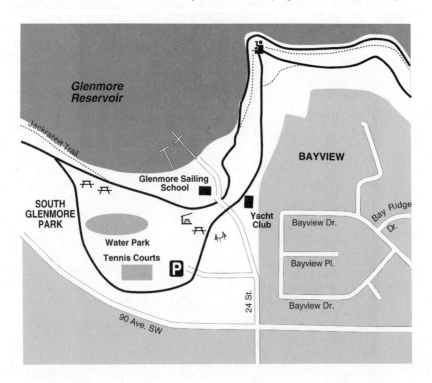

Icy shores—the Glenmore Sailing school in winter.

some of the nation's top sailors have been graduates from the Glenmore Sailing
School and even Olympic sailors have trained at the reservoir. Powerful winds
blast across the reservoir, challenging sailors of all abilities.

Would-be sailors can enrol in courses ranging from basic seamanship to advanced
boat handling in heavy winds. Courses run from May to August, and all are sanctioned
by the Alberta Sailing Association and the Canadian Yachting Association. Programs
are offered for sailors nine to 90 years old and a variety are offered for disabled,
special needs, and financially disadvantaged students. For further information, call
City of Calgary Recreation at 268-3800.

Rules of the Reservoir
The Glenmore Reservoir is patrolled by City of Calgary Recreation staff, which
strictly enforces the following rules:
- The public may only use non-motorized boats on the reservoir; inflatable
  craft are not allowed.
- Boaters must wear life jackets or PFDs (personal floatation devices) at all
  times.
- Alcohol consumption is not allowed.
- Pets are not allowed in the water or in boats.
- Swimming is not allowed in the reservoir.

For further rules and information, call Calgary Fire Department River Patrol at
287-4257 (on weekends call 264-1022).

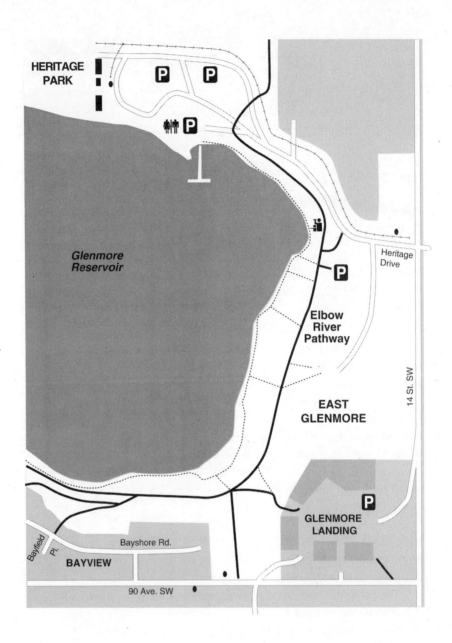

HERITAGE
PARK

Glenmore
Reservoir

Heritage
Drive

Elbow
River
Pathway

EAST
GLENMORE

14 St. SW

GLENMORE
LANDING

Bayfield
Pl.

BAYVIEW

Bayshore Rd.

90 Ave. SW

EAST GLENMORE PARK

EAST GLENMORE PARK AT A GLANCE

LOCATION	East shore of Glenmore Reservoir from 18 St. and 90 Ave. SW to Glenmore Tr. SW
HOURS	0600 to 2300 daily
TERRAIN	Open, grassy plateau above steep forested banks of the reservoir
ACCESS	90 Ave. and 18 St. SW (behind Glenmore Landing)
	Heritage Park (west end of Heritage Dr. SW)
	Rockyview General Hospital (west end of 75 Ave. SW)
	Elbow River Pathway
ACTIVITIES	Walking, hiking, cycling, bird and wildlife watching, dog walking, picnicking
FACILITIES	Seasonal washrooms
	Seasonal water fountains
DOGS	On leash
	Not allowed in reservoir
INFORMATION	268-3830
TRANSIT	#20
ADDITIONAL	No wading or swimming in reservoir
	No skating or walking on reservoir ice
	Do not pick or transplant any plants
	Stay on designated trails

Pathway Description—East Glenmore Park

East of the Sailing School in South Glenmore Park, the Elbow River Pathway is twinned. It makes a 90 degree turn and enters East Glenmore Park via a narrow ledge above the reservoir. As the surrounding cliffs soften into rolling hills, the berm that the pathway is constructed on widens.

Following the shoreline closely, the pathway gently winds around the bay. As it begins to swing north, the pathway begins to distance itself from the rocky shore; at this point, a connector pathway links to the community of Bayview.

Further east, another pathway links to the Glenmore Landing shopping centre. East Glenmore Park is open and often windswept; the reservoir is easily frothed by western gusts. Pathway users can expect blustery conditions on shore. After a long straight stretch, the pathway jogs and reaches the west end of Heritage Dr. SW, the entrance to Heritage Park.

From here, the pathway crosses the park's main parking lot. The route is somewhat difficult to follow; use the railway tracks as markers to find your way into Eagle Ridge. The on road route through Eagle Ridge becomes a dedicated pathway just south of the Rockyview General Hospital. As the pathway winds behind the hospital, expect to share it with hospital patients, visitors, staff, and physicians. For the next several hundred metres the pathway runs north, offering excellent views to the west. Past the hospital, the pathway narrows and twists in its descent to Glenmore Tr. SW, where it links to Glenmore Dam and North Glenmore Park.

Two new routes across Glenmore Tr. SW are being constructed in 2006/2007 as part of major roadway upgrades.

Glenmore Landing

The nautically themed Glenmore Landing at 90 Ave. and 14 St. SW features a wide variety of shops and services, including:

- The Good Earth—excellent coffee, tea, and generous portions of homestyle baked goods
- McDonald's—burgers, fries, and soft drinks
- Pizza Bank—takeout pizza in a hurry
- Patisserie du Soleil—sweet treats after a long walk or ride
- Gord's Running Room—athletic shoes, clothes, and advice
- Starbucks—the Seattle coffee chain that's caffeinating the world
- Jugo Juice—fruit, berries, and other good stuff blended to perfection

HERITAGE PARK

Since opening in 1964, Heritage Park (1900 Heritage Dr. SW) has been a stroll back in time. Dozens of authentic and replica buildings from the turn of the 20th century overlook the eastern shores of Glenmore Reservoir. The park's 150 exhibits include Peter Prince's sandstone home, the Wainwright Hotel, the Vulcan Ice Cream Parlour and the Antique Midway, North America's only antique midway.

The park also keeps alive the practices pioneers used in their daily lives. Visitors can see how women made bread, how farmers used grain threshing machines, or how a blacksmith pounded out his trade. And they can often join in the activities.

Heritage Park is open daily from Victoria Day weekend to Labour Day weekend, weekends from Labour Day weekend to Thanksgiving weekend and weekends in December. The Wainwright Hotel is open most Sundays throughout the year for brunch. For more information, call 268-8500 or visit www.heritagepark.ca.

Sam Livingston

The Peace Indians, far north of Calgary, called him Atomo-A-To (First Who Came), but he was baptized Samuel Henry Harkwood Livingston. When he died in 1897, he was one of the Northwest Territories' most memorable figures.

Sam Livingston was among the very first white settlers in Alberta. Before making the prairies home, the tall, handsome, golden-haired pioneer was an adventurous explorer, trapper, trader, and prospector. Born in Ireland to an Anglican rector, Livingston—or Livingstone, as he sometimes wrote his name—came to North America around 1848. He landed in Wisconsin but soon made his way west to the California Gold Rush of '49. There's some dispute as to whether he crossed over land or sailed around Cape Horn, but it's generally agreed he struck gold. Just how much is a mystery.

Sam Livingston
GLENBOW MUSEUM ARCHIVES

A victim of wanderlust and gold fever, Livingston made his way north, into Alberta's Peace River country, and is credited with being the first white man to see the Peace at its source. He explored the Jasper–Edmonton area, then headed south searching for gold along the Bow River.

He swore off gold prospecting after marrying and became a trader and buffalo hunter. Later, in the early 1870s, he became a farmer.

Livingston had planned to grow crops on the land at the confluence of the Bow and Elbow rivers, but that was the same place the North West Mounted Police wanted to build their fort. After reaching an amiable and mutual agreement with the Mounties, Livingston moved to what is now Heritage Park. Some of his land was the site of the Chinook Race Track and Polo grounds; in the 1930s, part of his land was flooded when the Glenmore Reservoir was built.

People often said that "the latch string was always out" at the Livingston Ranch. He welcomed many guests and friends to his home: Father Albert Lacombe, Reverend George McDougall, John Glenn, John Votier, and the Governor General, the Marquis of Lorne.

Livingston influenced friends and local politicians and was a progressive leader in new agricultural techniques, although he wasn't always the best of farmers. Today his memory lives on. A mountain range, a provincial fish hatchery, and a Calgary office tower bear his name.

A Brief History of a Historical Park

Heritage Park was first proposed in 1961 by lawyer and oil magnate Eric Harvie, and Eleanor Ingram. Both were members of the Woods Foundation when they met with the City of Calgary to discuss the historical village. Theme

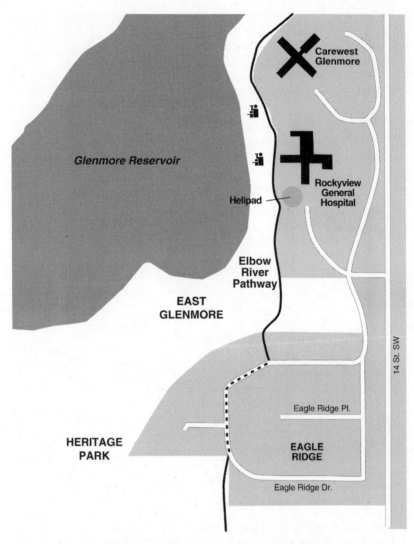

Glenmore Reservoir

Carewest
Glenmore

Rockyview
General
Hospital

Helipad

Elbow
River
Pathway

EAST
GLENMORE

14 St. SW

Eagle Ridge Pl.

HERITAGE
PARK

EAGLE
RIDGE

Eagle Ridge Dr.

parks were an established trend at the time and Calgary's Heritage Park was to have a distinct local personality recreating and preserving prairie life in and around the turn of the 20th century.

By 1963, park construction was underway, with funding for the giant-sized project coming equally from the City and the Woods Foundation. Most artifacts came from the Glenbow Museum, which Harvie founded.

As the make-believe town came to life, it reflected the flavour of several Alberta villages before it. Over the years, more and more buildings were added, many saved from a wrecker's ball. Now, some 40 years later, Heritage Park is one of Canada's largest historical sites.

Cool running—the Glenmore Reservoir's cleared paths accommodate joggers year-round.

GLENMORE ATHLETIC PARK

LOCATION	South of 50 Ave., between 16 and 19 St. SW
HOURS	Vary by facility and season
TERRAIN	Flat athletic fields
ACCESS	Lenton Ave. and 19 St. SW
	56 Ave. and 19 St. SW
	Elbow River Pathway
ACTIVITIES	Walking, cycling, track cycling, baseball, tennis, soccer, football, flag football, track and field, hockey, swimming, golf, safety education
FACILITIES	Big League baseball diamond—fenced
	Two softball diamonds—fenced
	Four soccer fields
	Two soccer/football fields—lit
	Six outdoor tennis courts
	Glenmore Track—A class
	Glenmore Velodrome
	Glenmore Pool
	Lakeview Municipal Golf Course

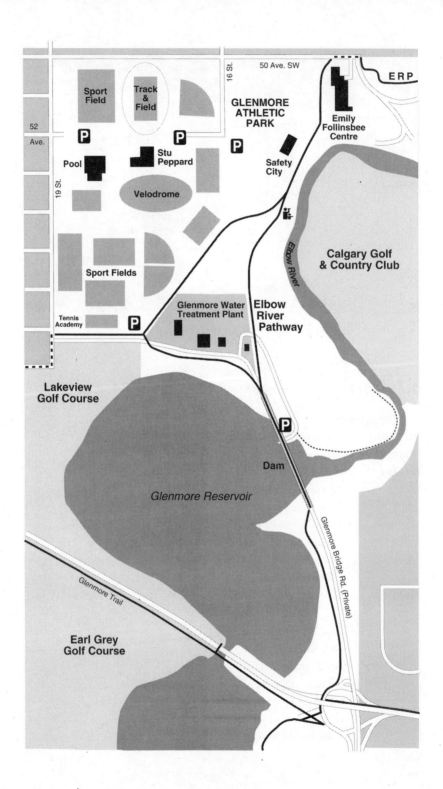

Stu Peppard Arena

Safety City

Seasonal washrooms and water fountains

Seasonal/event concession

DOGS　　　Not permitted on playing fields and athletic parks

INFORMATION　To book recreational facilities, call the City of Calgary's Event Service Production Coordinator at 268-4776.

TRANSIT　　#5, #13, #22

Pathway Description—North of Glenmore Resevoir

North of Glenmore Tr., the pathway descends to a service road across the Glenmore Dam causeway. A large pipe elevated across the dam road blocks any northeast views of downtown Calgary; views to the southwest are sweeping and worth stopping for.

Across the dam, the pathway forks: the north arm runs past the east side of Glenmore Athletic Park to link with River Park and Sandy Beach. The west arm climbs sharply in front of the Water Treatment Plant and joins an on road cycling route at 19 St. and 57 Ave. SW.

The Glenmore Velodrome

Cyclists eager to exceed pathway speed limits will find a little slice of nirvana at the Glenmore Velodrome, a permanent 400-metre concrete bicycle track at Glenmore Athletic Park (5300 – 19 St. SW).

Flag football is one of more than a dozen sports played at Glenmore Athletic Park.

"If you feel the need, the need for speed, track racing is for you! Velodrome racing is among the most exciting bicycle racing around, for both riders and spectators. Riders speed in excess of 30 mph (48 km/h) in points races," says the Calgary Bicycle Track League.

The track is owned by the City of Calgary; the Calgary Bicycle Track League runs races Thursday evenings (weather permitting) during the spring and summer. For information, visit www.acs.ucalgary.ca.

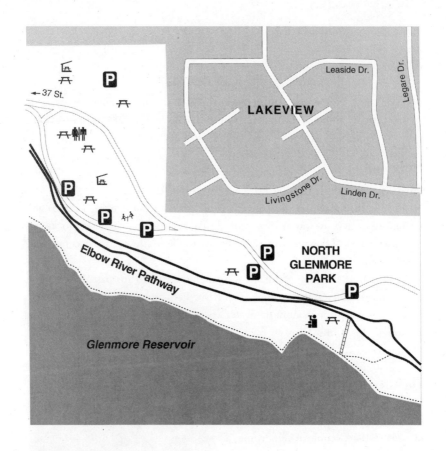

NORTH GLENMORE PARK

NORTH GLENMORE PARK AT A GLANCE

LOCATION	7305 – 24 St. SW (south end of Crowchild Tr. SW); north shore of Glenmore Reservoir between 37 St. and Crowchild Tr. SW
HOURS	0500 to 2300 daily
TERRAIN	Generally flat plateau dotted with trees and shrubs overlooking steep banks of Glenmore Reservoir
ACCESS	South end of Crowchild Tr. SW
	37 St. SW south of 66 Ave. SW
	Elbow River Pathway
ACTIVITIES	Walking, cycling, tennis, canoeing, rowing, kayaking, picnicking, cross-country skiing
FACILITIES	Playgrounds
	Seasonal washrooms and water fountains
	Calgary Canoe Club

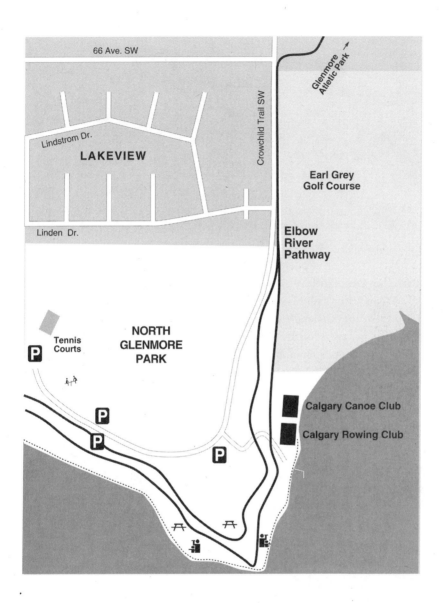

66 Ave. SW

Crowchild Trail SW

Glenmore Atletic Park

Lindstrom Dr.

LAKEVIEW

Earl Grey
Golf Course

Linden Dr.

Elbow
River
Pathway

Tennis
Courts

P

NORTH
GLENMORE
PARK

P

P

P

Calgary Canoe Club

Calgary Rowing Club

Calgary Rowing Club
BBQ pits (firewood provided when booked)
Tennis courts

DOGS   On leash
Not permitted in reservoir and some areas adjacent to the reservoir

INFORMATION   City of Calgary Event Service Production, 268-4776

TRANSIT   #18, #47, #63, #733

Now showing—North Glenmore is renowned for its dramatic views.

Pathway Description—North Glenmore Park

The Elbow River Pathway runs south along the east side of Crowchild Tr. past 66 Ave. SW into Glenmore Park. Near the Calgary Canoe Club and the Calgary Rowing Club (which share a clubhouse) and their adjacent parking lots, the pathway twins. As is often the case on Calgary's pathway system, the leg closest to the water's edge is designated for pedestrians and the leg furthest from shore is for cyclists and in-line skaters.

Scenic respite—the author takes a break at North Glenmore Park.

SHARMA CHRISTIE

Shortly after twinning, the pathway veers west past one of the best lookout sites on the reservoir, with views of Heritage Park, Bayview, and the Glenmore Sailing School, as well as the foothills and mountains to the west and the downtown core to the north. The pathways continue west across the flat, open plateau, where wind is almost a given. A string of breezy viewpoints and rest stops punctuates the escarpment.

Below the sharp escarpment, look for foot trails skirting the rocky shores of the reservoir. One is linked to the main pathway by a staircase, which also leads to a large barbecue pit/seating area/lookout point halfway down the escarpment.

The park road north of the pathways links the area's parking lots, picnic tables, tennis courts, playgrounds, and washrooms.

The North Glenmore Park section of the Elbow River Pathway ends at 37 St. SW, the east end of the Weaselhead Natural Area.

The Calgary Rowing Club

The Calgary Rowing Club, founded in 1966, offers learn-to-row programs, youth rowing camps, recreational and competitive programs, and rowing tours from its club headquarters on the northwest shores of the Glenmore Reservoir (6449 Crowchild Tr. SW).

For more information, call the Calgary Rowing Club at 249-2880, or visit www.calgaryrowing.com.

The Calgary Canoe Club

The endearing qualities of canoeing, one of Western Canada's oldest modes of transportation, are enthusiastically promoted and practised at the Calgary Canoe Club.

Since 1959, the club has offered touring and racing lessons, training facilities, equipment, and sightseeing tours for any level of paddler. The club also has kayaking and outrigger courses and training programs as well as Olympic sprint racing, whitewater racing, flat water paddling, junior development programs, stroke improvement, and river canoeing courses.

Located at the south end of Crowchild Tr. SW in North Glenmore Park, the Canoe Club offers memberships and equipment rentals. For information, contact the Calgary Canoe Club at 246-5757, or visit calgarycanoeclub.com.

RIVER PARK

RIVER PARK AT A GLANCE

LOCATION	4500 – 14A St. SW
HOURS	0500 to 2300 daily
TERRAIN	Gently sloping plateau overlooking river valley; thickly treed ravine at north end of park
ACCESS	50 Ave. and 14A St. SW
	Elbow River Pathway
ACTIVITIES	Walking, dog walking, cross-country skiing, picnicking
FACILITIES	Portable toilet
	Dog water fountain
	Cat Margetts Memorial Park
	Picnic tables
	Park benches
DOGS	Off leash
INFORMATION	City of Calgary 268-3800
TRANSIT	#13

Drink up—about half of all Calgarians get their
drinking water from the Glenmore Reservoir.

Oilman and businessman Eric Harvie—one of the most generous parks
supporters the city has ever seen—gave Calgarians a prime tract of the land he
owned overlooking the Elbow River (on the valley's west side between 38 Ave.
and 50 Ave. SW). To make sure a park was developed, Harvie also kicked in
$100,000, much of which went to flattening several steep ravines in the area.

Today, River Park is a popular dog walking area. It sits on a plateau above
the river and is criss-crossed with a series of well beaten foot trails. The park has
few facilities (an occasional picnic table at the north end, a small parking lot at

Urban canine—River Park is
one of Calgary's major
inner city off leash parks.

50 Ave. SW, and a smattering of benches), but it does
have exceptional views of downtown Calgary. And,
like other dog walking parks in Calgary, it is a very
social place—dogs are instant icebreakers.

Dogs are often the first feature you'll notice
about River Park, but another is River Park's rich
variety of trees and shrubs. Siberian larch, paper
birch, Sutherland caragana, and burr oak can easily
be spotted throughout the park's open areas. So can
Colorado spruce, laurel-leaved willow and American
elm. Originally, the north end of the park was an
arboretum featuring trees from the former Soviet
Union.

The park's south end is a grassy field; the north
end is lush with trees and dotted with picnic tables.
Also at the north end, several footbridges cross a tiny
brook, which is little more than a trickle, but provides
enough moisture to create a microclimate and denser

vegetation. As the brook trickles closer to the Elbow River, it cuts a pronounced ravine into the northeast corner of the park—and as ravines tend to be, this one is thick with natural and imported plant life, and populated by a number of species of birds.

Cat's Dog Park

The Cathryn (Cat) Margetts Memorial Park is named for Cat Margetts, a professional pet nanny who died in 2004 trying to rescue animals from her burning home. Her dogs Adamie and Max T Moose were found at her side.

The park-within-a-park features the city's only water fountain that serves dogs and people; it was built at one of Margetts' favourite dog walking areas, River Park, with donations from family and friends to the Parks Foundation, Calgary. The Memorial Park also includes new trees, flowers, and benches near the ravine midway through the park. The Cathrun Margetts Memorial Park opened on June 20, 2005, the day that would have been her 28th birthday.

For more information about the Cathryn (Cat) Margetts Memorial Park, visit www.catsdogpark.com.

Cat Margetts Memorial Park in River Park is home to Calgary's first dog fountain.
JERRILYN MARGETTS

SANDY BEACH

SANDY BEACH AT A GLANCE

LOCATION	4500 14A St. SW
HOURS	0500 to 2300 daily
TERRAIN	Narrow river valley with heavily forested riverbanks; steep escarpment levels into open, rolling field
ACCESS	50 Ave. SW east of 14A St. SW
	West end of Riverdale Ave. SW
	Elbow River Pathway
ACTIVITIES	Walking, picnicking, tobogganing, canoeing, rafting
FACILITIES	Seasonal washrooms
	Seasonal water fountains
	BBQ pits and picnic shelters
	Playground
DOGS	Rules vary throughout; on leash along pathways
	No dogs permitted within 20 metres of playgrounds
INFORMATION	City of Calgary 3-1-1
TRANSIT	#13

Tucked into a quiet section of the Elbow River Valley, just downstream of the Glenmore Dam, Sandy Beach is a summer escape and a winter retreat. The park's name is somewhat exaggerated: Sandy Beach has little sand or beach,

White on white—Sandy Beach under a blanket of snow.

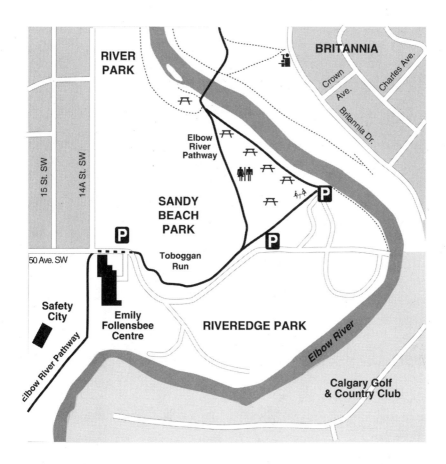

although it does have a flat, grassed area edged with a gravel shore where sunshine and water can be absorbed. A nearby "swinging" wooden suspension bridge—one of several along the river—lends nostalgic charm.

The park's natural features are complemented with variety of facilities: picnic tables, barbecue pits, ample parking spaces, indoor washrooms, and a children's playground. The park also provides an excellent launch point for canoeists and rafters and is riddled with well-established foot trails along the river and up and down its escarpment.

At 33 hectares, Sandy Beach is far from expansive, but it does have several natural communities: riverine forest, aspen woods, grasslands, and coniferous forests. Each blends seamlessly into the next.

Riveredge Park

Riveredge Park shares the Elbow River Valley with Sandy Beach. This secluded, blink-and-you'll-miss-it park is owned and operated by the City of Calgary,

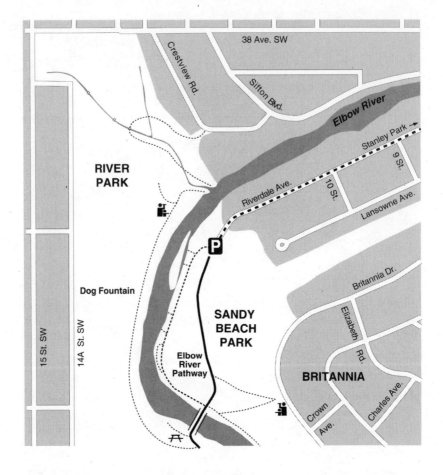

but users must book it in advance. Akin to a camp, and dedicated for outdoor education, activities, and adventures, the park has a kitchen shelter with wood-burning stove, firepit, picnic tables, and overnight tent site.

Used mainly by non-profit groups in the summers, the park is available for other users from mid-September to the end of June. For rates, booking, and further information, call the City of Calgary at 3-1-1.

Pathway Description—Glenmore Dam to Stanley Park

Travelling downstream, the Elbow River Pathway begins on the north side of the Glenmore Dam.

To reach the dam's spillway, take the access road on the south side of the Glenmore Water Treatment Plant. Depending on water levels, the spillway can be a mesmerizing sight as bluish-green water forcefully cascades into the typically sedate waterway below. Although the spillway is not an official park—and the access road is subject to closure—it's a haven for fishermen and a secluded launch point for rafters. A word of caution, however: water levels and currents can change quickly.

The Elbow River Pathway travels along the western escarpment of the river valley, skirting the east side of the Glenmore Water Treatment Plant—a pleasing and cohesive mix of new and Depression-era red brick architecture. To the east—and the opposite shore—are the achingly lush greens of the Calgary Golf and Country Club, and the posh residences of Britannia and Windsor Park.

The pathway continues north past Safety City (a traffic and bicycle education centre for children run by the Calgary Jaycees) and the Emily Follensbee Centre. Immediately past the special education school, the pathway reaches 50 Ave. SW, River Park, and Sandy Beach. River Park is at the crest of the hill; Sandy Beach is in the river valley.

Jaunty crossing—the Elbow River has a number of swaying pedestrian bridges like this one at Sandy Beach.

The Elbow River Pathway drops steeply into Sandy Beach. Near the base of the hill, the pathway forks. The main pathway and recommended route for cyclists swings north, skirting the picnic and playground area. As the pathway approaches the river, cyclists must dismount to cross a narrow wooden pedestrian bridge. On the east side of the river, the forest gives way to grassy areas flanked by forested slopes. A few metres later, the pathway reaches the west end of Riverdale Ave. SW. For about 1.4 kilometres, the route follows this canopied and stately street. The dedicated pathway resumes at 6A St. SW, drops under Elbow Dr. SW, and soon after (just east of 4A St. SW) enters Stanley Park.

STANLEY PARK

STANLEY PARK AT A GLANCE

LOCATION	4011 – 1A St. SW
	South–east bank of Elbow River
HOURS	0500 to 2300 daily
TERRAIN	Varied: flat, grassy riverbank at west end; steep, forested escarpment at north end; open, grass sports fields at south and east ends; sprinkled with stands of trees and shrubs throughout
ACCESS	East of 42 Ave. and Elbow Dr. SW

West of 42 Ave. and Macleod Tr. S

Elbow River Pathway

Heritage Escarpment Pathway

ACTIVITIES Walking, cycling, picnicking, canoeing, rafting, swimming, baseball, tennis, lawn bowling, rugby, grass volleyball, fishing, ice skating, tobogganing

FACILITIES Seasonal washrooms

Seasonal water fountains

BBQ pits and picnic tables

Playground

Outdoor swimming pool

Tennis courts

Baseball diamond

Sports fields (soccer, grass volleyball, football)

Stanley Park Lawn Bowling Club

Elboya Community Association Hall

DOGS Rules vary throughout; on leash along pathways

Not permitted on playing (sports) fields and within 20 metres of playgrounds

INFORMATION City of Calgary 268-3800

TRANSIT #3, #30, #419

Are we there yet? A young cyclist gauges the distance to his destination.

A shady stand of trees. A sun-drenched soccer pitch. A quiet river shore. A bustling public swimming pool. A lazy river. An exciting rugby match. Stanley Park offers all of this and more, making it one of Calgary's most diverse—and most visited—parks.

On muggy, sweltering summer days, thousands of people visit Stanley Park, where they wade in the river, walk through the trees, play on the tennis courts, or splash in the pool. The park is almost as busy on bright, crisp winter days, offering visitors an outdoor skating rink (near Elboya Community Hall), and toboggan runs.

Stanley Park's terrain is as wide-ranging as its facilities. Located on the Elbow River flood plain, it has wide open fields, shady riverbanks along the river, and a steeply

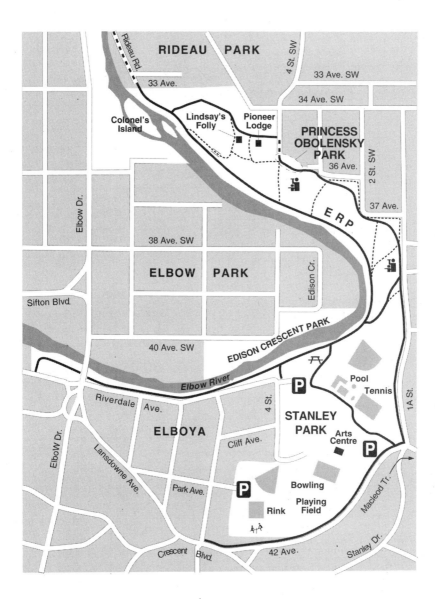

sloped grassy escarpment. The park includes the crumbling remnants of a dream started in boom times and forsaken in a bust (see sidebar: "Lindsay's Folly").

All of this is flanked by an eclectic array of new and old high-scale homes—many reminiscent of Victorian manors and English country estates—moments away from the downtown core.

Easy to reach, easy to enjoy, Stanley Park offers something for everyone.

Pathway Description—Stanley Park to Mission

East of Elbow Dr. SW, the Elbow River Pathway runs along the river and through the community of Elboya. It quickly reaches the west end of Stanley Park, where it meanders through the park's busiest sections: the main picnic area and the grassy riverbank beach.

A branch off the main route connects the park's west and east parking lots, swimming pool, tennis courts, and decorative garden. Cycling in this section is difficult during peak use, in summer or winter. Follow this pathway to reach the playing fields and playground located at the south end of the park. A pathway constructed in 2006 runs along the east side of the park.

Near the baseball diamond, the Elbow River Pathway bends north, and the park's picnic area and manicured grounds give way to riverine forest at the base of Parkhill Escarpment. The east riverbank becomes steeper and the

Benchmarks—Sharma Christie reads the commemorative plaque
on a Parks Foundation, Calgary, bench in Stanley Park.

pathway climbs slightly as it heads northward.

The pathway climbs slowly and steadily for a few hundred metres. Several viewpoints urge pathway users to take in the sights: the winding river valley, the natural habitats, the affluent neighbourhoods, and diverse fellow pathway travellers.

As the pathway descends, it passes through a dense riverine forest filled with red osier dogwood, white spruce, and in moist areas, black birch. Beyond the remains of a concrete bridge are the remains of Lindsay's Folly. A pathway also connects to the top of the escarpment, site of the Southern Alberta Pioneers Association Lodge and Princess Obolensky Park.

The Elbow River pathway leaves Stanley Park at Rideau Rd. and 33 Ave. SW and travels along Rideau Rd. SW for several hundred metres. The dedicated pathway resumes near 32 Ave. SW and crosses the river via a narrow, wooden (and bouncy) suspension bridge into Woods Park and a recently widened and realigned twinned section of the pathway. One branch follows the riverbank and the other follows along Elbow Drive. Both amble north past Gerry Shaw Garden, a playground, and a gently sloped grassy beach. Near 29 Ave. SW, the pathways join and follow the river east to 4 St. and 26 Ave. SW, the southern gateway to the community of Mission.

High times—the Elbow River at Woods Park, hours after flooding in June 2005.

WOODS PARK

WOODS PARK AT A GLANCE

LOCATION	Elbow Dr. and 32 Ave. SW
	West bank of Elbow River
HOURS	0500 to 2300 daily
TERRAIN	Gently sloped forested riverbank with formal gardens and playground
ACTIVITIES	Walking, cycling, dog walking, picnicking, river wading/ viewing
FACILITIES	Playground
	Gerry Shaw Gardens
	Picnic tables
DOGS	On leash
INFORMATION	City of Calgary 268-3800
TRANSIT	#3

Gerry Shaw Gardens

Gerry Shaw and Mike Stafford met at the age of four, forming a friendship that survived even after Gerry's death from kidney cancer in 1995.

"Gerry went down fighting," says Mike of his friend's last battle. "While Gerry was alive a group of us decided we wanted to do something for him. We considered a chair at the University of Calgary, but Gerry wanted something with more legs."

Mike Stafford led the campaign to build a garden for his late friend ,Gerry Shaw.

Gerry's friends, however, chose something with roots: a public garden just downstream of the swinging wooden bridge in Woods Park (at Elbow Dr. and 30 Ave. SW). Overlooking the Elbow River, Gerry Shaw Gardens is only a few blocks from where Gerry grew up in Elbow Park and just a short walk from his last home on Rideau Rd. SW.

Gerry, who played nine seasons with the Calgary Stampeders Football Club and also ran a brokerage office, died before seeing the formal riverside garden his friends planned for him. Mike's fundraising efforts netted $440,000 for the project (and turned him into a decade-long volunteer with the Parks Foundation, Calgary). An agreement for the garden was struck within six weeks of Gerry's death, and the garden opened six months to the day after Gerry's passing. To this day, the garden is maintained using funds from the endowment fund created in Gerry's name.

Gerry Shaw Gardens.

ELBOW ISLAND PARK

An often overlooked destination—and among the only islands of consequence on the Elbow River—Elbow Island Park at the south end of Mission Bridge (4 St. and 26 Ave. SW) is a cool, lush oasis in a dense riverine forest.

Marathon Realty, a subsidy of Canadian Pacific Railway Ltd., donated the island to Calgarians for the city's 1975 centennial.

The bulk of the park is located west of the bridge, with a small section to the east. The narrow paths are not easily reached or navigated by bicycle, wheelchairs or baby strollers; this is a walking park. Thick undergrowth makes exploring anything off the paths difficult. The park has little more added to it than a few garbage bins and benches, but is home to a wide variety of trees, shrubs, flowers, birds, and, during damp summers, mosquitoes.

LINDSAY PARK

LINDSAY PARK AT A GLANCE

LOCATION	2225 Macleod Tr. S
HOURS	0500 to 2300 daily
TERRAIN	Riverine forest wrapping around the Talisman Sport Centre
ACCESS	Talisman Centre parking lot
	22 Ave. and Erlton St. SW
	19 Ave. and 1 St. SW
	Elbow River Pathway
ACTIVITIES	Walking, cycling, picnicking, fishing; swimming, fitness, sports, and recreation at Talisman Centre
FACILITIES	Picnic tables
	Benches
	Playground
	Talisman Centre (includes washrooms, concessions, and a wide range of sports, fitness, and recreation facilities)
DOGS	On leash along pathway
	Not permitted within 20 metres of playground
INFORMATION	For park inquiries, call the City of Calgary at 268-3800
	For Talisman Centre, call 233-8393 or visit www.talismancentre.com
TRANSIT	South C-Train (Erlton Station)
	#10, #30, #770, #772

Pathway Description—Mission to Fort Calgary

The Elbow River Pathway continues east along a grassy knoll overlooking the river

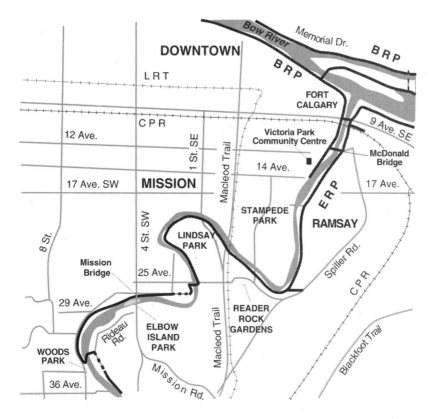

DOWNTOWN

Bow River

Memorial Dr.

BRP

BRP

LRT

FORT
CALGARY

9 Ave. SE

CPR

12 Ave.

1 St. SE

Macleod Trail

Victoria Park
Community Centre

14 Ave.

McDonald
Bridge

17 Ave. SW

MISSION

17 Ave.

STAMPEDE
PARK

ERP

RAMSAY

4 St. SW

LINDSAY
PARK

8 St.

Mission
Bridge

25 Ave.

Spiller Rd.

CPR

29 Ave.

Rideau Rd.

ELBOW
ISLAND
PARK

READER
ROCK
GARDENS

Macleod Trail

Blackfoot Trail

WOODS
PARK

36 Ave.

Mission Rd.

to the end of 26 Ave. SW, where it turns north for 200 metres to the 25 Ave. SW bridge. After entering the community of Erlton, the pathway runs north along the east riverbank behind a row of condominiums and into Lindsay Park.

As the Elbow River Pathway leaves Lindsay Park, it drops under 1 St. SE (Patterson Bridge), rises slightly, and drops again, under the northbound Macleod Tr. S (Victoria Bridge) and north and southbound C-Train bridges. As it climbs a short steep pitch, it levels and enters the south end of Stampede Park at the south entrance bridge.

As the pathway enters Lindsay Park, it forks in several directions to the heart of the park, the riverbank and the Talisman Centre. The main route follows the riverbank, curving from west to north to east. Along the way it passes a children's playground,

Lindsay Park is just a short
walk from the city's core.

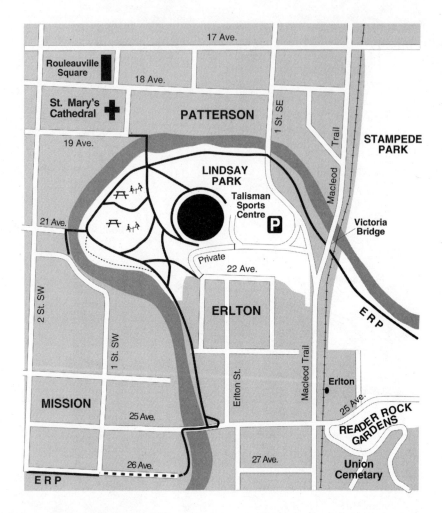

a large outdoor playing field, several picnic sites and two pedestrian bridges, one located west of the sports centre and the second (an old railway bridge) northwest of the centre to Rouleauville Square.

Near the horse barns, the pathway turns north and continues along the river for about 800 metres to MacDonald Bridge. (This section is subject to closure during the Stampede's annual ten-day event every July.) About 400 metres north, the pathway ducks under a low railway bridge and the 9 Ave. SE bridge to join the Bow River Pathway at the site of Fort Calgary and the confluence of the Bow and Elbow rivers.

Dominated by the Talisman Centre (previously the Lindsay Park Athletic Centre), Lindsay Park is a few short blocks south of downtown Calgary. Dotted with trees and picnic tables, the park also features a very kid-friendly playground, complete with a giant "spider web."

For decades, the slow-moving currents and occasional deep pools along this section of the river have lured summer swimmers. Although a popular "swinging tree" at the south end of the park was cut down more than 15 years ago, daredevils and dabblers still find cool relief and good fun in the river's waters.

With the explosion of condominiums in Mission and Erlton in the past two decades, Lindsay Park has become a well-travelled commuter route for workers walking and cycling to and from their jobs in the city's central core. For this reason, the pathway through the park is lined with lights.

STAMPEDE PARK

Open 365 days a year, Stampede Park welcomes more than one million visitors every July during the ten-day long Calgary Stampede, "The Greatest Outdoor Show on Earth." The park's current facilities include the Big Four Building, Roundup Centre, Pengrowth Saddledome (home of the Calgary Flames NHL Hockey Team), Stampede Corral, Stampede Grandstand, Rotary House, and the Archie Boyce Pavilion.

"The Greatest Outdoor Show on Earth"—Stampede Park is best known for its annual ten-day festival every July.
CALGARY EXHIBITION AND STAMPEDE

Although more parking lot than park, the exhibition grounds nonetheless have pockets of trees and shaded benches and a variety of relaxing features, such as the riverine forest along the Elbow River, a children's play area outside the Archie Boyce Pavilion, and a water fountain in front of the Big Four Building. And with thousands of events staged here every year—ranging from rodeo and rock 'n' roll to hockey and home shows—this is a park well worth visiting.

During the next decade the organizers of the Stampede will create a more park-like environment, including extensive restoration and reclamation along the riverbank.

For information about the Calgary Stampede and Stampede Park, call 261-0101 or visit www.calgarystampede.com. For information about events at the Pengrowth Saddledome, call 777-4636 or visit www.pengrowthsaddledome. com.

NOSE CREEK PATHWAY

A major part of Calgary's pathway system, Nose Creek Pathway runs from along West Nose Creek in the far northwest to the Bow River. At first glance, the Nose Creek Pathway appears to be a poor country cousin to the Elbow River and Bow River pathways: it meanders through large tracts of industrial land and sections of recently reclaimed industrial sites, and has far fewer facilities and attractions.

In the past decade, the Nose Creek Valley has seen a number of improvements and additions. The pathway has become a well-established commuter and recreational route. And the surrounding open spaces are coming into their own. As a park, West Nose Creek has nothing to apologize for.

Still, it's not an area that's always immediately embraced. But Nose Creek nonetheless has a gritty beauty and a never-say-die naturalness that is regaining its footing. Traffic is a constant in the valley, but even so the gentle rustling of aspen leaves spinning in the breeze can be heard, and once neglected areas are being replaced by new forests, revitalized natural areas, and community open spaces.

Nose Creek is also home to Swainson's hawks, Richardson's ground squirrels (good old gophers), mallards, geese, red foxes, muskrats, weasels, and a surprising number of beavers that have built several dams along the creek (hence the name of the nearby Beaver Dam Rd. NE).

WEST NOSE CREEK CONFLUENCE PARK

WEST NOSE CREEK CONFLUENCE PARK AT A GLANCE

LOCATION	Beddington Tr. and Centre St. N
HOURS	0500 to 2300
ACCESS	Beddington Tr. west of Deerfoot Tr. NE
	Beddington Tr. and Centre St. North
	Nose Creek Pathway
	Beddington Tr. and Berkshire Blvd. NW
ACTIVITIES	Walking, hiking, cycling, picnicking, bird and wildlife watching
FACILITIES	Washrooms
	Benches and seating
INFORMATION	City of Calgary 3-1-1
DOGS	On leash
TRANSIT	#46

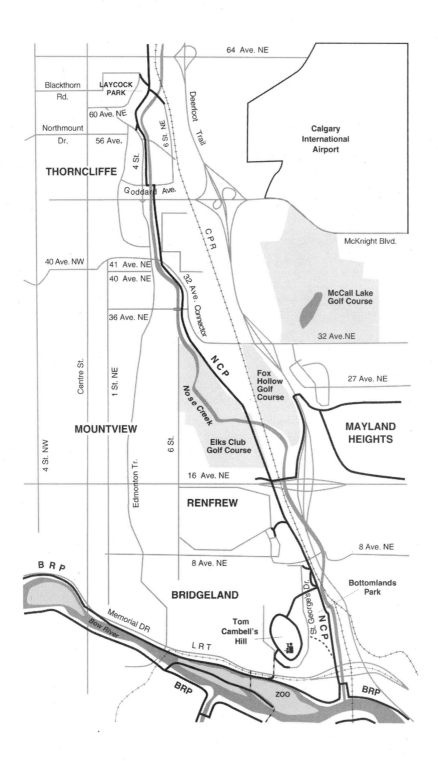

Rock and roll—traffic rolls by the glacial erratic
at West Nose Creek Confluence Park.

Tens of thousands of years before the CPR and CN arrived, Western Canada had an "erratic train," a slow-moving glacier that carried and deposited large quartzite rocks—some the size of a barn—from Jasper National Park southeast to the Montana–Alberta border about 17,000 years ago.

In the Calgary area, the erratic train stopped to drop cargo at Nose Hill Park, Fish Creek Park, Okotoks, and West Nose Creek. The Big Rock at Okotoks may be the largest, but the Split Rock at West Nose Creek (featured on the cover) is the most symmetrical. As its name implies, the large rock is split right in half, resulting in a narrow passage between the two pieces.

The erratic train didn't need rails, bridges, or switching stations; it pushed across the prairies millimetre by millimetre, creating West Nose Creek and Nose Creek with ice and meltwater. And then the erratic train—and its glacial engine—stopped.

Today, the creeks are much smaller than the valleys they occupy. On the prairies, however, even a small creek delivers big benefits. For instance, West Nose Creek. Typically only a metre or two wide, this twisting, turning waterway feeds and cleans a number of ponds and wetlands, brings moisture and nutrients to farms and ranches, and catches and carries snowmelt and rainwater.

The riparian areas or green zones along West Nose Creek support all kinds of soft, lush vegetation and are highly productive, says the Nose Creek Watershed Partnership. The park's habitat also includes native and non-native grasslands, riverine tall shrubs, low shrublands, and some small aspen and balsam poplar stands.

As well, West Nose Creek runs atop an important regional aquifer, the Paskapoo Formation, which, says Natural Resources Canada, "dates back to the Early Tertiary (Paleocene). This cliff was excavated as a potential sandstone quarry, one of many quarries from which Calgarians acquired the sandstone blocks used to construct many of the older heritage buildings that still exist in the downtown area." The sandstone formation is on the north side of the creek valley about a kilometre east of Centre St./Harvest Hills Blvd. N.

"The interpretive value of this valley is spectacular," says Bill Morrison, a volunteer with the Parks Foundation, Calgary, and the Calgary River Valleys Committee who helped create the park. Part of his work involved transplanting lady slipper orchids and wild roses and western wood lilies disturbed during the construction of Stoney Tr. NW to the park. "Humans have been leaving marks on the surrounding rocks for millennia."

Other features and treasures within the park include the creek's many oxbows which sometimes create pint-size sandy shores, and the airplanes—the park is under the Calgary International Airport flight path, and arriving and departing planes seem close enough to touch. As well, park users can enjoy the lookout point east of the Split Rock, which is

The long and winding trail—Leads through West Nose Creek Confluence Park.

most impressive and colourful in the fall, and the park's bridges—some would say there are too many of them, but these seven "human markers" have come to define the park and provide maximum contact with this fascinating creek.

Pathway Description—West Nose Creek Confluence Park

The communities of Beddington, MacEwan, Hidden Valley, Hanson Ranch, Panoramic Hills, Country Hills Village, Country Hills, Coventry Hills, and Harvest Hills have a well-defined network of pathways that tie into West Nose Creek Confluence Park at Beddington Tr. and Country Hills Blvd. NW and at Beddington Tr. and Centre St. N.

From the park's western boundary at Beddington Tr. NW and Berkshire Blvd. NW, follow the pathway east along Beddington Tr. NW on the south side of West Nose Creek. Near Centre St. N, the pathway turns north to cross the creek and then travels under Harvest Hills Blvd. About a kilometre along is the Split Rock. Here the pathway is twinned, running along both sides of the creek valley. Both routes travel through a variety of terrain, sometimes along the

Clematis tangutica grows in larges patches at West Nose Creek Confluence Park.

valley's shoulders and sometimes along the valley floor. The valley is not grand, but it is beautiful in an understated way—and anyone who has lived on a farm or ranch in southern Alberta will instantly recognize, and be soothed by, its sights, sounds, and smells.

The north pathway links to a parking lot off Beddington Tr. west of Deerfoot Tr. NE. Upstream of the confluence with Nose Creek, the pathways merge; the actual confluence is for the most part visually lacklustre, although significant to water management in the Calgary area. The park ends at Beddington Tr. NE and the pathway continues south to the Bow River along the Nose Creek Pathway.

Morning stroll—rolling through West Nose Creek Confluence Park.

Pathway Description—Nose Creek Pathway South of West Nose Creek Confluence Park

South of West Nose Creek Confluence Park, the Nose Creek Pathway follows Nose Creek on its journey south to the Bow River. The pathway is typically wide, open, and pleasant. The valley's western shoulder is covered in vegetation, which comes alive with the colours of fall.

Shortly after passing under Beddington Tr. NE, the pathway connects to another regional pathway that runs about 4 kilometres west to the top of Nose Hill.

Around the bend—riding in unison on Nose Creek's winding, open pathway.

On the north and south side of 64 Ave. NE, the pathway connects to the community. South of 64 Ave. NE (about 200 metres), the pathway also connects to Laycock Park of Thorncliffe Heights.

The pathway climbs at the south end of Laycock Park and the crest of the hill offers one of the most encompassing views of the creek valley and the mixture of activities that take place in it: industry, transportation (ground and air), and nature (especially beavers). Beyond the crest of the hill, the pathway descends as it approaches an underpass at Beaver Dam Rd. NE.

Continuing south, the pathway travels through Skyline Industrial Park, dropping under Goddard Ave. NE and McKnight Blvd. NE.

From Goddard Ave. NE to midway through the Elks Golf Course, the pathway runs along the east shore of the creek. As well, south of 36 Ave. NE, the pathway is cleared during winter months.

Until the pathway reaches the golf course, expect the route to be utilitarian with a few well-placed benches for rest stops. The pathway, however, is not overly demanding or strenuous—its entire length can for the most part be covered (there and back again) in an afternoon or evening. But if you really want a break— or a treat—stop by the Confetti Ice Cream Factory at 4416 – 5 St. NE.

One of the pathway's greenest sections is located away from the creek and along the eastern edge of the Elk Golf Course and the western edge of Fox Hollow Golf course, although the route is bounded by chain-link fences. After crossing Nose Creek via a pedestrian bridge, the pathway runs adjacent to the valley's railway line.

At the north side of 16 Ave. NE, the pathway reaches an important intersection with a connection west along 16 Ave. NE to the community of Mountview and a connection to the east (and then north) along the east side of Fox Hollow Golf Course and via a pedestrian bridge over Deerfoot Tr. NE into the community of Vista Heights.

About 300 metres south of 16 Ave. NE, the Nose Creek Pathway connects to the community of Renfrew; the connecting pathway is steep and switch-backed. A number of well-established foot trails also lead up and down the valley's west side.

Four hundred metres south of the connection, the pathway travels under 8 Ave. NE. This section of the Nose Creek Pathway runs through Bottomlands Park and has seen considerable cleanup and development in recent years: two pathways link to St. George's Heights, Bridgeland/Riverside, and Tom Campbell's Hill. The city's newest planned attraction, the Telus World of Science, will also be located in this section of Nose Creek Valley, north of the zoo parking lot and animal hospital and at the end of St. George's Dr. NE. The new science centre is expected to open in 2010.

Nose Creek Pathway ends at the confluence of Nose Creek and the Bow River. From Beddington Tr. NE to the Bow River, the pathway covers 15.6 kilometres.

LAYCOCK PARK

LAYCOCK PARK AT A GLANCE

LOCATION	Blackthorn Rd. east of 4A St. NE
HOURS	0500 to 2300 daily
TERRAIN	Generally flat lawn areas with sloping hills to the west
ACCESS	Blackthorn Rd. and 60 Ave. NE
	64 Ave. east of 4A St. NE
	Nose Creek Pathway
ACTIVITIES	Walking, cycling, picnicking, playing
FACILITIES	Benches
	Picnic shelter
	Playground
DOGS	On leash on pathway and within 20 metres of playground
INFORMATION	268-3800
TRANSIT	#4, #5, #32

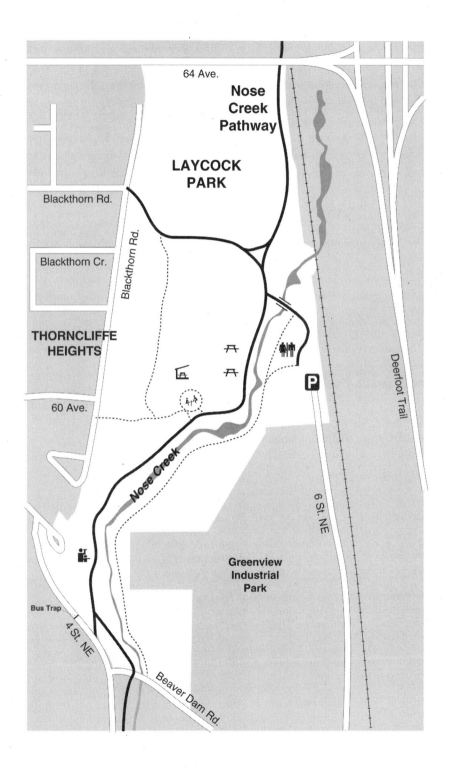

Laycock Park is built on a small piece of land once part of a large farm owned by the Thomas Laycock family. Laycock immigrated to Calgary from England in 1888 and set up a grain and cattle farm in 1892 that was eventually passed on to one of his sons, Thomas Hayes Laycock.

Before his death in 1920, the elder Laycock was known throughout the Alberta cattle industry as a pioneer breeder of Holsteins. He often put his knowledge of cattle to use in his position as a judge at the Calgary Exhibition, which later became the Calgary Stampede. The family's cattle herd continued to thrive over the years and Hayes Laycock showed the animals at fairs and exhibitions throughout Western Canada.

Hayes and his wife Violet worked the Nose Creek farm until it was sold in 1957. The couple then retired to the Thorncliffe district; Hayes died in March 1988.

The recreational park commemorating the Laycock family was built with funds raised by the Thorncliffe/Greenview community, and subsidies from the City of Calgary, and lottery funds from the provincial government. The park includes picnic tables, a playground, and a parking lot on the east side of Nose Creek with connecting pathways to the community of Thorncliffe/Greenview.

BOTTOMLANDS PARK

BOTTOMLANDS PARK AT A GLANCE

LOCATION	300 Saint George's Dr. NE
HOURS	0500 to 2300 daily
TERRAIN	Rolling creek valley with extensive landscaping, reclaimed natural areas, playground, and soccer pitches
ACCESS	North of zoo parking lot on Saint George's Dr. NE
	13 A St. and 7 Ave. NE
	Nose Creek Pathway south of 8 Ave. NE
	Nose Creek Pathway north of Bow River
ACTIVITIES	Walking, cycling, picnicking, wildlife viewing, birdwatching, soccer
FACILITIES	Benches and picnic tables
	Playground
	Seasonal washroom and water fountains
	Two soccer pitches
DOGS	On leash on pathway
	Off leash area as posted
	Not allowed on playing fields or within 20 metres of playgrounds

INFORMATION 268-3830

TRANSIT Northeast C-Train (Zoo Station)
#19, #119, #743, #745

A red-light district in Calgary's earliest days (see sidebar: "Red Lights on Nose Creek"), little more than a sooty railway corridor throughout much of the first part of the 20th century, and a garbage dump after the second World War, Bottomlands Park has survived its share of dirt and grime to re-emerge as a well-used and increasingly appreciated green space and reclaimed natural area in the Nose Creek Valley.

This is one of Calgary's newer parks and is located north of the Calgary Zoo's main parking lot on Saint George's Dr. NE, east of Tom Campbell's Hill, and adjacent to a community park in nearby Regal Park.

From Deerfoot Tr. NE, Bottomlands Park's two soccer pitches look as though they slope upward with the creek valley, but it's a trick of perspective and the fields are regulation flat.

The east-facing slope of Bottomlands Park is more natural—dense with native and introduced shrubs and thick with a variety of birds and small mammals. Years ago, two to three pairs of breeding red foxes lived along the hill and/or on Tom Campbell's Hill. However, increased use in the valley—by both humans and their dogs—has made sightings of these animals precariously rare both here and elsewhere in the city's river valleys. Among the wildlife more commonly spotted in Bottomlands Park are Swainson's hawks, grey partridge, cliff swallows, black-billed magpies, American crows and white-tailed jackrabbits.

Bottoms up—Bottomlands Park along Nose Creek is one of Calgary's newer parks.

Red Lights on Nose Creek

Stroll down the Nose Creek Valley and you're not likely to hear much more than the constant hum of travel. It was a different tune a century ago. In his 1971 book, *Red Lights on the Prairies*, author and historian James H. Gray wrote that the sounds of piano playing and singing in Nose Creek could be heard as far as Scotsman's Hill.

The source of serenading was scandalous: eight or nine bordellos on what today is the zoo parking lot. "Stutterin' May," "Diamond Dolly," Lila Wilson, and Madge Jennings were among the women who ran rowdy and raunchy bordellos along the valley—and lit their porches with a red light.

Catering to hard-working, hard-playing men who worked on the nearby railway line, they prospered because their bawdy establishments were outside of the existing city limits. Calgary police were powerless to shut them down. The RCMP knew of the red-light district but it took several raids and some stiff fines to close the three-storey houses. Presbyterian and Methodist clergymen were appalled at the business conducted overlooking the banks of Nose Creek. They wrote to Superintendent Richard Burton Deane complaining the women of Nose Creek were "prejudicially affecting the morals and welfare of the community at East Calgary."

As the years passed, it became tougher for "Stutterin' May" and "Diamond Dolly" to do business anywhere, and their red lights on the prairies were extinguished.

Houses of ill repute—the lower reaches of Nose Creek once comprised a red-light district.
GLENBOW MUSEUM ARCHIVES

DOWNTOWN PARKS

DOWNTOWN'S +15 WALKWAYS

by Richard White, former Executive Director of the Calgary Downtown
Association

When you think of parks and pathways in Calgary, you probably don't think
about the 16 kilometres of downtown's +15 walkways as pathways. Yet they
are the most travelled walkway system in the city. Literally more than 100,000
people use them every work week.

Calgary's above ground walkways are on par with Toronto's and Montreal's
underground systems. And Calgary's +15 walkways link more shopping (1,000-
plus shops, restaurants, food courts, and services), more tourist attractions (six)
and more hotel rooms (4,000) than West Edmonton Mall.

The father of the city's +15 walkway system was Harold Hanen, who
worked for the City of Calgary's Planning Department from 1966 to 1969. He
conceived the idea of a network of mid-block bridges, 15 feet off the ground,
connecting all downtown buildings. The first bridge was built in 1970 and
the office building boom of the '70s saw the system grow rapidly. By 2007,
60 bridges will connect more than 100 buildings in a network more than 17
kilometres long. A memorial in the +15 walkway between the Epcor Centre
for the Performing Arts and the Calgary Municipal Building Parkade captures
Hanen's vision and the system's growth.

The system is not totally integrated, so gaps exist, and because the system
links old and new buildings, the routes have lots of twists and turns, sometimes
making them an adventure to navigate.

The longest contiguous leg runs east–west from The Bay at 1 St. SW to
the Western Canadian Centre at 6 St. SW. It takes you through Scotia Centre,
TD Square, Calgary Eaton Centre, Sears, Watermark Tower, and Centennial
Parkade. Along the way you will encounter two food courts, four indoor
shopping centres, two department stores, Devonian Gardens, and the Udderly
Art Pasture.

The Art Pasture is the legacy of the Colourful Cows for Calgary art project
in 2000. At the time, more than 100 moulded-plastic cows were decorated by
local artists then auctioned off for charity. Today, 15 of the cows are permanently
located in the +15 level of the Centennial Parkade along 9 Ave. between 5 and
6 St. SW.

The most "cultured" section of the +15 system begins at the Olympic
Plaza and radiates to the Palliser Hotel, Calgary Tower, Glenbow Museum,

The Udderly Art "herd" in the Centennial Parkade on 9th Avenue is one of the many attraction along the +15 walkway network.

Telus Convention Centre, Hyatt Regency Calgary, and Epcor Centre for the Performing Arts, as well as the Calgary Municipal Building, Calgary City Hall, W. R. Castell Public Library, and numerous other buildings. The Glenbow Museum is the largest museum in Western Canada and the Epcor Centre is Western Canada's largest performing arts centre.

The hidden gem of the +15 cultural district is the Police Interpretive Centre just east of the W. R. Castell Library. Kids love riding the police motorcycle, dressing in police uniforms and using a computer to solve a crime.

The best north–south route goes from Gulf Canada Square on 9 Ave. SW to the Ernst Young Tower in Eau Claire (2 Ave. SW). This route passes the still controversial "big white trees" on Stephen Ave. When the idea to enclose the block between Bankers Hall and TD Square proved unfeasible, these complex metal structures were created. They have been nicknamed "trees" for the flora they replaced, but in reality they have no name. The "trees" were conceived by architects as an element for the proposed Bankers Hall galleria. Some call them futuristic, some call them prehistoric, and others call them "the world's largest pooper scoopers!" People seem to either love them or hate them.

Also along the north–south leg of the system is the "Stampede Poster" exhibition between First Canadian Centre and the Centrum office building. It is interesting to see how these posters have evolved over the past century. The early posters are just packed with information while the current ones are much more visual.

Another east–west link runs on the north side of downtown along 4 and 5 Ave. SW. This leg connects Sun Life Plaza, Petro-Canada Towers, Trans Canada Towers, Bow Valley Square, and Energy Plaza on the east side with the Westin and International hotels, as well as Shell and Calgary Place offices and McDougall Centre further west.

This leg of the system could be nicknamed "Food Court Alley" as nearly every building has a food court on the +15 level. At lunchtime, these courts swarm with activity. This is also the site of Lunchbox Theatre, located in the Bow Valley Square. Lunchbox Theatre is the longest running lunchtime theatre in the world. Nearby is Art Central, which can be reached via the Petro-Canada and Hanover Place +15. Art Central has about 15 art galleries, as well as a great diner (Siding Café) and great café (The Palette).

Check out downtown's +15 walkway for something different to do.

DEVONIAN GARDENS

DEVONIAN GARDENS AT A GLANCE

LOCATION	4th level, Toronto Dominion Square, 317 – 7 Ave. SW
HOURS	0900 to 2100 (closed occasionally for private events)
ACCESS	Toronto Dominion Square, 317 – 7 Ave. SW
	+15 Walkway
	Eaton Centre Food Court
ACTIVITIES	Self-guided walking tour, indoor picnicking, tours, field trips, weddings, receptions
FACILITIES	Washrooms
	Benches and seating
	Playground
	Gardens
	Stage
	Wheelchair accessible
INFORMATION	Bookings and rental rate 268-3830
	Guided group tours 221-3782
	Event planning 221-4274
	Park brochure available at www.calgary.ca
DOGS	Not permitted
TRANSIT	C-Train (all lines) 3 St. SW Station
	#2, #10, #24, #107
ADDITIONAL	Free admission. Donations welcome
	Postcards and pins available from park office

A tropical oasis in downtown Calgary and one of the world's largest indoor parks, Devonian Gardens is located on three floors and occupies 10,500 square metres of TD Square. Here water fountains gurgle, 20,000 native and imported plants thrive, and giant koi fish nibble.

Devonian Gardens lies at the heart of Calgary's +15 walkway system, making it a favourite lunchtime escape for hundreds of office workers every

Olymipic Plaza—where Calgary celebrates.
CALGARY TOURISM PHOTO

Monday to Friday. The gardens are equally busy on mornings, afternoons, and weekends with school field trips, family outings, and weddings.

One of the many projects built for Western Canadians by the Devonian Group (funded by the Eric Harvie family), the gardens also feature 1.6 kilometres of walkway, a stage and exhibit area, a reflecting pool, playground, water gardens (with koi), a sun garden, and a sculpture court and creek bed.

OLYMPIC PLAZA

For the past 20 years, when Calgarians have had something to celebrate, they have headed to Olympic Plaza at the east end of Stephen Avenue Walk.

The plaza is where up to 60,000 people a night welcomed medal winners each night of the Olympic Winter Games in 1988. The next year, Calgarians gathered on a rain-soaked Saturday to greet the Calgary Flames hockey team after they won the Stanley Cup in 1989. In 1990, people lined the plaza to see Queen Elizabeth during her visit to Alberta.

More recently, a lunchtime crowd of about 50,000 gathered on the plaza to welcome the Calgary Flames Hockey Club home after they lost Game seven of the 2004 Stanley Cup Finals to the Tampa Bay Lightning.

Summer or winter, rain or shine, day or night, the Olympic Plaza is a favourite gathering point.

Located on Stephen Avenue Walk between 1 St. and Macleod Tr. SE, the plaza occupies nearly a full city block and is surrounded by the Glenbow Museum, the W. R. Castell Central Library, the Centre for Performing Arts, the Municipal Building, and City Hall. The plaza's southwest corner is ringed in winter with bright lights and in summer with colourful flowers; the plaza has a central stage, wading pool/skating rink, terraced viewing and seating areas, washrooms, and an outdoor concession.

Look for the Famous Five sculptures in the plaza's southwest corner. These statues commemorate the work of the five formidable women who struggled to make Canadian women recognized as "persons." Until 1929—and the Famous Five's "persons" case brought forward by Emily Murphy, Henrietta Muir Edwards, Irene Parley, Louise McKinney, and Nellie McClung—women in Canada could not hold elected or appointed office. The statues were unveiled in 1999 on the 70th anniversary of the landmark court case; identical versions of the sculptures are located on Parliament Hill. Both sets owe their existence to Frances Wright.

A number of restaurants and cafés surround the plaza, including Teatro in the old Toronto Dominion Bank Building at the plaza's west end and the Good Earth Café on the main level of the W. R. Castell Library.

One of the plaza's enduring features is the bricks used to pave the walkway around the wading pool/skating rink and central stage. The custom-engraved bricks sold for $19.88 in a pre-Olympic promotion and thousands of people jumped at the chance to buy a little piece of Calgary's largest-ever international event.

SHAW MILLENNIUM PARK

SHAW MILLENNIUM PARK AT A GLANCE

LOCATION	1220 – 9 Ave. SW
HOURS	24/7 daily
TERRAIN	Urban skateboard, in-line skate, and BMX bike park surrounded by largely open landscaped space
ACCESS	9 Ave. and 12 St. SW
ACTIVITIES	Skateboarding, in-line skating, "acrobatic" biking, basketball, beach volleyball, playing, hangin'
FACILITIES	Stage and amphitheatre
	Mewata Armoury
	Waterfall
	Millennium clock tower
	Basketball courts
	Beach volleyball courts

Children's waterworks play area
Concession (seasonal, independently operated)
Washrooms (open year-round, 0800 to 2000 daily)
Benches

DOGS	On leash
INFORMATION	268-3830
TRANSIT	#10, #11, #18, #31
ADDITIONAL	Free
	Dedicated website: www.gov.calgary.ab.ca/skatepark
	Lessons available

Nothing makes me feel older and more out of touch than a trip to Shaw Millennium Park. And that's exactly the point. This park is not for people of "my generation." It's for today's generation—although the City of Calgary does bill it as "a family activity park and special event venue."

Easy landing—making the difficult look non-chalant at Shaw Millennium Park.

This is North America's largest skateboarding/in-line skating park—and it's the world's biggest free outdoor skate park. If you don't wear plaid boxer shorts, a capped skewed on brim to back and super baggy pants, you may not be cool enough to truly enjoy Shaw Millennium.

Built as one of the city's millennium projects—after all, not everything was about Y2K—the park welcomes more than 1,000 skaters a day during the summer as well as spectators and basketball and volleyball players.

This is the only public park in Calgary open 24 hours a day and while some people may complain about the "kids that hang around there," this is a home away from home for thousands of city youth.

For "hipper" information about the park, visit: www.gov.calgary.ab.ca/skatepark.

NORTHEAST PARKS AND PATHWAYS

JIM FISH RIDGE

JIM FISH RIDGE AT A GLANCE

LOCATION	Centre St. and Samis Rd. NE
HOURS	0500 to 2300 daily
TERRAIN	Landscaped bench overlooking Centre St. and downtown Calgary
ACCESS	Centre St. and Samis Rd. NE
	1 St. and 6 Ave. NE
ACTIVITIES	Walking, sightseeing, picnicking
FACILITIES	Benches
	Viewpoints
	Gardens
DOGS	On leash on pathway and in park unless otherwise noted
INFORMATION	268-3830
TRANSIT	#2, #3, #17, #62, #64, #109, #116, #142, #301

From 1973 to 1988, the Devonian Foundation—the charity established by Eric Harvie—was quietly influential. Its last executive director, Jim Fish, was no different. Like his employers (first Eric and later his son Donald), Fish seldom sought publicity and spoke on relatively few occasions about the money and gifts bestowed by the Devonian Foundation.

Instead, he worked behind the scenes and over the years he reviewed, approved, and funded millions of dollars worth of park and pathway projects in Calgary and throughout Western Canada.

Fish started his career as an accountant with one of Harvie's companies and in 1951 he was charged with looking after the Harvie family's fortune. He would work for and with the family and its charitable foundation—launched originally as the Harvie Foundation with $100,000—for his entire career.

On one rare occasion, as quoted in Fred Diehl's book *A Gentleman from a Fading Age: Eric Lafferty Harvie*, Fish recalled the publicity-averse Harvie "Eric ran his charitable organization with

On the edge—downtown Calgary looms at Jim Fish Ridge.

the same meticulous precision and dedication as he had characteristic of all facets of his various endeavours. There was perhaps one difference. He enjoyed it more . . . It allowed him to be extravagant on behalf of others—never on himself. He could indulge in a favourite hobby whenever he felt like it. He could 'spend money like water' when it had purpose for the benefit of others."

Projects supported by the Harvie and Devonian foundations included:

- Canadian Geographic magazine—one of the Devonian's first projects was to give $100,000 "in order to save and rejuvenate a Canadian magazine in trouble."
- Donating extensive collections to the Glenbow and Alberta Provincial museums.
- 22 kilometres of pathways along the Bow River in Calgary—a 1975 centennial gift.
- Another centennial gift in 1975—the $3.2 million Century Garden Park at the corner of 8 St. and 8 Ave. SW.
- Research on the sexual prowess of beluga whales.
- Devonian Gardens—an ambitious $6-million glassed-in park in Oxford Square (now TD Square) that many Calgarians feared would be a costly albatross.
- Purchase of the Clearwater lands on the Elbow River west of Calgary.
- Five million dollars for main street beautification projects in 162 towns across Alberta.
- Purchase of 25 hectares of land at Bearspaw Reservoir northwest of the city along the Bow River.

In 1988, the Devonian foundation ceased operations, after having given away $89 million. Fish's calm demeanour and still-as-deep-water resolve impressed many people, including a number of volunteers with the Parks Foundation, Calgary, who thought it fitting to acknowledge his "first-class contributions to Calgary's parks and pathway system." The idea and construction costs were supported by the Crescent Heights Community Association. Jim Fish Ridge, at the edge of the escarpment overlooking the Centre Street Bridge and Samis Ridge and at the south end of Rotary Park, was named in his honour.

In 2004, *Fast Forward* magazine named the eastern edge of Jim Fish Ridge (Samis Road and 1 St. NE) one of Calgary's best summer make out spots, describing it as "an impressive variation that moves away from the category of obvious . . . same idea but without being so already-done-that."

No wonder. It takes a whiteout or blackout to ruin the view and the vibrant fuchsia rose bushes add a dash of romance. The landscaping creates just the right amount of privacy . . . well, you get the picture. For something other than smooching, delve into the interpretive signs detailing the growth of Calgary's downtown core and its every-changing skyline.

The north end of Jim Fish Ridge melds into Rotary Park (617 – 1 St. NE), a well-established community park with a small but somewhat dated wading pool, tennis courts, and seasonal washrooms and water fountains. Note: dogs are not allowed at the north end of Rotary Park.

TOM CAMPBELL'S HILL

TOM CAMPBELL'S HILL AT A GLANCE

LOCATION	Child Ave. and Centre Ave. NE
HOURS	0500 to 2300 daily
TERRAIN	Grassy bluff with treed plateau
ACCESS	St. George's Dr. and 12 St. NE
	13 St. south of Child Ave. NE
	Nose Creek Pathway south of 8 Ave. NE
ACTIVITIES	Walking, cycling, picnicking, sightseeing, birdwatching, wildlife viewing
FACILITIES	Benches
	Interpretive structure and displays
	Viewpoints
DOGS	On leash on pathways
INFORMATION	268-3800
TRANSIT	C-Train Northeast leg (Bridgeland/Memorial Station)
	#9

West of the confluence of the Bow River and Nose Creek sits Tom Campbell's Hill—a grassy protruding thumb of a hill overlooking downtown Calgary. Once the property of the Calgary Zoo, the open expanses of the hill held an enclosure for deer and buffalo, reindeer and zebras. Limited space and complaints from people who found the animals' breeding habits offensive forced zoo administrators to move the animals. In 1979, the land was turned over to the City of Calgary by the Devonian Group.

Although designated as parkland the same year, Tom Campbell's Hill—named for the Calgary hat maker whose sign was perched on the hill for many years—sat almost untouched for almost a decade. In the later 1980s, local residents in the community of Bridgeland/Riverside lobbied the city to have the hill preserved as a natural area and in July 1990 the City agreed to their request. Over the course of five years, the park was created. Among the most ambitious

A hat maker's sign has long since been replaced with
interpretive signage at Tom Campbell's Hill.

undertakings on the windswept bluff were efforts to restore the park's prairie
flora. Today the park features a mix of native and non-native grasslands,
including a good section of fescue in the northeast end. The park's aging hilltop
poplars—planted in a poker-straight line to form a wide allée—attract a wide
variety of bids.

The park's most outstanding feature is the panoramic view it offers of the
Bow River, the zoo, downtown Calgary, and nearby foothills and mountains. The
view is both impressive and dramatic—and best enjoyed on a warm summer's
night when you want to just sit and look for a while.

PRAIRIE WINDS PARK

PRAIRIE WINDS PARK AT A GLANCE

LOCATION	223 Castleridge Blvd. NE
HOURS	0500 to 2300 daily
TERRAIN	Rolling landscaped park with engineered hills and creek and playing field and courts
ACCESS	54 Ave. west of Castleridge Blvd. NE
	Castleridge Blvd. north of 54 Ave. NE
ACTIVITIES	Walking, cycling, picnicking, playground, baseball, soccer, tennis, playing, wading, tobogganing, ice skating, cross-country skiing

FACILITIES	Concession (seasonal)
	Washrooms and water fountains (seasonal)
	Playgrounds
	Outdoor skating rink
	Wading pool
	Spray pool
	Soccer pitch
	Baseball diamond
	Tennis courts
	Toboggan hill
	Engineered creek
	Kiddie train ride ($2)
	Grant MacEwan Grove and Gazebo
	Picnic tables and shelter
	Benches
DOGS	As posted
	On leash on pathways
	Not permitted within 20 metres of playgrounds and sports fields
INFORMATION	City of Calgary 3-1-1
	For booking and programming call 268-3800
TRANSIT	#21, #55, #71, #755

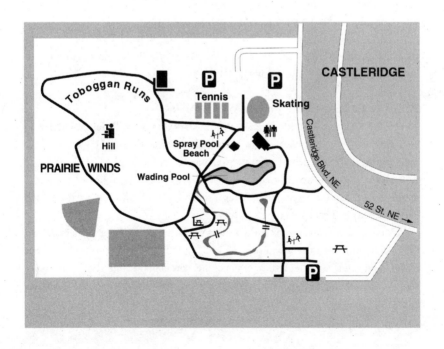

Northeast Calgary's first major park, Prairie Winds Park opened in 1990. This regional northeast park is the result of a long, hard political fight by local residents to bring green space to the communities of Rundle, Whitehorn, Falconridge, Castleridge, and Taradale. Once the battle was won, the City's Parks and Recreation department faced the formidable task of building a park on a piece of land that was flat and almost featureless.

In a feat of architectural landscaping, hills and a creek were sculpted onto the site. The summit of the highest hill, which rises about 30 metres, offers one of the most panoramic views in the city; the mountains butt up against the downtown core and flight pathways of the Calgary International Airport pass directly overhead. At dusk, this is one of the most thrilling places in town to watch planes land and lights sparkle. On a snowy winter's day, the hill is transformed into a toboggan run.

Another notable park feature is the gazebo in the heart of Grant MacEwan Grove, in the park's northeast corner. Ninety trees were planted in the grove to celebrate MacEwan's 90th birthday. MacEwan was born Aug. 12, 1902, and died June 15, 2000. In the years in between, he filled his life with teaching, writing and public service. A former dean, professor of animal husbandry, and director of the School of Agriculture at the University of Saskatchewan, MacEwan was a Calgary alderman from 1953 to 1958 and was elected to the Alberta Legislature in 1955. He became the mayor of Calgary in 1963 and was appointed lieutenant-governor of Alberta in 1965 (he held the office until 1974). MacEwan also wrote 49 books, many about agriculture and prairie history.

While Prairie Winds Park has yet to rival the longevity of MacEwan, its trees and grounds are rapidly maturing and its facilities have become among the most widely used and enjoyed in the city.

Pathway Description—Prairie Winds Park

Wide and easily travelled, Prairie Winds Park has a well-defined network of pathways. Travelling west from the south parking lot off 54 Ave. NE, the main pathway runs past the soccer pitch and skirts home plate of the baseball diamond. As it turns north it runs along the bottom of the largest of the park's engineered hills (Toboggan Hill). After a sharp jog east and then northeast, the pathway travels through MacEwan Grove.

After turning east, the pathway travels past a parks storage and maintenance yard and connects to the north parking lot. It winds and braids around the large playground south of the tennis courts, the spray pool, and the concession/washroom building. Several connecting pathways also wrap around the creek and picnic shelter area before the main pathways return to the south parking lot.

AIRPORT PATHWAY

Proof that if you build it people will come, the Airport Pathway is a seven kilometre long rambling thread of asphalt adjacent to the growing network of pathways in northeast Calgary. Although not directly linked to the network—the closest connection is across Barlow Tr. at 48 Ave. NE—the route is well travelled throughout much of the year.

The pathway originates near the Aerospace Museum just north of Barlow Tr. at McCall Way NE, and travels northeast along McCall Way for a few hundred metres. At Palmer Rd. NE, it jogs east to Barlow Tr. and then turns north to run along that road all the way to the main terminal of the Calgary International Airport. This is one of the few places in the world you can walk out of an airport terminal and onto a multi-use pathway.

Wide open, curvy and virtually runway-flat, the pathway is ideal for cycling, jogging, in-line skating, and plane watching. The views of the city, Nose Hill, mountains, airport, and surrounding prairie make this route more than just a "transportation corridor"—it is a destination unto itself. Small landscaped nodes provide places to absorb the surroundings and take a breather. Although the pathway can seldom be described as peaceful, it has a distinctive industrial beauty that is enjoyed by airport users and workers as well as people from across the city.

In 2005, a new section was completed along Barlow Tr. between Airport Rd. NE and Country Hills Blvd. NE.

Window seat—views from the Airport Pathway include fields, runways, downtown buildings, and not-so-distant mountains.

Don Skinner: A "Selfish" Pathway Builder

A long-time supporter of Calgary's parks and a volunteer with the Parks Foundation, Calgary, Don Skinner was instrumental in building the pathway along Barlow Tr. NE between McCall Way and the Calgary International Airport.

Skinner has always viewed the pathway as a "great way to enter Calgary" and an exciting vantage point for watching arriving and departing aircraft.

Working with the Calgary Airport Authority's then director of Community Development Myrna Dubé, and its then Board Chairman Tommy Walsh, Skinner convinced the federal, provincial, and municipal governments to fund pathway construction in the late 1990s.

Skinner's donation of $70,000 to the project generated substantial matching dollars and enthusiasm from the governments.

"I've used the pathways selfishly for years and still cover more than 50 kilometres in a day," says the developer and property manager about his motivation to create a new stretch of recreational pathway. "What I like about the whole concept of Calgary's pathways is that the whole city can take advantage of them."

Now well into his 70s, Skinner still "selfishly uses" the pathways regularly. And when he takes to the pathway he helped create, he, like many of its users, prefers to cover ground on in-line skates.

Don Skinner regularly uses the pathway he helped create at the Calgary International Airport.

ROTARY CHALLENGER PARK

ROTARY CHALLENGER PARK AT A GLANCE

LOCATION	3688 – 48 Ave. NE
HOURS	Vary seasonally
TERRAIN	Open rolling, landscaped space with plaza, play areas, and playing fields
ACCESS	Barlow Tr. and 48 Ave. NE

FACILITIES	**Barrier-free Alberta Centennial Centre**: baseball centre (including slo-pitch and softball), stadium seating, player and officials change rooms, concession (seasonal, independently operated), first aid centre, elevator, and home of Special Olympics Calgary
	Barrier-free Jim and Pearl Burns Centre: parks offices, Social Heart (foyer); dining, meeting and special event facilities; weight machines; home of Cerebral Palsy Association in Alberta
	Barrier-free Canada–Alberta Century Field House: eight-lane track; Gene Filipski Memorial Football Field, track and field facilities; stadium seating, washrooms, lockers rooms, first aid and soccer pitch
	Other barrier-free outdoor features: patio and plaza, picnic area, specialized playground, tennis courts, basketball courts Summer camps
DOGS	Not allowed on playing fields (except for working guide dogs)
INFORMATION	250-2707
TRANSIT	#55, #71, #428, #436
ADDITIONAL	Dedicated website: www.challengerpark.com
	Facilities rates (non-profit, corporate, and tournament) may apply

I still marvel at how Rotary Challenger Park was able to come to life. Although it bears the name and undeniable "stamp" of several local Rotary International clubs, the park really owes its existence to Myrna Dubé of the Calgary Airport Authority.

Dubé—whom I worked with on this project and many others—headed up the majority of the park's fundraising activities and government relations. She worked with Calgary's and Airdrie's Rotary Clubs and countless donors to raise several million dollars (more than $8 million in all) of additional funding from the Government of Canada, the Province of Alberta, and the City of Calgary. The $14-million park is located on Calgary Airport Authority land near McKnight Blvd. and 36 St. NE and is also a Parks Foundation, Calgary, project.

An official Alberta Centennial project, Rotary Challenger was designed and constructed to meet the needs of people of any ability. The park is particularly geared to wheelchair users, people with visual and cognitive impairments, and/or with limited mobility. It includes baseball diamonds and a baseball complex, tennis and basketball courts, an eight-lane track, and the Jim and Pearl Burns Sr. Centre.

"I have long been a supporter of the Rotary Club's many good works, but I have to admit that Challenger Park is one of my favourite Rotary projects," said the Honourable Norman (Normie) L. Kwong, Lieutenant Governor of Alberta at the drizzly park opening in September 2005. "As an advocate of fitness and healthy lifestyles, it's wonderful to see this terrific facility, which will provide disabled Albertans with a safe environment for sporting activities."

The park's executive director, Jim Zackowski, describes this special park as "a model of community inclusiveness where people with disabilities can play next to and with their able-bodied peers."

Putting wildlife in your sights
Quick tips for increasing your chances of seeing wildlife in Calgary.
- Know where to go. Habitat, wildlife, and opportunities for viewing differ by park and natural area.
- Know what you're looking for. Check out the Alberta Wildlife List Generator at www.weaselhead.org to learn where species thrive.
- Know when to go. Wildlife movement and habitat can vary with the seasons and the time of day. Generally, the best time to spot wildlife is in the early morning or at dusk. Many species are also active after heavy rainfall, winds, and snowfall.
- Know what to do. Quiet steps and calm movements are less likely to startle wildlife. Frequently stopping to look and listen for wildlife will also help.
- Know what to bring. A pair of binoculars, a camera, a field guide, a knowledgeable friend or guide. All can make wildlife viewing more enjoyable.

Starlings at Tom Campbell's Hill.

NORTHWEST PARKS

RILEY PARK

RILEY PARK AT A GLANCE

LOCATION	800 – 12 St. NW
HOURS	0500 to 2300
TERRAIN	Flat grasslands surrounding by mature trees and flower gardens; slopes upward at north end
ACCESS	10 St. north of 6 Ave. NW 8 Ave. and 12 St. NW
ACTIVITIES	Walking, picnicking, band concerts (summer), wading pool, cricket
FACILITIES	Picnic tables Washrooms and water fountains (seasonal) Benches Wading pool Concession (seasonal) Cricket pitches Band stage Large playground Flower gardens Senator Patrick Burns Memorial
DOGS	On leash
INFORMATION	City of Calgary 268-3800
TRANSIT	North Leg C-Train (Sunnyside Station) #4, #5, #9, #145, #405, #411, #419

One of the city's oldest and most charming parks, Riley Park is a place of simple but deliberate beauty located in Hillhurst below the Southern Alberta Institute of Technology Polytechnic and the Alberta College of Art and Design. The park's open fields are rimmed by graceful stands of trees, brilliantly coloured flower gardens and picnic tables and benches. The setting is relaxed and inviting with a hint of English tradition and formality, especially when the cricket pitches and concert band stage are in use. The park also has

A quite moment in between cricket matches at Riley Park.

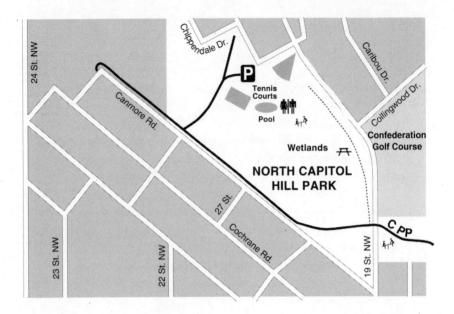

elements of pure fun such as a wading pool, a mainstay for Calgary families for
more than 40 years, and the large treed playground in the southwest corner.
There's no better place to take a picnic blanket and a bucket of fried chicken
and potato salad on a hot summer afternoon.

About six city blocks square, Riley Park is generally flat and easily travelled
by foot, cycle, and stroller. The northeast corner of the park, along the 10 St.
NW hill, is the Senator Patrick Burns Memorial Park.

Riley Park was once part of the 146,000-hectare Cochrane Ranch. In
1888, Thomas and Georgina Riley and their family of 10 children homesteaded
the land, and in 1909 following Thomas' death their land was left to the City
of Calgary.

Senator Patrick Burns Memorial Park
Senator Patrick Burns's name is dotted across the city, but on nothing quite as
genteel and pastoral as this flower and rock garden along the west side of the 10
St. NW hill (between about 8 Ave. and 13 Ave.).

A series of narrow brick and flagstone walkways meanders through
fastidiously tended flower displays. At the base of the gardens is the marigold
symbol Burns used as a brand on thousands of cattle in his ranching empire.

The gardens were constructed in the 1950s with more than 20,000 pieces
of flagstone from the senator's demolished mansion, which once stood near the
Colonel Belcher Hospital along 4 St. SW.

NORTH CAPITOL HILL PARK

LOCATION	19 St. and Canmore Rd. NW
HOURS	0500 to 2300
TERRAIN	North-facing slope overlooking wetlands and gentle treed knolls
ACCESS	19 St. and Canmore Rd. NW
	19 St. and Collingwood Dr. NW
	Chippendale Dr. west of 19 St. NW
	27 St. and Canmore Rd. NW
	Pathway from Confederation Park
ACTIVITIES	Walking, cycling, birdwatching, tennis, wading pool, picnics
FACILITIES	Picnic tables
	Washrooms and water fountains (seasonal)
	Benches
	Wading pool
	Tennis courts
	Playground
DOGS	On leash on pathways
	Not permitted within 20 metres of playground
INFORMATION	City of Calgary 268-3800
TRANSIT	#407, #449

North Capitol Hill Park is a quiet, well-treed park in northwest Calgary linked to the Confederation Park Municipal Golf Course and Confederation Park.

Thick groves of trees grow along the north-facing slopes of the park, providing a cool escape in summer and, in years of good snowfall, cross-country ski trails in the winter. Several foot trails criss-cross the park, weaving in and out of the park's lush stands of trees. A forested knoll is scattered with picnic tables, and the adjacent wetlands are thick with bulrushes and willows. North of the knoll, the park flattens, creating the setting for three tennis courts, a playground, a parking lot, and indoor washrooms.

Pathway Description—North Capitol Hill Park

An on road cycling route at the west end of Cochrane Rd. NW becomes a pathway through North Capitol Hill Park. A pathway runs atop the park's woodlands; at 28 Ave. NW, a feeder pathway linked to a number of foot trails branches north down a gently sloping hill to the park's tennis courts, playground, and washrooms.

The park's main pathway runs east along Canmore Rd. NW; near 27 Ave.

NW, it steers northeast, gradually dropping into an open field and marshy area. After cutting through the field, it quickly reaches and crosses 19 St. NW to run on the south side of Confederation Golf Course.

CONFEDERATION PARK

CONFEDERATION PARK AT A GLANCE

LOCATION	30 Ave. and 10 St. NW
	24 Ave. and 14 St. NW
HOURS	0500 to 2300
TERRAIN	Mature stands of native and introduced trees and shrubs in a coulee
ACCESS	30 Ave. and 6 St. NW
	30 Ave. and 10 St. NW
	24 Ave. and 14 St. NW
	14 St. and Roselawn Dr. NW
	9 St. north of 27 Ave. NW
	Pathway from Queen's Park Cemetery
	Pathway from North Capitol Hill
ACTIVITIES	Walking, cycling, golf, tennis, baseball, picnicking, tobogganing, cross-country skiing, orienteering, birdwatching, Christmas light viewing
FACILITIES	Picnic tables
	Washrooms (open year-round in park office)
	Benches
	Confederation Park Municipal Golf Course (3204 Collingwood Dr. NW)
	Tennis courts
	Baseball diamonds
	Orienteering track
	Playground
	Lions Club Festival of Lights
	Confederation Park Senior Citizens' Centre (2212 – 13 St. NW)
DOGS	On leash
INFORMATION	City of Calgary 268-3830
	Alberta Orienteering Association (for maps) 453-8577
	Confederation Park Municipal Golf Course (tee times) 221-3510
	Confederation Park Senior Citizens' Centre 289-4780
TRANSIT	#4, #5, #89, #145, #414

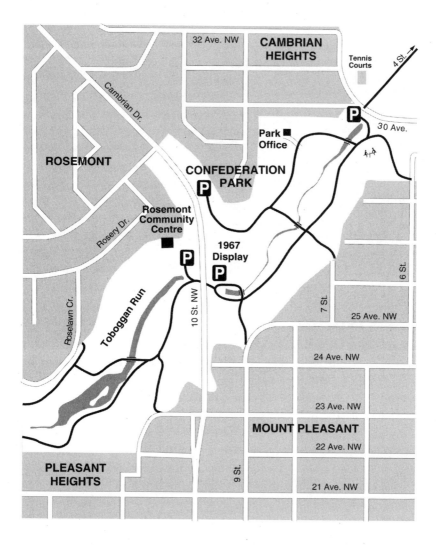

As the name suggests, Confederation Park commemorates the birth of Canada as a country. The park opened in 1967, the year of Canada's centennial.

A testament to what was dubbed at the time "people participation," countless people, clubs, associations, and community groups helped build Confederation Park in the 1960s under the banner of the Ravine Park Society.

Originally a natural prairie coulee, over the past 35 years or so the park has matured into a gracious urban park. It evolved substantially in 2005 and 2006 with the restoration of wetlands in the coulee bottom. The City of Calgary's Parks and Wastewater departments worked with the community of Rosemont to restore the terrain around a small creek that runs through the park as well as a

A touch of white—over the past 35 years Confederation Park
has matured into a gracious urban area.

pond created during initial construction. The wetlands will greatly improve the
quality of water that flows through the park and eventually into Nose Creek.

Used as enthusiastically—and almost as much—during winter as in the
summer, the park's north-facing slopes and coulee floor hold snow well,
much to the enjoyment of cross-country skiers and tobogganers. When snow
conditions allow, cross-country ski trails are groomed in the park.

Another wintertime ritual at Confederation Park is the Lions Club Festival
of Lights at the east end of Confederation Golf Park Municipal Course (24 Ave.
and 14 St. NW). Some 75,000 lights are turned on for nightly viewing every
holiday season, usually from mid-December to the first week of January, making
this the city's largest free Christmas light display.

Confederation Park Senior Citizens' Centre

Formed more than 30 years ago, the Confederation Park Senior Citizens'
Centre is one of the most active and engaged clubs of its kind in Calgary.

More than 1,500 seniors (over the age of 55) belong to the club, including
the 400 volunteers who organize and stage club functions. The club offers
drop-in activities such as quilting, floor hockey, whist, bridge, crib, and dancing.
Weekly dances are held every Saturday and every season features a special
dinner, exhibit, or outing.

The centre is open every day and most evenings; membership is $20 a year.

Located at 2212 – 13 St. NW; for further information, call 289-4780 or
visit http://members.shaw.ca/confedparksrcentre.

Pathway Description—Confederation Park

From 19 St. NW near Canmore Rd. NW, the Confederation Park pathway runs along the south side of Confederation Park Municipal Golf Course. As the pathway winds east, it climbs, drops, and turns between the golf course and a City maintenance yard. At 14 St. NW, the pathway drops into a tunnel under the road, emerging on the east side into Confederation Park.

Through the park, the pathway is often twinned, with routes on either side of the watercourse and numerous connections into the surrounding communities of Rosemont, Cambrian Heights, North Mount Pleasant, Pleasant Heights, and Mount Pleasant.

The coulee walls rise as the pathway continues east, and the park's best toboggan runs flank 10 St. NW. The pathway crosses 10 St. NW by another tunnel and its eastbound route continues past a Confederation display to the north. Past the park's east parking lot, the pathway crosses 30 Ave. and 6 St. NW, and turns northeast through Queen's Park Cemetery to 40 Ave. and 4 St. NW.

Also, a regional pathway runs along 24 Ave. NW to 14 St. NW and north from 24 Ave. NW along 14 St. SW.

UNIVERSITY OF CALGARY

UNIVERSITY OF CALGARY AT A GLANCE

LOCATION	2500 University Dr. NW
HOURS	24/7
TERRAIN	Rolling park-like campus with extensive building and development; West Campus at end of 24 Ave. NW has open grasslands overlooking Bow River Valley
MAIN ACCESS	24 Ave. and University Dr. NW
	24 Ave. and University Gate. NW
	32 Ave. and Campus Dr. NW
	32 Ave. and Collegiate Blvd. NW
ACTIVITIES	Walking, hiking, cycling, dog walking (West Campus), sports, recreation, arts, and culture
FACILITIES	MacEwan Hall Student Centre
	Olympic Oval
	Playing fields
	Rozsa Centre
	Nickle Arts Museum
DOGS	On leash on Main Campus
INFORMATION	www.ucalgary.ca, click on News/Events

North Leg C-Train (University Station)
#9, #19, #20, #37, #43, #72, #73, #119, #137, #810

The University of Calgary campus covers 123 hectares of land. Campus life features an endless array of activities, sights, and events throughout the year, including sports, entertainment, arts, debates, guest speakers, and, of course, the pursuit of knowledge.

Easily reached by major roads such as Crowchild Tr., Shaganappi Tr., and 24 and 32 Ave., the campus is criss-crossed with walking and cycling routes. With its wide sidewalks, mature trees, and rolling lawns, the university is like a park with classrooms.

You'll find a complete self-guided walking tour posted on the University of Calgary's website (www.ucalgary.ca). Simply search for "walking tour." Aimed at new students, it's nonetheless a great way to get acquainted with the campus. The 90-minute tour starts at MacKimmie Library (the largest of the U of C's on-campus libraries and home to nearly seven million books, journals, air photos, and other materials), and ends at the Rozsa Centre (a fine arts hall).

For a real insider's guide to campus sites and legends, see "A Conversation with Campus Culture Walking Tour" (also posted on the University's website), which highlights "eight points of 'interest' where campus culture can be seen." Points of interest include Leon the Frog (which has supposedly lived in a Social Sciences Building for a couple of decades or more), The Rock (a once holy university icon that's now a graffiti-emblazoned sounding board) and the myth of Bob Boston (rumour has it if you rub his face three times and simply answer C on any multiple-choice exam, you will be right 25 per cent of the time). For food, refreshments, games, and the campus bookstore, check out Mac Hall (the MacEwan Hall Student Centre) in the middle of the campus.

University of Calgary Outdoor Centre

The University of Calgary's Outdoor Centre in the Kinesiology Complex has it all—from hiking to mountaineering, canoeing to sea kayaking, bike repair clinics to avalanche awareness programs. Expert guides and a comprehensive rental program, combined with its prime location near the Rockies, make it one of the best outdoor programs in North America.

Focused on introducing people to outdoor activities, the centre offers courses for all kinds of skiing, hiking, climbing, mountaineering, ice-climbing, kayaking, and canoeing, as well as safety and first aid courses for wilderness survival. All activities and programs are open to the public. For information, call 220-5038 or visit camprec@ucalgary.ca.

Peregrine Falcons

Peregrine falcons are striking birds of prey occasionally spotted on the prairies. In Calgary, they are most often seen at the University of Calgary's Craigie Hall and the Telus Building in downtown Calgary. (Oddly, falcons also nest on the Telus Building in Edmonton.)

These birds are sparse housekeepers: they use no nesting materials and lay their eggs in holes or recesses. Their affinity for office towers stems from their usual nesting sites of crevices and ledges on cliffs and contributes to a high rate of fledgling mortality—some chicks do not survive their inaugural flights.

Peregrine falcons have distinctive black hoods over their faces, which accent their large brown eyes. Their sharply hooked beaks rip into their prey, usually caught in mid-flight with powerful talons. Falcons have narrow wings and a streamlined body. The species flies to South America for winters.

Although now outdated, the University of Calgary maintains a peregrine website at www.ucalgary.ca/~tull/falcon/.

Peregrine falcon.

KEN RICHARDSON

NOSE HILL PARK

NOSE HILL PARK AT A GLANCE

LOCATION	North of John Laurie Blvd. and south of MacEwan Glen Dr. NW between 14 St. and Shaganappi Dr.
HOURS	0500 to 2300
TERRAIN	Large prairie plateau with native, non-native, and disturbed grasslands at summit; surrounding slopes are a mix of grasslands, ravines, shrubs, and aspen woods
ACCESS	Calgary Winter Club (14 St. north of John Laurie Blvd. NW)
	John Laurie Blvd. and Brisebois Dr. NW (pedestrian overpass)
	Shaganappi Tr. and Edgemont Blvd. NW (barrier-free pathway trailhead)
	MacEwan Glen Dr. west of 14 St. NW
	14 St. and Berkley Gate NW
	14 St. south of Berkley Gate NW (pedestrian underpass)
	14 St. and 64 Ave. NW
	14 St. and Norfolk Way NW (pedestrian underpass)
	14 St. and Quarry Road

ACTIVITIES	Walking, hiking, cycling, mountain biking, dog walking, birdwatching, sightseeing, wildlife viewing, orienteering
FACILITIES	Washrooms (seasonal at Shaganappi Tr. and Edgemont Blvd. NW) Picnic tables and benches
DOGS	As posted On leash as designated
INFORMATION	City of Calgary 268-3830 Natural Areas Adopt-a-Park Program 221-4668 Alberta Orienteering Association (for maps) 453-8577
TRANSIT	#64, #89, #449, #812

From a distance it looks like a big, bald hill on the prairies. At more than 11 kilometres square (1,127 hectares), Nose Hill Park is undeniably large. But it is far from bald. One of the defining geographical features of Calgary, Nose Hill Park is covered in prairie grasses, dotted with stands of aspen, wrinkled with valleys and ravines, scoured by westerly winds, and travelled by thousands of people every day.

Like many features on the prairies, Nose Hill's attractions are—to the unappreciative eye—subtle, but they warrant more than a passing glance. It's easy to overlook a delicate blooming crocus, a fleeting hawk, or a centuries-old tipi ring. These must be sought.

End of your nose—downtown Calgary appears to hover on the tip of Nose Hill.

Nose Hill Park also has some very obvious features, none more so than its views of downtown Calgary, the Calgary International Airport, the Rocky Mountains, Nose Creek Valley, and Bow River Valley. About ten per cent of the park's visitors never even leave their cars, preferring to stay inside sipping a coffee and/or munching a burger while absorbing the sights.

An environmental treasure and the largest municipal park in Canada, Nose Hill Park has seven distinct areas. Clockwise from the north, they are: Aspen Grove, Porcupine Valley, Rubbing Stone Hill, Mule Deer Plateau, Wintering Hill, Many Owls Valley, and Meadowlark Prairie. These areas are a mix of natural, naturalized, and disturbed parkland and grassland with dozens of species of native vegetation, birds, and mammals.

Social climber—few can resist scrambling on the glacial erratic at Nose Hill.

Discovering Nose Hill Park is an admirable undertaking. For all its vastness the park has very few formal pathways. Countless foot trails, however, weave and wander across the park. The trails provide some direction and endless variety, but their proliferation has scarred the hill. The City of Calgary has extensive restoration plans for the park. Its 247-page Nose Hill Trails and Pathways Plan addresses "declining park health due to trail proliferation, habitat deterioration, and wildlife disturbance; increasing volume and diversity of park users; limited public accessibility, and lack of a user-friendly trail and pathway network."

Expect to see a number of changes at Nose Hill Park in coming years: some trails will be paved, some gravelled, and others closed. Work will also include parking lot upgrades, improved signs, and vegetation restoration. Dog and mountain bike use could also change, and responsible park use and stewardship will be promoted to park visitors of every kind.

Nose Hill Park is a grand place where solitudes collide: the commitment of environmentalists is pitted against the pressures of urban growth; dog owners and their pets often conflict with wildlife and other park users; mountain bikers raise the ire of hikers (and vice versa); and the open prairies contrast with crowded city streets. These encounters and variances are sometimes hotly contested, but they serve only to emphasize the park's diversity and its users' passions.

Miraculously, through all of this, Nose Hill Park endures.

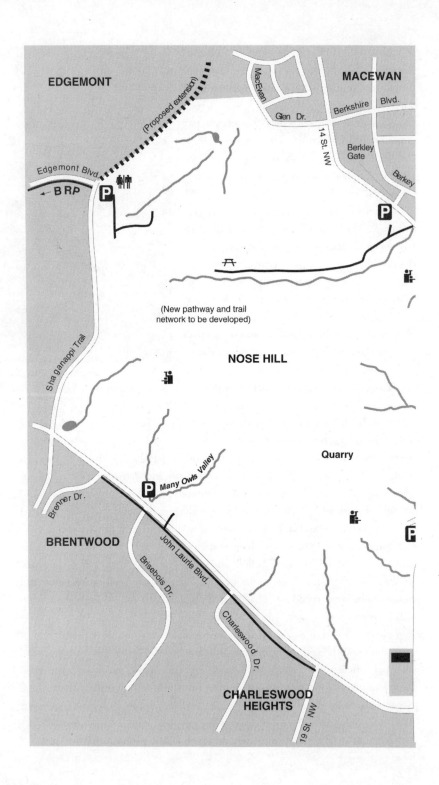

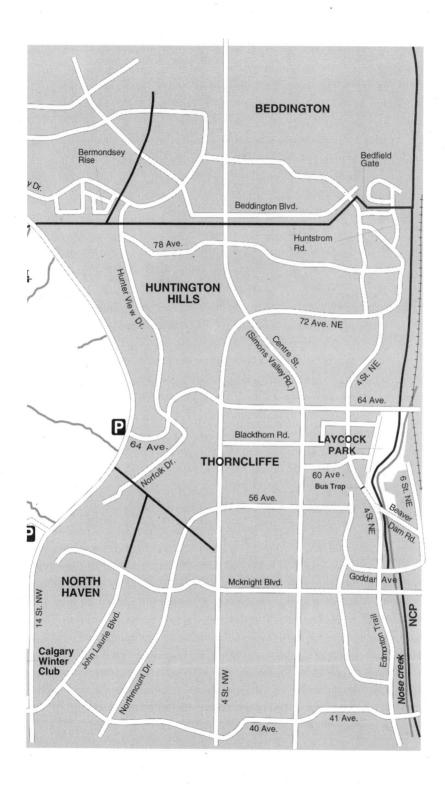

Where the prairie meets the sky—grass and clouds collide at Nose Hill.

The Naming of Nose Hill

Three stories exist on the naming of Nose Hill. The first claims a woman's nose was cut off following a drunken melee by a group of Indians. The second story says the name came from the Blackfoot custom of cutting off the noses of women who were unfaithful to serve as a reminder to other women. The punishment was enforced until the 1900s and then outlawed. The third story is the most accepted—and least offensive—and says the Blackfoot Indians thought the hill closely resembled the nose of the chief. Today, the city of Calgary is a flowing beard beneath that nose.

History Carved Onto a Hill

When the last Ice Age retreated about 15,000 years ago, what is now Calgary sat in a glacial lake. Five thousand years later, the lake drained leaving behind a number of features: the Bow River, the Elbow River, Broadcast Hill, and Nose Hill.

Buffalo found Nose Hill ideal for their needs. The windswept grasslands remained clear of snow when everything else would be buried. In turn, Native tribes were attracted to the hill where they found a year-round source of buffalo meat. Numerous tipi rings—most located in Wintering Hill—still exist, and archaeological studies have documented a kill site, campsite, and isolated finds on the hill. Nose Hill also has a dramatic glacial erratic on its east side, rubbed smooth over the centuries by bison scratching their dry, dusty coats.

Like a number of glacial erratics in Calgary, notably those at West Nose

Calgary's skyline from Nose Hill Park around 1975.
GLENBOW MUSEUM ARCHIVES

Creek Park and Fish Creek Provincial Park, this large quartzite boulder was dragged across the prairies from Mount Edith Cavell near Jasper about 17,000 years ago.

Much later in history, two early European explorers visited Nose Hill from the other direction (east). In the 1790s, Peter Fidler travelled to Nose Creek during a balmy chinook. David Thompson referred to the hill in a visit through the area in 1800 while he was working for the North West Company.

Eight decades later, with the arrival of European settlers and the demise of the buffalo, Nose Hill found a new purpose for cattle grazing. Calgary's meat packing millionaire Pat Burns bought two sections of land on the hill. In the 1960s the land was mined for gravel; two abandoned gravel pits sit on the east side of Nose Hill.

In 1973, the Calgary Planning Commission recommended that 1,659 hectares of Nose Hill "be preserved as natural prairie parkland and that all urban development be restricted." A series of debates followed about the location and size of the park, and the park size was later reduced.

At the time, critics argued the park was too removed from Calgary, as it was adjacent to only a handful of communities. Today the park is completely surrounded by development and visited in the summer by 5,000 people a day.

Pathway Descriptions—Nose Hill Park

Nose Hill Park's pathways and trails are expected to change dramatically in coming years. For pathway updates and additions, visit the City of Calgary website at www.calgary.ca and follow links from City Living to Nose Hill Park.

Currently, the trail heads to the park's established paved/hard-surfaced pathways are at:

- Edgemont Dr. and Shaganappi Tr. NW—this site has the park's only washroom, a parking lot, and a 1.7 kilometre, barrier-free interpretive pathway.

- John Laurie Blvd. east of Brisebois Dr. NW—a new barrier-free pedestrian overpass provides a safe entrance to Many Owls Valley and links to the regional pathway on the south side of John Laurie Blvd. NW. The pathway in Many Owls Valley winds north into the park for just a few hundred metres before branching into a number of foot trails. One of the most established routes leads to one of the two old gravel pits in the park.

- 14 St. south of Berkley Gate NW—a pedestrian underpass at 14 St. NW offers safe passage into the park and connects to a nearby parking lot off Berkley Gate NW. The pathway climbs west to the summit of Nose Hill through Porcupine Valley. This is one of the park's oldest and most travelled routes, overlooking Porcupine Valley, a lush ravine thick with aspens, and flanked by rough fescue grasslands. Travellers can expect a rather demanding ascent, exceptional views, and abundant wildlife. The pathway is overgrown in many sections and ends about two-thirds of the way across the park. East of 14 St. NW, the pathway runs through the communities of Huntington Hills and Beddington, linking with the Nose Creek Pathway near Deerfoot Tr. and Beddington Tr. NE.

CANADA OLYMPIC PARK

CANADA OLYMPIC PARK AT A GLANCE

LOCATION	88 Olympic Park Rd. NW
HOURS	Vary through the year
TERRAIN	North-facing ski slope with natural vegetation in ravines and along eastern and western edges (Paskapoo Slopes)
ACCESS	85 St. and Canada Olympic Dr. SW
	Canada Olympic Dr./Bowfort Rd. and Trans-Canada Hwy NW
	Pathway from 83 St. NW
ACTIVITIES	Alpine skiing, snowboarding, cross-country skiing, cycling, mountain biking, bobsled, luge, ski jumping, elite training, summer camps, ski lessons, special events, Olympic history tours, Sunday Brunch, sightseeing
FACILITIES	Day lodge (equipment rentals, concession, lounge, shop)
	Olympic Hall of Fame
	Ski and snowboard hill
	Cross-country ski track
	Ski jumps
	Bobsled/luge track
	Training facilities
	Mountain bike course
	Naturbahn Teahouse
	Eurobungee trampoline
	Climbing wall
DOGS	No dogs
INFORMATION	Call 247-5452 or visit www.canadaolympicpark.ca
TRANSIT	#408

Olympic tradition all but dictates that one host city must outdo the last host city, thus Olympic Park was one of the most ambitious venues ever built for a Winter Olympic Games.

Until Calgary was named the host city of the 1988 Winter Games, Canadian Olympic Park (COP) was called Paskapoo Ski Hill. The small but thriving ski school tutored thousands of Calgary skiers and was affectionately and jokingly nicknamed "Poo Glacier."

A $72 million facelift transformed COP into a world-class sports facility, complete with refrigerated and lit bobsled/luge track; a practice push track; 15, 30, 50, 70 and 90 metre ski jumps; a renovated day lodge; an Olympic Hall of Fame; an Olympic Training Centre; an Olympic Visitors Centre; an

Snow wonder: Canada Olympic Park is Calgary's winter sports headquarters.
DAVID BUSTON, CODA

equipment warehouse; a naturbahn luge track; and a teahouse.

These facilities were once the very best of their kind and are still world-class. Canadian Olympic Park's operator, the Canada Olympic Development Association, has slated another major facelift for them. Meanwhile, the park continues to attract tens of thousands of grassroots athletes and recreational users every year. Among the most popular attractions at COP are the ski hill, the cross-country ski track, the mountain bike course—the only such course in Calgary accessible via a quad chair lift—and the minigolf course. As well, the park hosts countless special and community events of all description throughout the year.

TWELVE MILE COULEE

TWELVE MILE COULEE AT A GLANCE

LOCATION	West of Stoney Tr. between Tuscany Blvd. and Nose Hill Dr. NW
HOURS	0500 to 2300 daily
TERRAIN	Narrow, heavily vegetated stream valley with grassy escarpments
ACCESS	Tuscany Blvd. and Tuscany Mews NW
	Tuscany Ravine NW
	Tuscany Mews NW
	Stoney Tr. and Nose Hill Dr. NW
	Regional pathway from Scenic Acres and Bow River
ACTIVITIES	Walking, hiking, cross-country running, mountain biking, birdwatching, wildlife viewing, picnicking, sightseeing

FACILITIES	Benches
	Viewpoints
DOGS	On leash on pathway and in ravine
INFORMATION	Adopt-a-Park Program 268-3830
TRANSIT	#130, #421

This rich, compact valley was once a buffalo hunting ground. Today, it is poised to become Calgary's newest natural environment park. Currently, the section of Twelve Mile Coulee adjacent to Stoney Tr. NW is part of a provincial right-of-way, but it is also on the City of Calgary's list of planned parks and a management plan for the area is being drafted.

Meanwhile, local residents in Tuscany and Scenic Acres—as well as park users from across the city—have embraced Twelve Mile Coulee. The paved pathway running along the western shoulder of the valley links to an impressive array of local pathways in the hill communities and all are faithfully travelled by walkers, hikers, cyclists, and strollers year-round. Mountain bikers particularly adore and recommend this area. The moist valley floor is rich with wildlife and wetlands. The small stream that winds through Twelve Mile Coulee is seldom wider than a hop, skip, and a jump. This is a fine place for puddle jumping, although increased use of the valley in recent years has led to considerable creek bed damage.

Officially, no designated trails exist in the valley floor. Unofficially, you can find trails that have been travelled by wildlife, cattle, hunters, ranchers, and recreational users for centuries. Archaeological studies have unearthed a variety of artifacts from native people. Further archaeological and environmental studies are planned to determine Twelve Mile Coulee's role and importance.

As the valley opens to the south, the surrounding hillsides make a transition from aspen and spruce forests to grasslands, and every undulating peak offers a stop-in-your-tracks view of the Bow River Valley, the Keith CPR yards, Valley View Golf Course, Canada Olympic Park, the Rocky Mountains and, surprisingly, downtown Calgary.

For a further taste of the area's beauty and diversity, see the winning entries of the City of Calgary's Twelve Mile Coulee photo contest at www.calgary.ca (type "twelve mile" in search).

Hidden valley—Twelve Mile Coulee is poised to become Calgary's newest natural environment park.

SOUTHEAST PARKS

WESTERN IRRIGATION DISTRICT (WID) CANAL PATHWAY

WID CANAL PATHWAY AT A GLANCE

LOCATION	Headworks: Across from Pearce Estate
HOURS	24/7
TERRAIN	Typically open and flat with some forested areas and escarpments
ACCESS	Below Max Bell Arena south of Memorial Dr. and Barlow Tr. SE
	17 Ave. and Deerfoot Tr.
	Bow Waters Canoe Club at 17 Ave. and 28 St. SE
	Access road to Inglewood Golf and Curling Club
	50 Ave. SE and WID Canal
	52 St. SE and WID Canal
	South end of Chestermere Lake
	Bow River Pathway near headworks
ACTIVITIES	Walking, hiking, cycling, bird and wildlife watching, dog walking, cross-country skiing, picnicking
FACILITIES	Interpretive display at headworks
	Picnic tables
	Benches
DOGS	On leash
INFORMATION	Western Irrigation District 934-3542
	City of Calgary 3-1-1
TRANSIT	Northeast C-Train Barlow/Max Bell Station
	# 23, #24, #72

One of the longest, but perhaps least travelled, pathways in Calgary is the Western Irrigation District (WID) Canal Pathway in the city's southeast. Running from the WID headworks to Chestermere Lake well east of the city limits, the pathway covers 26 kilometres one way.

In her 2000 report to the Alberta Trailnet Society, "Two Successful Rural Trails," Linda Strong-Watson describes the canal's origins:

"In 1903, the Canadian Pacific Railway received its land grant (an area totalling 3 million acres) in the heart of the Palliser Triangle, the area east and south of Calgary bounded by the Bow and Red Deer Rivers. In return the CPR agreed to develop an irrigation system to bring water to this fertile but arid area."

When completed in 1906, the canal was one of the world's largest water diversions—second only to the Nile River. Although it appears to meander lazily in its western section, the canal is a hard-working waterway that serves some

38,445 hectares of farmland between Calgary and Cluny. It also collects the majority of stormwater runoff for northeast Calgary and the Village of Chestermere Lake.

Throughout much of its history, the canal has only been used sporadically for recreation. The exception, however, is along the shores of Reservoir No. 1, Chestermere Lake, where urban and rural dwellers have boated, swam, fished, and picnicked for a century.

Within Calgary city limits, the WID Canal Pathway is often gritty and noisy, running adjacent to Deerfoot Tr. and then along the CPR's Ogden Shops and the industrial districts of Foothills and South Foothills.

The pathway and canal are not always a serene retreat, but they offer a number of dramatic scenic views, wildlife viewing areas, and an award-winning interpretive display (near the canal's headworks).

Low head room—bridge crossings on the WID can present a vertical challenge.

From the headworks near Max Bell Arena, the paved WID Canal pathway runs most often along the seasonal waterway's east–north shore. The gravelled pathway along much of the canal's opposite (west–south) bank doubles as a maintenance access road.

Water from the Bow River is diverted into the canal and Chestermere Lake from May until September annually and the waterways are drained every fall until the following spring.

Pathway Description—WID Canal

The Irrigation Canal Pathway begins at the headworks of the Western Irrigation District Canal across from Pearce Estate and quickly passes a pedestrian bridge over Deerfoot Tr. SE.

Downstream of the pedestrian bridge the pathway branches, with one branch climbing to the nearby communities of Albert Park and Radisson Heights, the intersection of Memorial Dr. and Barlow Tr. NE, the Barlow/Max Bell C-Train station, and the Max Bell Arena.

The WID pathway winds through a number of picnic sites above the canal, offering well-deserved resting spots with good views of downtown, the Bow River Valley, and the Calgary Zoo.

Shortly after, the pathway connects to 17 Ave. SE, proceeding south past the Bow Waters Canoe Club and below Slater Park.

With a paddle—school students learn the basics of canoeing on the WID Canal at the Bow Water Canoe Club.

About 1.3 kilometres south, the pathway goes under Deerfoot Tr. SE; extremely low headroom and a tight winding route force most cyclists to dismount. After crossing the access road to the Inglewood Golf and Curling Club, the pathway enters its noisiest section, an isolated stretch adjacent to Deerfoot Tr. SE.

At Bonnybrook Bridge, the pathway passes once again under Deerfoot Tr. SE and travels east, then south, around the CPR Ogden Shop to 50 Ave. SE and through the light industrial areas of Foothills and South Foothills. This section is not often busy, but it is used regularly.

Past the city limits at 85 St. SE, the pathway and canal travel through pastures, grain fields, and acreages for more than a dozen kilometres. The surrounding land is privately owned and pathway users must respect landowners' property, livestock, and crops.

The route is typically open, straightforward and flat, although the wind can make it feel like you're going uphill, whether you're travelling upstream or downstream. The pathway ends 26 kilometres after it began at the south end of Chestermere Lake.

READER ROCK GARDENS

READER ROCK GARDENS AT A GLANCE

LOCATION	Southeast corner of Macleod Tr. and 25 Ave. SE
HOURS	Park 0500 to 2300 daily
	Reader House and Café, spring to end of December, hours to be announced
TERRAIN	Steep, winding flagstone trails through a variety of forests and gardens with native, non-native, and rare plants overlooking Stampede Park and downtown Calgary
ACCESS	Macleod Tr. and 25 Ave. SE
	Through Union Cemetery
ACTIVITIES	Walking, picnicking, self-guided trails, interpretive displays, dining, picnics, educational programs (for school groups and adults), sightseeing, birdwatching

FACILITIES	Gardens: South Slopes, Nana's Gardens, High Rockery, West Slope, West Garden
	Reader House Café and interpretive centre (café open spring to end of December for lunch, afternoon tea, and dinner; picnic lunches also available)
	Picnic tables
	Indoor washrooms (open spring to end of December)
	Benches and gazebos
	Meeting and events facilities
	Numerous viewpoints
DOGS	Not allowed
INFORMATION	City of Calgary 3-1-1
	For booking and programming 221-4500
TRANSIT	South Leg C-Train (Erlton Station)
	#10, #30, #403, #433, #770, #772
ADDITIONAL	Monthly tours scheduled throughout 2006
	Past adult education programs include: Sketching Garden Flowers, How to Plan a Rock Garden, and Gardening for Birds and Butterflies. For current program offerings, call the City of Calgary at 268-3800

The King's Gardener

Ninety years ago, Calgary had few trees, even less shade, and scant idea how to get either.

Enter William Reader, a landscaper who in 1913 became the superintendent of Calgary's Parks department. For the next 29 years he coloured the city green. He created Central Park (now Memorial Park) as well as parks on St. George's, St. Patrick's, and St. Andrew's islands. But his greatest achievement was Reader Rock Gardens.

He painstakingly built the rock gardens on a sandy hill at the entrance to Union Cemetery. Over the years, he constructed an intricate and peaceful hillside garden using some of the rarest and finest rock and alpine plants he could find. And while he had a fondness for the plants of Western Canada and the Rockies, he also imported flora from around the world.

Calgarians and visitors alike, including the wife of the Governor General, Viscountess Byng of Vimy, who toured the gardens several times with Viscount Byng, delighted in Reader Rock Gardens. When the Byngs returned to England, rumours swirled that she tried to recruit Reader to tend her gardens across the Atlantic.

King's gardener—William Reader created a world-famous garden in Calgary in the early 1900s.

GLENBOW MUSEUM ARCHIVES

Early maturity Reader Rock
Gardens circa 1959.

GLENBOW MUSEUM ARCHIVES

Reader, however, was firmly rooted in Calgary. And he already worked for nobility: Reader planted a simple garden for Edward, Prince of Wales, at his ranch southwest of Calgary. (Edward, who would later abdicate his crown for Wallis Simpson, officially opened Reader Rock Gardens in the 1930s.)

The gardens enthralled Reader, perhaps because they were literally in his backyard. His home and the Parks department's main operations were both based at the cemetery.

When Reader died in January 1943, he was buried in Union Cemetery, only a stone's throw from the rock gardens he loved. W. Ingverson wrote this tribute to him in the Gardeners' Chronicle of England:

"Reader had to contend with a climate which dropped the thermometer to 40 degrees and 50 degrees below zero during the winter, often with little snow to protect plants. What courage that man must have had to continue in the face of continual disappointments! How often he must have had to start over again and what pride must have been his in later years as he surveyed the beauty he had created."

Once almost overgrown, the beauty of Reader Rock Gardens continues. Both Reader's home and the rock gardens have been lovingly and meticulously restored with support from Calgary Chapter of the North American Rock Garden Society, the Parks Foundation, Calgary, the City of Calgary, and Infrastructure Canada–Alberta Program. The gardens will feature self-guided tours of five different areas and the house will become a café, interpretive centre, and special events venue.

ELLISTON REGIONAL PARK

ELLISTON REGIONAL PARK AT A GLANCE

LOCATION	2020 – 60 St. SE
HOURS	0900 to 2200 daily
TERRAIN	Engineered hill and stormwater retention pond with maturing landscaped grasslands, trees, shrubs, and rose gardens
ACCESS	17 Ave. and 60 St. SE
ACTIVITIES	Walking, hiking, cycling, fitness, picnicking, birdwatching, tobogganing
FACILITIES	Lake Elliston (stormwater retention pond; park may close when pond fills)
	Picnic tables and shelters
	Benches
	Outdoor amphitheatre

	Interpretive displays
	Rose gardens
	Washrooms (year-round)
	Youth fitness equipment
DOGS	On leash on pathways
	Otherwise as posted
INFORMATION	Elliston Park 268-3830
	GlobalFest International Fireworks Competition
	www.globalfest.ca or 569-9679
TRANSIT	#45, #126

A testament to imagination and environmental reclamation, Elliston Park is right next to a city landfill. Some day, the landfill could even become part of the park, but for now Elliston Park is better known as the first BP BirthPlace Forest and the site of the annual and breathtaking GlobalFest International Fireworks Competition. It is also a prime birdwatching and recreational area, featuring fitness equipment designed especially for kids 10 to 15 years old.

With each passing year, this young park with its restored windmill becomes a little more known, a little more used, and a little more "grown in." The trees seem a little fuller and the rose gardens a little more colourful.

The park has two distinguishing landmarks: a 20 hectare stormwater retention pond (Elliston Lake, the largest stormwater lake in Calgary), and an

In bloom—roses are the most abundant bloom at Elliston Park.

engineered hill, the crest of which offers a 360 degree view of east Calgary and points beyond. The park's wide open spaces—which are numerous—give it a true prairie character: windswept, lush, and rolling.

Five generations of the Ellis family have lived in and around the park since Shepard S. Ellis, his wife, and their nine children left Ontario to homestead in the West in 1912. The park was named in 1995 after the family's many contributions to and activities in East Calgary, Conrich, and Chestermere Lake.

An environmental project initiated in 2000 by the Friends of Elliston Park Society and funded by the federal government has helped restore five hectares of the park back to native grassland/prairie habitat. Interpretive displays at the park's northwest corner highlight this habitat as well as how people through the ages have lived—and can continue to live—on and next to it. The displays also reflect how people have derived energy from land, primarily through wind power (hence the windmill) and other forms of alternative energy. A sundial, complete with instructions, lets park visitors test the reliability of the very first "clocks."

Elliston Lake

During heavy rain, up to 37,000 litres of water per second can pour into Lake Elliston, a stormwater retention pond that collects runoff from a 30 square kilometre area in southeast and northeast Calgary. Water levels can rise as much as 30 centimetres an hour and three metres in all.

Given the risk runoff can pose, the park may close during heavy rainfall. A siren warns park visitors to leave immediately.

Attractive to many kinds of birds and waterfowl, Elliston Lake is off limits to people and dogs. Park rules prohibit swimming, wading, sailing, fishing, and drinking lake/pond water.

Calgary has a growing number of stormwater retention ponds, which are used to hold stormwater runoff during heavy rainfall and reduce the burden on underground pipelines, water treatment plants, and local waterways.

VALLEYVIEW REGIONAL PARK

VALLEYVIEW REGIONAL PARK AT A GLANCE

LOCATION	28 St. and 30 Ave. SE
HOURS	0900 to 2300 daily
TERRAIN	Reclaimed field with athletic fields, playgrounds, and engineered wetlands; natural area across Barlow Tr. on bench overlooking Bow River Valley
ACCESS	28 St. and 30 Ave. SE
	28 St. and 32A Ave. SE
	Barlow Tr. SE between 30 Ave. and 34 Ave. SE
	Dovista Close SE
	Valleyview Park SE
ACTIVITIES	Walking, cycling, beach volleyball, soccer, baseball, picnicking, birdwatching, tobogganing
FACILITIES	Picnic tables and benches

12 beach volleyball courts (operated by Calgary Beach
Volleyball Association)
Baseball diamond
Two soccer pitches
Water park
Natural area
Engineered wetlands

DOGS On leash on pathways
Not allowed within 20 metres of playing fields and playgrounds
Otherwise as posted

INFORMATION 268-3830
Calgary Beach Volleyball Association info@cbva.ca

TRANSIT #26, #57

Long time Dover resident George Trotter is credited with rallying the community support needed to turn a once neglected flat field into a $5 million rolling park with a little bit of everything for everyone. The park has both "passive" and "active" features. Those features include a natural area on the west side of Barlow Tr.—named for Mary Dover, whose grandfather, Col. J.F. Macleod, named Calgary and whose father, A.E. Cross, was one of the Big Four founders of the Calgary Exhibition and Stampede.

The park opened in 2003, but its development is ongoing. In 2004, a group of volunteers and the City repaired the pathways at the south end of

Water ahead—wetlands at Valleyview Regional Park.

the park that link to the Valley View Senior Lodge, making the pathways safer and more enjoyable to use. In 2006, a water park opened. Valleyview Park has also sparked interest in the community of Dover and a number of residential building projects—including some affordable housing—are being constructed around and adjacent to this 13 hectare park, one of only a handful of regional parks in this part of the city.

Although easily reached from Deerfoot Tr. via 17 Ave. SE or Peigan Tr. SE, Valleyview Park is not overly crowded. In fact, it is a park waiting to be discovered—both by those living around it and those looking to discover the variety of Calgary's parks.

SOUTHWEST PARKS

CENTRAL MEMORIAL PARK

CENTRAL MEMORIAL PARK AT A GLANCE

LOCATION	1221 – 2 St. SW
HOURS	0500 to 2300 daily
TERRAIN	Formal gardens surrounded by mature shade trees; commemorative statues and cenotaph at west end, library at east end
ACCESS	12 Ave. between 2 St. and 4 St. SW
ACTIVITIES	Walking, strolling, Remembrance Day gatherings, library, picnicking
FACILITIES	Benches
	Washrooms (in library)
	Memorial Park Library
	Cenotaph
DOGS	On leash
INFORMATION	Park 268-3800, Library 221-2006
TRANSIT	#3, #6, #7, #13, #403, #433

Central Memorial Park is Calgary's oldest park and one of the most important open spaces in the Beltline. The Federal Government set aside the land for the Park in 1899 and by 1912 Central Memorial Park was a civic showplace. It has also been used as a holding ground for thousands of imported trees Calgarians could plant. At the turn of the century, spruce trees from Canmore cost 10 cents, maple trees from Manitoba sold for 15 cents and local cottonwoods (balsam poplars) commanded a price of 20 cents.

One of Calgary's earliest and most influential citizens, William Pearce, conceived the notion for the Beltline park and in 1899 he convinced the Dominion Government to donate a square of parkland to the city. By 1912, the park was considered a civic showcase and was home to Alberta's first public library. Park grounds were modelled after a formal Victorian garden and featured geometric pathways, elaborate garden beds, and rows of imported and native trees. At the west end, backing onto 4 St. SW and Patrick Burns's home, was a wooden bandstand styled after one in New York's Central Park.

When Calgary's Central Park was renamed Memorial Park in 1928, the old bandstand was torn down. By then, a statue of a mounted soldier already stood in the park to commemorate the local men who fought and died in the Boer War and a cenotaph was erected for those who had fallen in the first World War. Additional memorials followed the second World War.

Also in 1928, the park became the site of the city's benchmark elevation point designated by the Federal Geodetic Survey branch. A concrete column marked the "reference point for all precise levelling benchmarks in Calgary and vicinity." The survey indicated the benchmark as 1,048.41 metres or 3,439.66 feet above sea level.

Like the eye of a storm, Memorial Park is a calm centre in a flurry of change. Over the years, Burns's mansion was demolished to make way for the Colonel Belcher Hospital. More recently, the Colonel Belcher Hospital was demolished to make way for the Sheldon Chumir Health Centre. Traffic has thickened and the surrounding buildings have grown taller.

Memorial Park is also a Provincial Historic Resource and will become a Municipal Historic Resource.

Central Memorial Library

As Calgarians marched boldly into the 20th century, they were determined to bring culture to the city. An energetic group of women petitioned American philanthropist Andrew Carnegie to build a library in Calgary. Carnegie was perhaps the richest man of his time. In the early 1900s, he'd sold off his huge steel production holding for nearly half a billion dollars. Some of his vast fortune went to fund 2,800 public library buildings in North America, including the first public library in Alberta.

The Carnegie Foundation donated $80,000 toward the cost of the then $100,000 library. The decision to build the library at the east end of Central Park was made by a plebiscite in 1908. Prior to the library's opening in 1912, the city hired Alexander Calhoun to organize the library. Calhoun arrived in Calgary during a balmy chinook and said, "I strolled over to Central Park to find my future home well on the way to completion, Central Park was . . . an unsightly wilderness of sand and scrub."

Landscaping aside, the library was an instant hit. Within months of opening, more than 8,000 cardholders were borrowing just 5,000 books.

JAMES SHORT SQUARE

JAMES SHORT SQUARE AT A GLANCE

LOCATION	115 – 4 Ave. SW
HOURS	0500 to 2300 daily
TERRAIN	Formal gardens surrounded by mature trees in downtown core
ACTIVITIES	Walking, strolling, picnicking
FACILITIES	Benches
	+15 connections

	Playground
DOGS	On leash
INFORMATION	268-3800
TRANSIT	#2, #3, #19

In 1904, the James Short School was constructed in what today is the heart of the city. When the school was demolished decades later, the only thing salvaged was its cupola, which was moved to Prince's Island Park in the 1970s. The school site became a Greyhound bus station.

In more recent years, Greyhound moved its station to downtown's west end and the James Short School cupola was returned to its first home in 1990, newly named James Short Square. A new addition—one of the city's oldest tower clocks—was also built in 1904. Salvaged by the Parks Foundation, Calgary, from an antique store in 1990, the clock was lovingly restored by members of the Calgary Watch and Clock Collectors Association.

The clock's face remains hidden behind the cupola, but it chimes four times an hour. The clock has been wound by hand every week since 1991 by Parks Foundation, Calgary, volunteer Doug Sinclair, with assistance in more recent years from City of Calgary employees.

The cupola at the corner of 4 Ave. and Centre St. SW is the anchor to a very urban park. James Short Square is fashioned after the semi-formal garden of the Edwardian period. About a half city block in size, it is a relief to the rows of concrete and glass lining Calgary's core. It also links the SunLife Building and Petro-Canada Centre via the +15 walkway system.

The raised and enclosed walkway curves around the circle of trees in the centre of the park. A Chinese-style gateway at the northeast corner leads to Chinatown's busy streets. A series of bricks running along a grid throughout the park provides a checkerboard pattern among the trees and concrete walkways that is best viewed from high above in one of the surrounding buildings.

ROULEAUVILLE SQUARE

ROULEAUVILLE SQUARE AT A GLANCE

LOCATION	17 Ave. and 1 St. SW
HOURS	0500 to 2300 daily
ACCESS	17 Ave. and 1 St. SW
	19 Ave. and 1 St. SW
	Elbow River Pathway north of Lindsay Park
TERRAIN	Formal gardens surrounded by interpretive displays
ACTIVITIES	Walking, strolling, sitting, historical learning

FACILITIES	Benches
	Gardens
	Interpretive displays
DOGS	On leash
INFORMATION	268-3800
TRANSIT	#6, #7

In the 1990s, this half-acre site was a gravel parking lot in Victoria Crossing, west of Stampede Park and north of Lindsay Park. But nine decades before, it had been the heart of a thriving French Catholic community south of Calgary called Rouleauville.

Terry Hawitt, a parishioner of St. Mary's Church and a founding director of the Parks Foundation, Calgary, believed the small site could be transformed into a more suitable neighbour to the nearby St. Mary's parish—a way of remembering the contributions of the city's early French-speaking settlers.

Rouleauville Square was viewed as more than just a beautification project—it was going to be a catalyst to revitalize an area that had lost its connections with history, heritage, and people.

"The church warmed to the project when it was proposed some of the park's features extend across the street to the front entrance of the church," recalls Hawitt, who marked his 20th anniversary with the Parks Foundation, Calgary, in May 2005.

Although divided by 19 Ave. SW, today the park and church grounds are

Norm Harburn and Terry Hawitt of the Parks Foundation, Calgary, survey the pedestrian bridge that links Rouleauville Square and Lindsay Park.

decidedly united by their colourful gardens filled with marigolds (donated by the Marigold Foundation) and a number of other amenities.

Rouleauville Square features a sculpted brick monument at the 17 Ave. SW entrance and 12 interpretive panels highlighting the area's history. Flanked by St. Mary's Church and the old railway station that houses the Alberta Ballet, the pint-sized park marks the transition between downtown and uptown: to the north is the central core's skyline and to the south is an old railway bridge across the Elbow River that links to Mission and the Elbow River Pathway.

French Catholics in Calgary

The story of French Catholics in Calgary begins with Pére Leon Doucet, an Oblate priest credited with meeting Inspector Ephrem Brisebois and his troop of North West Mounted Police as they crossed the confluence of the Bow and Elbow rivers in 1875.

Brisebois was a native of Quebec and his troop included a number of Métis who drove the troop's oxen wagons. As Brisebois set out to construct the wooden fort that briefly bore his name—and later became Fort Calgary—he hired more "local" Métis, who had been living in the area as interpreters for missionaries and traders, to work as labourers. For a time, French was spoken as often as English in the fledgling town.

By 1882, a new chapter in French Catholic Calgary began with the arrival of Father Albert Lacombe. In his book *The Franco-Calgarians: French Language Leisure and Linguistic Life-style in an Anglophone City*, Robert A. Stebbins writes "Lacombe dreamed of founding the 'Quebec of the West' on the Elbow." He tried recruiting Quebecers to the remote Western outpost, although his efforts were never as successful as he had hoped. Nonetheless in 1883 and 1884, a number of *cheminots*, or Quebec labourers, arrived to help construct the Canadian Pacific Railroad.

A few professionals also arrived, among them Charles Borronée Rouleau, a judge who would become a Chief Justice, and, later, his brother Édouard Hector, a surgeon for the NWMP. By this time Lacombe had already convinced the government in Ottawa to set aside two sections of land south of Calgary for a francophone settlement and had established the Notre Dame de la Paix parish. The community and the parish thrived and were incorporated in 1889 as Rouleauville. That same year the parish was renamed St. Mary's. The church was rebuilt in 1955 and was designed by Maxwell Bates, an architect who became a well-known painter.

Rouleauville continued to grow but by 1893 the community's and the parish's predominant language was English. By the turn of the century, less than three per cent of Rouleauville's population was considered francophone. When Calgary annexed the area in 1907, the name Rouleauville disappeared from Calgary maps for almost 90 years until Rouleauville Square was constructed in 1996.

The French Catholic community, however, never completely died and was kept alive by families such as the Rouleaus and the St. Jean-Baptiste Society; brother Édouard Rouleau served as the first president of the international francophone association's Calgary chapter.

APPENDIX

Cleared Pathways

During winter—a season that occasionally descends on Calgary—the City of Calgary's Parks department clears ice and snow from about 95 kilometres of pathways on a priority basis. Cleared sections include:

- Bow River Pathway north shore, Montgomery Rd. NW to Nose Creek
- Regional pathway between Prince's Island (north) pedestrian bridge and Crescent Rd. NW
- Bow River Pathway south shore, Sovereign Cr. SW to St. Monica Ave. (Inglewood) SE
- Nose Creek Pathway and connectors between Bow River and 32 Ave. NE, including the Deerfoot Tr. NE pedestrian overpass at 25 Ave. NE
- Most of Confederation Park
- Elbow River Pathway from 4 St. SW to Fort Calgary
- Elbow River Pathway from Sandy Beach to Eagle Ridge
- Southland Natural Area
- Carburn Park
- South Glenmore Park from 37 St. SW to Heritage Park
- North Glenmore Park from 37 St. SW to Crowchild Tr. and 66 Ave. SW
- Marlborough Park NE
- West side of pathway along Nose Hill Dr. NW from Country Hills Blvd. to John Laurie Blvd.
- Parts of the Ranchlands regional pathway
- Vista Heights regional pathway from 25 Ave. NE pedestrian overpass to Barlow Tr. NE
- Regional pathways connecting to C-Train stations

For additional pathways information, visit www.calgary.ca/parks.

INDEX

"Diamond Dolly", 182
"F" Troop, 61
"Stutterin' May", 182
+15 Walkways, 183
2000 Millennium Committee, 5
33rd Engineer Squadron of the Canadian
    Armed Forces Reserves, 2
Aerospace Museum, 195
Airport Pathway, 4, 195
Al Azhar Shrine Centre, 14
Alberta College of Art & Design, 199
Alberta Foundation for Environmental
    Excellence, 85
Alberta Orienteering Association, 202, 208
Alberta Science Centre, 47
Alberta Sustainable Resource Development,
    73, 234
Alberta Trailnet Society, 218
Alkali buttercup, 27
Alpine skiing, 215
American Birding Association, 79
Amphitheatre, 15, 19, 21, 101, 117, 187,
    223
Amusement rides, 15
Anderson, Del, 65
Anemone, Cut-leaved, 40, 140
Annie's Bakery & Café, 126
Art Central, 185
Aspen Grove, 209
Avens, Three-flowered, 40
Baker Centre, 21
Baker Memorial Sanatorium, 21
Baker Park, 13-4, 16, 19, 21-2, 27
Baker, Dr. A.H., 21
Bankers Hall, 184
Bankside, 66, 103-4, 106, 108, 110
Barclay Parade, 58
Baseball, 30, 32, 149, 162, 164, 192-4, 197,
    202, 224-5
Basketball, 30, 187-8, 197
Bat, Little brown, 105
Beach volleyball, 187, 224-5
Bearspaw East, 12-4
Bearspaw Legacy Park, 13-4
Beaulieu Gardens, 4
Beaver, 53, 27-4, 79, 84, 87-8, 99, 105, 131,
    137, 140, 172, 177

Beaver Dam Flats, 2, 85-90, 92
Bebo Grove, 103, 113-4, 118, 120
Bikes and C-Trains, 7
Bird Alert, 77, 81-2, 94
Bird monitoring, 80
Bird watching, 12, 63, 69, 97, 129, 180,
    191, 201-2, 208, 216, 220, 222, 224
Blackfoot Indian, 212
Blue jay, 105
Boat ramp, 113
Boating, 16, 49, 87, 90, 101, 111
Bobsled, 215
Bonnybrook Water Treatment Plant, 85
Boothman, Harry, 36
Bosco Sacro, 48
Boston, Bob (rumour of), 206
Botanical Gardens, 66-8
Bottomlands Park, 178, 180-1
Bow Habitat Station, 60-71, 73, 234
Bow River, 49, 52, 55, 57, 60-1, 68, 71, 76,
    87, 84, 87-8, 93-5, 97, 100, 103-6,
    108-9, 111, 113, 124-6, 128-132, 142,
    147, 172, 176, 178, 180, 190-2, 212,
    216, 219, 232
Bow River Lumber Co., 49, 55
Bow River Pathway (BRP), 49, 53-4, 56-8,
    60, 64-6, 69, 76-7, 85-7, 89, 94-6, 98-
    9, 106, 108,170, 172, 218, 232
Bow River Valley, 81, 205, 209, 217, 219,
    224
Bow Valley Ranch Visitor Centre, 101, 106,
    116, 123-7
Bow Valley Ranche House, 121, 124, 126
Bow Valley Square, 184-5
Bow Waters Canoe Club, 218-9
Bowmont Natural Environment Park
    Management Plan, 25
Bowmont Park, 18, 22, 24, 26-8
Bowness Park, 2, 14-5, 17-9, 21
BP BirthPlace Forests, 98
BP Canada Energy Company, 73, 98
Bragg Creek, 132
Brickburn, 36
Bridgeland/Riverside Community
    Association, 3
Brisebois, Éphrem A., 61-2, 231
Bronconnier, Dave, 14
Brook stickleback, 105
Browning, Gary, 130
Brunch, 146, 215
Buffalo jumps, 35

Bufflehead, 81

Burnco Rock Products, 95

Burns, Michael John, 127

Burns, Senator Patrick (Pat), 195, 199-200

Burnsmead, 103, 106, 108, 110-1, 128

Calgary Airport Authority (The), 4, 196-7

Calgary Area Outdoor Council, 7, 47

Calgary Beach Volleyball Association, 225

Calgary Bicycle Track League, 151

Calgary Bird Banding Society, 80, 234

Calgary Board of Education, 94

Calgary Canoe Club, 152, 154-5

Calgary Curling Club, 54

Calgary Eaton Centre, 183

Calgary Field Naturalists Society, 41, 93,
    138

Calgary Flames Hockey Club, 186

Calgary Folk Festival, 51

Calgary Golf & Country Club, 161

Calgary Health Region, 98

Calgary International Airport, 81, 175,
    194-6, 209

Calgary Jaycees, 161

Calgary Municipal Building, 183-4

Calgary Parking Authority, 2

Calgary Place, 184

Calgary Planetarium, 47

Calgary Power, 55

Calgary Rowing Club, 153-5, 234

Calgary Stampede, 167

Calgary Tower, 183

Calgary Watch & Clock Collectors
    Association, 229

Calgary Zoo, Botanical Gardens and
    Prehistoric Park, 3, 52, 56-8, 64, 66-9,
    181, 191, 219

Calgary Zoological Society, 64, 68

Calgary's Coney Island, 18

Calgary's Name, 62

Calhoun, Alexander, 228

Campbell, Tom, 3, 178, 181, 191, *192, 198*

Canada buffaloberry, 25

Canada Day, 51

Canada Olympic Park, 27, 215-7, 235

Canadian Migration Monitoring Network,
    80

Canadian National/CN, 174

Canadian Pacific Railway/CPR, 25, 27, 36,
    38-9, 43, 61, 69, 168, 174, 217-8, 220

Canadian Wilds, 67-8

Canoeing, 15, 35, 49, 137, 152, 155, 158,
    162, 206, 220

Caragana, Sutherland, 156

Carburn Park, 72, 88-95, 97, 232

Carnegie Foundation, 228

Carnegie, Andrew, 228

Cat's Dog Park, 157

Catbird, Gray, 80

Cedar waxwing, 80

Centenary Park, 56, 58, 63-5

Centennial Parkade, 183

Central Memorial Library, 228

Central Park (New York), 71, 221, 227-8

Centrum Building, 228

Century Garden Park, 190

Chestermere Lake, 10, 57, 76, 218-20, 224

Chevron Learning Pathway, 49

Chevron Learning Pathway, 5, 53-4

Chickadee, Black-capped, 41, 80-1, 93, 105,
    137

Chinatown, 58-9, 229

Chinese Cultural Centre, 58

Chinook Ridge, 103

Choke cherries, 41, 123

Christie, Nat, 46-7

Christie, Sharma, xii, *165*, 234

City Hall, 32, 184, 187

City of Calgary Information, 7, 22, 46, 90,
    98, 134, 143, 151, 153, 155, 158, 160,
    162, 166, 172, 178, 181, 185, 188,
    189, 191, 193, 199, 201, 202, 208,
    221, 223, 225, 227, 229, 230

Cleared Paths, *149*

Clearwater Park, 14, 133

Clearwater Tipi Park, table of contents

Climbing wall, 215

Cochrane Ranch, 25, 200

Colonel's Island, 15

Colorado spruce, 22, 156

Cominco, 96

Concessions, 168

Confederation Park, 201-5, 232

Confederation Park Municipal Golf Course,
    201-2, 205

Confederation Park Senior Citizens' Centre,
    202, 204-5

Conrich, 224

Cormorant, Double-breasted, 88, 93

Cow parsnip, 41

Coyote, 79, 88, 93, 99, 105-6, 109, 136

Craigie Hall, 207

Crescent Heights Community Association,
    5, 190

Cricket, 199

Cross, A.E., 73, 225
Cross-country skiing, 192, 202, 215
Crow, American 80, 181
Crowchild, David, 46
Currey, Fred, 68
Cycling, xii, 12, 15, 19, 22, 27-8, 30, 33,
    35, 47, 49, 60, 63, 69, 77, 85, 87, 90,
    97, 99, 101, 106, 111, 114, 123, 125,
    128, 131, 133, 137, 140, 145, 149,
    151-2, 162, 164, 168, 171, 178, 180,
    184, 191-2, 195, 201-2, 205-6, 108,
    214-5, 218, 222, 224
D'Amore, Louis J., 48
Deane House, 60, 62-3, 69
Deane House murder mystery dinner
    theatre, 63
Deane, Richard Burton, 62, 182
Deer, Mule, 68, 79, 105, 209
Deer, White-tailed, 27, 68, 88, 93, 105
Deerfoot Meadows, 95-7
Destination Africa, 66-8
Devonian Foundation, 52, 75, 189-90
Devonian Gardens, 183, 185, 190
Diamond Bakery, 59
Disc golf, 63-4
Distance Charts, 10-1
Dog walking, 40, 97, 101, 133, 137, 140,
    145, 155-7, 166, 205, 208, 218
Dogs, parks and pathways, 18
Dogwood, Red osier, 25, 63, 92, 165
Doucet, Pére Leon, 231
Douglas Fir Trail, 17, 35-6, 38-41, 43
Dover, Mary, 225
Dragon City Mall, 59
Dubé, Myrna, 196-7
Duck, Wood, 79, 93
Ducks Unlimited, 4, 70, 73
Eagle, Bald 53, 79, 81, 84, 88, 92-4, 105,
    137
Eagle, Golden, 93-4
Early cinquefoil, 25
East Calgary, 182, 223-4
East Glenmore Park, 136, 142, 145
Eau Claire Lumber Co. of Wisconsin, 49, 55
Eau Claire Market, 49, 55
Educational programs, 60, 66, 77, 114, 121,
    127, 220
Edward, Prince of Wales, 222
Edwards, Henrietta Muir, 187
Edworthy Park, 10, 30, 33, 35-6, 38, 40-3
Edworthy, George, 37

Edworthy, Thomas, 36
Elbow Island Park, 167-8
Elbow Lake, 131
Elbow River, 131-8, 147, 156-7, 161-2,
    164, 166-7, 170-2, 190, 212, 231
Elbow River Conservancy, 2
Elbow River Valley, 131-2, 158-9
Elbow Valley Constructed Wetlands, 4
Elderberry, Red, 27
Elite training, 215
Elks Golf Course, 177
Ellis, Eileen, 139,
Ellis, Shepard S., 223
Elliston Lake, 223-4
Elliston Regional Park, 222
Elm, American, 156
Elphinstone, Dave, 82
Emerald Award, 85
Emily Follensbee Centre, 161
Emperor Seafood Restaurant, 58
Energy Plaza, 184
Epcor Centre for the Performing Arts,
    183-4
Ernst Young Tower, 184
Eurobungee trampoline, 215
Evamy Ridge Park, 5
Evamy, Michael, 5
Evening grosbeak, 41
Extreme Bean, 43
Falcon, Peregrine, 207
Famous Five, 187
Federal Geodetic Survey, 228
Fern, Fragile, 27
Ferret, 42
Fidler, Peter, 213
Fire Department (Calgary), 95-6, 143
First Canadian Centre, 184
Fish Creek Environmental Learning Centre,
    114, 116-7
Fish Creek Park, 3, 127, 174
Fish Creek Restoration Society, 125
Fish Creek Valley, 104, 113, 117-8, 120-1,
    123-6
Fish, Jim, 5, 52, 189
Fishing in Calgary, 9
Fleabane, 25
Flicker, Northern, 80-1, 105
Floods of 2005, 13, 93-4, 97, 116
Flycatcher, Least, 81
Football, 30, 32, 149, 151, 162, 167, 197
Forever Green program, 98

Fort Calgary, 10-1, 56, 58, 61-2, 65, 69, 168, 170, 231-2
Fort Calgary Preservation Society, 62
Fox Hollow Golf Course, 178
Fox, Red, 136
French Catholics in Calgary, 231
Friends of Elliston Park Society, 224
Friends of Fish Creek, 3
Frog, Boreal chorus, 105, 136
Fushimi, Prince, 62
Gardens, 66-8, 166-7, 183, 185-6, 189-90, 199-200, 220-3, 227-8, 230-1
Garter snake, Red-sided, 105
Garter snake, Wandering (common), 105, 136
Gasser, Ellen, 73, 234
Gerry Shaw Garden, 3, 165-7
Gilchrist, John, 52
Glacial erratics, 212
Glenbow Museum, 148, 183-4, 187, 234
Glenmore Athletic Park, 20, 136-7, 149, 151
Glenmore Dam, 52, 131, 142, 146, 151, 158, 160
Glenmore Landing, 145-6
Glenmore Park, 3, 20, 136-7, 140, 142, 145-6, 152, 154-5, 232, 235
Glenmore Pool, 149
Glenmore Reservoir, 8, 132-3, 136, 138, 140, 143, 145-7, 149, 152, 155-6
Glenmore Reservoir rules, 143
Glenmore Sailing School, 137, 142-3, 154
Glenmore Track, 149
Glenmore Velodrome, 149, 151
Glenmore Water Treatment Plant, 160-1
Glenn, Adelaide (Belcourt), 121, 124
Glenn, John, 121, 124, 147
Glennfield, 103, 123-5, 128
GlobalFest International Fireworks Competition, 223
Gold Inn Restaurant, 59
Golden Acre Garden Sentres Ltd., 98
Golden Happiness Bakery, 59
Goldeneye, Common, 79, 81, 137
Goldenrod, 25
Goldfinch, American, 80, 105
Goose, Canada, 93, 105
Gopher, Pocket, 105
Grand Trunk Pacific Railway, 62
Grass, Awnless brome, 125
Grass, Blue grama, 125
Grass, June, 25, 125

Grass, Needle, 25
Grass, Parry's oatgrass, 25
Grass, Rough fescue, 25, 126, 192, 214
Grass, Wheat, 25, 125
Graves Landing, 95-6, 113
Gray, James H., 3, 182
Grayling, Arctic, 73
Griffith Woods, 1, 5, 14, 131, 133-6
Griffith, Wilbur, 134
Grouse, Ruffed, 105
Gulf Canada Square, 184
Gull, Franklin's, 93
Gull, Glaucous-winged, 81
Gull, Iceland, 81
Gull, Mew, 81
Gull, Ring-billed, 93
Gull, Thayer's, 81
Hanen, Harold, 183
Harburn, Norm, xii, 1, *130*, *230*, 234
Hare, Snowshoe, 105
Harvie Passage, 5, 57, 75
Harvie, Don, 52
Harvie, Eric, 75, 90, 95, 97-8, 147, 156, 186, 189
Haultain School Park, 5
Hawitt, Terry, 230, 234
Hawk, Red-tailed, 105
Hawk, Swainson's, 105, 136, 172, 181
Heffler, Howard, 76
Helmet law, 6
Heritage Day, 51
Heritage Escarpment, 2, 162
Heritage Park, 20, 55, 136-7, 145-8, 154, 232
Heron Flats, 103
Heron, Great blue, 93, 105, 125-6
Hextall, John, 15, 18
Higgins, Sue, 3, 99, 106
Hiking, 12, 14-5, 22, 35, 41, 47, 49, 87, 90, 101, 111, 114, 123, 128, 133, 137, 140, 145, 172, 205-6, 208, 216, 218, 222
Honsun, Chu, 59
Howell, Sal, 52
Hull, William Roper, 121, 124-5, 127
Hull's Wood, 103, 108, 110-1, 121
Hull's Wood & Sikome Lake, 108, 111
Hummingbird, Rufous, 136
Hyatt Regency Calgary, 184
Inglewood Bird Sanctuary, 3, 57, 76, 77, 79-82, 84-5, 93-4, 96, 99, 234

Inglewood Bird Sanctuary Nature Centre, 77, 82
Inglewood Community Association, 2
Inglewood Golf & Curling Club, 84, 220, 218
Inglewood Wildlands Park, 85
Ingram, Eleanor, 147
Ingverson, W., 222
In-line skating, xii, 187-8, 195
International Hotel, 184
Interpretive displays, 69, 77, 220, 223-4, 230
Interpretive trails, 35, 60, 69, 70
Jackrabbit, White-tailed, 181
James H. Gray Park, 3
James Short School, 2, 229
James Short Square, 228
Jim & Pearl Burns Centre, 197
Jim Fish Ridge, 1, 5, 189-91
Johannsen, Jackrabbit, 140
Juniper, 25, 140
Kananaskis Country, 132
Kayaking, 75, 152, 155, 206
Kensington at Louise Crossing, 43
Kestrel, American, 81, 136
Killdeer, 81
King, George Clift, 61
Kingbird, Eastern, 81
Kingfisher Seafoods Restaurant, 59
Kingfisher, Belted, 81
Klein, Premier Ralph, 96
Klippert Construction, 28
Kwong, Honourable Norman (Normie) L., 198
Lacombe, Father Albert, 147, 231
Lafarge Canada Construction, 98-9, 130
Lafarge Meadows, 129-30
Lagoon Café & Cappucino Bar, 15, 17
Lakeview Municipal Golf Course, 149
Lawn bowling, 162
Lawrey Gardens, 35-6
Laycock Park, 117, 178, 180
Laycock, Thomas, 180
Laycock, Thomas Hayes & Violet, 180
Leavitt's Ice Cream Store, 43
Leslie, Jack, 52
Lily, Western wood, 40
Lindsay Park, 131, 168-71, 230
Lindsay, Dr. Neville James, 164
Lindsay's Folly, 164-5
Livingston, Sam, 70-1, 73, 147

Loaf and Jug, 5
Lougheed family, 4
Louise Crossing, 43, 47
Lowery Gardens, 2, 35-6, 38, 40-1, 43, 46
Luge, 215-6
Lunchbox Theatre, 185
Lupine, 25
MacEwan Hall Student Centre, 205-6
MacEwan, Grant, 55, 194
Mackay, A.S., 32
MacKimmie Library, 206
Macleod, Colonel James, 62, 225
Magpie, Black-billed, 80, 181
Mahaffey, Pat, xii, 234
Mallard, 66, 81, 106, 172
Mallard Point, 99, 103, 106, 110
Mannix family, 117
Many Owls Valley, 209, 214
Maranatha Church, 28
Margetts, Cathryn (Cat), 155, 157, 164
Marquis of Lorne, 3, 12, 104-5, 111, 113, 128-130, 147
Marshall Springs, 103, 114, 118
Marshall, E.T., 118
Mary Dover, 224
Mawson, Thomas, 49-51
Max Bell Arena, 57, 218, 219
McCall Lake Golf Course, 98
McClung, Nellie, 187
McDougall Centre, 184
McDougall, Reverend George, 147
McHugh Bluffs, 46, 54
McInnes & Holloway, 123
McKenzie Meadows Golf Course, 101, 109, 128, 130, 235
McKinney, Louise, 187
Meadowlark, Prairie, 209
Meikle, Wayne, 103, 105, 235
Memorial Forest, 123
Memorial Park, 71, 221, 227-8
Memorial Park Library, 227
Merganser, Common, 81, 93, 105
Mewata Armoury, 47, 187
Midnapore Woollen Store, 123
Milne, Bill , 95
Minigolf, 15, 216
Montgomery Flats, 24
Moose, 136
Morrison, Bill, 175, 234
Morrow, E. Joyce, 50
Moss phlox, 88

Mountain biking, 40, 208, 209, 215-7
Mule Deer Plateau, 209
Municipal Historic Resource, 228
Murphy, Emily, 187
Muskrat, 79, 105, 136, 140, 172
Nat Christie Park, 46-7
Natural Areas Adopt-a-Park Program, 208, 217
Natural Resources Canada, 132, 174
Naturalist for Hire, 79
Nature Calgary, 79
Nickle Arts Museum, 205
North Capitol Hill Park, 201-202
North Glenmore Park, 20, 136, 146, 152, 154-5, 232
North West Mounted Police, 60, 61-2, 124, 147, 231
Northeast Regional Park Committee, 2
Northern bedstraw, 25
Nose Creek, xi, 3, 20, 56, 57, 172, 174, 176-82, 191, 204, 213, 232
Nose Creek Pathway. 20, 156, 172, 176, 178, 180, 191, 214, 232
Nose Creek Valley, 172, 178, 181, 182, 209
Nose Hill Park, 3, 103, 174, 207-16
Nose Hill Park Board, 3
Nose Hill Park studies, 214
Novak, Len, 85
Nuthatch, Red-breasted, 41, 80, 88, 105
Nuthatch, White-breasted, 81
Obolensky, Princess Tania, 164
Old Refinery Park, 86
Olympic Plaza, 183, 186
Oriole, Baltimore, 80, 81
Outdoor Resource Centre, 46
Outwest Park, 2
Owl, various, 68, 79, 88, 93, 105
Paddle boats, 15, 16
Palliser Hotel, 183
Parks Foundation, Calgary, 1, 2, 3, 5, 53, 75, 85, 89, 130, 134, 157, 165, 167, 175, 190, 196, 197, 222, 229, 230, 231, 234, 235
Parley, Irene, 187
Partridge, Gray, 79, 81, 181
Paskapoo Formation, 47, 174
Pathway Etiquette, 33, 36
Pathway Hotline, 86
Patterson Homestead Park, 4
Peace in the Parks, 98
Peace Park, 2, 47-8

Pearce Estate Park, 57, 69-72, 73, 75, 76, 113, 218, 219
Pearce, William, 71
Pelican, American white, 72-3, 88, 93, 137
Pengrowth Saddledome, 131, 171
Petro-Canada4, 85
Petro-Canada Bird School, 77
Petro-Canada Towers, 184, 185, 229
Pheasant, Ring-necked, 79, 105
Pickering, George, 84
Picnic shelters, 15, 101, 106, 111, 114, 124, 158, 178, 194
Picnicking, 15, 49, 66, 101, 106, 111, 133, 137, 140, 145, 152, 155, 158, 162, 168, 172, 178, 180, 185, 189, 191, 192, 199, 202, 216, 218, 220, 222, 224, 227, 229
Pike, Northern, 43, 93
Pinel, Harold, xii, 235
Pintail, Northern, 81
Playgrounds, 1, 8, 15, 17, 30, 31, 32, 35, 37, 38, 47, 53, 54, 63, 65, 67, 68, 87, 89, 90, 94, 101, 111, 112, 137, 140, 152, 154, 158, 159, 161, 162, 164, 165, 166, 168, 169, 170, 178, 180, 185, 186, 192, 193, 194, 197, 199, 200, 201, 202, 224, 225, 229
Porcupine, 9, 105, 140
Porcupine Hills Formation, 118, 120
Porcupine Valley, 209, 214
Prairie crocus, 25, 27, 40, 88, 208
Prairie fires, 126
Prairie Winds Park, 2, 192, 194
Pratt, Bill, 20
Prehistoric Park, 56, 66-7, 68
Prince, Peter, 49, 52, 55, 146
Prince's Island, 1, 5, 20, 42, 46, 47-51, 52, 53, 55, 56, 58, 59, 232
Prince's Island Park, 5, 54, 229
Princess Obolensky Park, 164, 165
Provincial Historic Resources, 228
Provincial Museum of Alberta, 74, 190
Public art, 49, 54
Pumphouse Theatre, 46
Queen Elizabeth, 186
Queen's Park Cemetery, 202, 205
Raspberries, Wild, 41, 68, 92
Raven, 117
Raven Rocks, 103, 118, 120, 121
Reader Rock Gardens, 220, 221-2
Reader, William, 68, 221-2

Red Light District, 181-2
Riley Park, 199-200
Riley, Thomas and Georgina, 200
River Café (The), 49, 52, 53
River Park, 131, 151, 155-7, 161, 164
River Valleys Committee, 2, 3, 5, 89, 95,
        136, 175
Riveredge Park, 159
Riverine forest, 94, 96, 97, 98, 100, 103,
        106, 108, 111, 114, 118, 121, 123,
        125, 131, 159, 165, 171, 174
RiverWatch, 76, 94
Robertson, Anna, 120
Robin, American, 80
Rocky Mountain whitefish, 46
Rocky Mountains, 41, 118, 129, 132, 209,
        217
Rose, Common Wild, 92, 175
Rose, Prickly, 92
Rotary Challenger Park, 1, 5, 196, 197
Rotary Chinook Natural Area, 103, 109
Rotary Chinook Nature Park, 128, 129, 130
Rotary Club of Calgary, 4, 85, 129, 197
Rotary Park, 5, 190, 191
Rouleau, Charles Borronée, 231
Rouleau, Édouard, 231
Rouleauville Square, 3, 4, 190, 229, 231
Roxboro Community Association, 3
Royal Astronomical Society of Canada, 118,
        235
Royal Canadian Legion, 3
Royal Canadian Mounted Police, 60
Rozsa Centre, 205, 206
Rubbing Stone Hill, 209
Safety City, 151, 161
Sagewort, 25
Salamander, Tiger, 105, 136
Sam Livingston Fish Hatchery, 70, 71, 73
Sam Livingston Fish Hatchery Volunteer
        Society, 73
Sandhills cinquefoil, 85
Sandpiper, Spotted, 81
Sandy Beach Park, 52, 131, 151, 158-61,
        232
Sapper's Bridge, 2, 89
Saskatoon (berry), 25, 68, 92, 123
Scaup, Lesser, 81
Scotia Centre, 183
Seinfeld, Jerry, 85
Senator Patrick Burns Memorial Park, 200
Shannon Terrace, 101, 103, 113-4, 116-8

Shannon, Joseph & Margaret, 116
Shaw Millennium Park, 5, 47, 187-8
Shaw, Helen, 122
Shaw, Samuel (Sam), 121-2
Shaw's Meadow, 121
Shell Place, 184
Shepard Wetlands, 14
Shouldice Arena, 30
Shouldice Park, 28, 30, 31-2, 33, 52
Shouldice Swimming Pool, 30, 32
Shouldice, James, 32
Shrews, 105
Sien Lok Park, 20, 58-9
Sien Lok Society, 59
Sightseeing, 155, 189, 191, 208
Sikome Lake, 10, 101, 103, 108, 110, 111-3
Silver Dragon, 59
Silver Springs Golf & Country Club, 28
Simonot, John, 5, 136
Simpson, Wallis, 222
Sinclair, Doug, 229
Skateboarding, 187-8
Skating, Ice, 15, 16, 18, 92, 112, 137, 141,
        145, 162, 187, 192, 193
Skating, In-line, xii, 187-8, 195
Ski jumping, 215
Ski lessons, 215
Skinner, Don, 4, 196, 234
Slater Park, 219
Smart, Fire Chief James "Cappy", 68
Soccer, 30, 32, 149, 162, 180, 181, 192,
        193, 194, 197, 224, 225
South Glenmore Park, 136, 137, 140, 142,
        145, 232
Southern Alberta Institute of Technology,
        199
Southland Natural Park, 90, 95, 96, 97-100,
        232
Southwest Community Association, 3
Sparrow, Chipping, 80
Sparrow, White-crowned, 81
Sparrow, White-throated, 81
Split Rock, 174-5
Squirrel, Eastern grey, 93
Squirrel, Red, 105, 140
Squirrel, Richardson ground, 105, 172
St. Mary's Church, 230, 231
Stafford, Mike, 166-7, 234
Stampede Park, 131, 169, 171, 220, 230
Stanley Park, 131, 160-4
Stanley Park Lawn Bowling Club, 162

Stargazing, 118
Starling, 80, 198
Stebbins, Robert A., 231
Stephen Avenue, 186, 187
Strong-Watson, Linda, 218
Stu Peppard Arena, 151
Sturgeon, 73
Sucker, Longnose, 117
Summer camps, 197, 215
Sun Life Plaza, 184
Swallow, Cliff, 93, 181
Swallow, Tree, 93
Swan, Tundra, 137
Swimming, 30-2, 68, 71, 77, 111-2, 137,
    141, 143, 145, 162, 164, 168, 224
T.B Riley Junior High School, 94
Talisman Centre, 168-9, 170
Telus Building, 207
Telus Convention Centre, 184
Tennis, 30, 31, 32, 140, 141, 149, 152, 153,
    154, 162, 191, 192, 193, 194, 197,
    201, 202
The Bay, 164, 183
Thompson, David, 213
Tidswell, Lt. Col. J.E.H., 3
Tidswell, Mrs. J., 3
Tobogganing, 38, 158, 162, 192, 193, 194,
    202, 204, 205, 222, 224
Tom Campbell's Hill, 3, 178, 181, 191-2, 198
Toronto Dominion/TD Square, 183, 185, 190
Tours, 60, 69-70, 77-9, 82, 127, 155, 185,
    215, 222
Trans Canada Trail, 20, 104
TransCanada, 94, 184
Tree, Aspen, 123
Tree, Balsam poplar, 25-6, 82
Tree, Bur oak, 156
Tree, Colorado spruce, 22
Tree, Douglas fir, 22
Tree, Flowering crabapple, 22
Tree, Green ash, 22
Tree, Hawthorn, 22
Tree, Larch, 156
Tree, Laurel-leaved willow, 156
Tree, Lodgepole pine, 22
Tree, Manchurian elm, 22
Tree, Manitoba maple, 22
Tree, May Day, 22
Tree, Mountain ash, 22
Tree, Paper birch, 22, 156
Tree, Poplar, 22, 123
Tree, Scots pine, 22

Tree, Siberian larch, 156
Tree, Trembling aspen, 26
Tree, Water birch, 25
Tree, Weeping birch, 22
Tree, White spruce, 22, 123, 125
Trotter, George, 225
Trout Unlimited, 46
Trout, Brook, 73
Trout, Brown, 9, 46, 64, 73, 93, 105
Trout, Bull, 46, 73
Trout, Cutthroat, 73
Trout, Rainbow, 9, 46, 73, 93, 105
Tsuu T'ina (Sarcee), 46, 103, 124, 132, 134,
    138
Tufa, 27
Twelve Mile Coulee, 216-7
U of C Archaeological Field School, 101,
    121, 125
Udderly Art Pasture, 183, 184
Union Cemetery, 220, 221-2
University of Calgary, 206, 207
University of Calgary Outdoor Centre, 206
Urban Park Master Plan, 21
Using Calgary's Natural Areas, 82
Valley Ridge Golf & Country Club, 13
Valleyview Regional Park, 224-6
Variety Club Spray Deck, 137, 141, 142
Vicountess Byng of Vimy, 221
Vireo, Red-eyed, 136
Vole, Meadow, 105
Von Kunig, Count Leo, 164
Votier Flats, 121, 122
Votier, James, 121
W.R. Castell Library, 184, 187
Wading, 112, 166, 187, 191, 192, 199, 201,
    224
Walde, Dale, 125
Walker House, 77, 82
Walker, Colonel James, 77, 84
Walker, Selby, 84
Walking, xii, 12, 15, 19, 22, 30, 35, 49, 60,
    63, 66, 69, 77, 87, 90, 97, 101, 106,
    111, 114, 122, 123, 128, 131, 133,
    137, 140, 145, 149, 155, 158, 162,
    166, 168, 171, 172, 178, 180, 185,
    188, 191, 192, 199, 201, 202, 205,
    206, 208, 216, 218, 220, 222, 224,
    227, 229, 230
Walsh, Tommy, 196
Warbler, Orange-crowned, 80
Warbler, Tennessee, 80
Warbler, Yellow, 81

Warbler, Yellow-rumped, 80
Washrooms, 14, 15, 19, 30, 35, 49, 60, 67,
    77, 87, 88-90, 95, 101, 106, 111-2,
    114, 117, 123, 125, 133, 134, 137,
    141, 142, 145, 151, 152, 154, 158,
    159, 162, 168, 172, 185, 187-8, 191,
    193, 197, 199, 201, 202, 208, 221,
    223, 227
Wasyliw, Larry & Mitzie, 127
Water fountains, 19, 30, 35, 46, 49, 54, 60,
    77, 87, 90, 101, 106, 111, 114, 123,
    127, 145, 151, 152, 155, 157, 158,
    162, 171, 180, 185, 191, 193, 199,
    201
Waterfall Valley, 27-8, 120
Weasel, Long-tailed, 79
Weaselhead Flats Natural Area, 20, 136,
    137-8, 142, 154
Weaselhead Society, 138, 235
Weasels, 79, 105, 172
West Nose Creek, xi, 20, 172, 174, 175
West Nose Creek Confluence Park, 172,
    174, 175, 176
Western Irrigation District, 5, 71, 75, 218,
    235
Western Irrigation District (WID) Canal, xi,
    75, 76, 95, 218, 219, 220
Western Irrigation District (WID) Pathway,
    57, 76, 218-20
Western Irrigation District (WID) Weir, 57,
    69, 70, 72
Western Irrigation District (WID) Weir
    Safety, 75
Westin Hotel, 184
Wetlands, 1, 5, 12, 13, 35, 53, 69, 73, 76,
    88, 89, 93, 100, 104, 122, 128, 129,
    130, 133, 134, 135, 136, 137, 138,
    140, 174, 201, 203, 204, 217, 224,
    225
White, Richard, 183, 235
Whitefish, 46, 64
Wildlife checklists, 93, 105
Wildlife watching/viewing, 66, 77, 101,
    106, 111, 114, 123, 128, 129, 133,
    137, 140, 145, 172, 180, 191, 198,
    208, 216, 218, 219
Willans Ranch, 117
Willans, Maud and Norman, 117
Willow, Wolf, 25, 40, 92, 123
Wilson, James Lewellyn, 127
Wilson's snipe, 81

Wilson's warbler, 81
Wood's Douglas Fir Trails, 16, 17
Woodpecker, Black-back, 136
Woodpecker, Downy, 80, 105
Woodpecker, Hairy, 105
Woodpecker, Pileated, 105
Wood-pewee, Western, 81
Woods Foundation, 147, 148
Woods Park, 131, 165, 166-7
Wren, House, 80
Wright, Frances, 187
Zackowski, Jim, 198

ACKNOWLEDGEMENTS

Thanks to those who accompanied me on walks and served as willing or reluctant photo subjects: Norm Harburn, Sharma Christie, James Mahoney, Sean Mahoney, Mike Stafford, Bill Morrison, Don Skinner, Arielle Hofmeister Bullick, Terry Hawitt, Tanya Kahanoff, Nicky Blackshaw, Kal Dhanda, Jennifer Allford, Jean and Niall Roe.

I would also like to thank and acknowledge the many people and organizations who provided and/or verified information, images, sources, and mapping data:

Lorna Allen, Alberta Parks and Protected Areas

Ken Ashmead, Data Service Analyst, Corporate Data Access & Marketing, City of Calgary

Chris Ballard, Corporate Data Access & Marketing, City of Calgary

Ken Bendiktsen, External Relations, University of Calgary

Calgary Public Library, Humanities Reference Desk

Calgary Rowing Club

Calgary Exhibition & Stampede

City of Calgary webspace

Amanda Cole, Inglewood Bird Sanctuary

Eric Collins, Geomatics Manager, Enviro-Tech Surveys Ltd.

Douglas Collister, Calgary Bird Banding Society

Lindsay Anne Dann, Executive Producer, GlobalFest

Ellen Gasser, Visitor Service Coordinator, Bow Habitat Station, Alberta Sustainable Resource Development

Graham Gerylo, Natural Areas Project Coordinator, Parks Natural Areas, City of Calgary

Glenbow Museum Archives

Norm Harburn, Parks Foundation, Calgary

Vlad Ianev, Enviro-Tech Surveys Ltd.

Andrea Kingwell, Saloon Communications

Jack Leslie, former Mayor, City of Calgary

Jean Leslie, Author, Three Rivers Beckoned

Wayne Logan, Volunteer, Parks Foundation, Calgary

Joan Macleod, Corporate Data Access & Marketing, City of Calgary

Pat Mahaffey, Parks, City of Calgary

Jerrilyn Margetts

H. David Matthews

Dave McKee, Aldermanic Office, City of Calgary

Doug McIntyre, Calgary Olympic Development Association/Canada Olympic Park
McKenzie Meadows Golf Club
Wayne Meikle, Urban Planning Specialist, Fish Creek Provincial Park, Alberta Community Development
Sherry Mumford, Connections Desktop Publishing
George Nelson, Enviro-Tech Surveys Ltd.
Harold Pinel, Pathway Coordinator, Parks, City of Calgary
Calgary Chapter, Royal Astronomical Society of Canada
Brenda Smyth, Parks Foundation, Calgary
Jennifer Symcox, Natural Areas Project Coordinator, Parks, City of Calgary
Irene Till, Fish Creek Provincial Park
Dale Walde, University of Calgary Archaeology Field School
Weaselhead Glenmore Park Preservation Society
Jim Webber, General Manager, Western Irrigation District
Richard White, former Executive Director, Calgary Downtown Association
Bob Willgress, Enviro-Tech Surveys Ltd.
Peter Wilson, Chief Structures Engineer, Roads, City of Calgary

Terry Bullick is a writer and communications consultant based in Calgary, Alberta, who has written about everything from pathways to parenting during the past two decades.